This book describes the history, scope, problems, and present state of the study of language and communication—and, in particular, the field of linguistic science—in America.

Mr. Carroll takes up, one by one, the approaches to the study of language that have been developed in linguistics, psychology, philosophy, anthropology, sociology, education, and communication engineering. He shows that these approaches have evolved relatively independently and with little cognizance of developments in other fields, but he also points out that, if they were properly fitted together, there would emerge a broad and unified science of language and communication with numerous applications in education and in the social sciences.

The major portion of the book is devoted to linguistic science, a field that is not widely known either to scholars in other fields or to the general public. Mr. Carroll demonstrates how linguistic science studies and compares, from both descriptive and historical points of view, the structures and characteristics of language systems, whether of the well-known languages like English, French, and German, or of the less-known languages such as Burmese, Navaho, and Bantu. He describes many procedures of linguistic methodology; he shows, for example, how linguistic science has developed units of

Continued from front flap

analysis such as the phoneme—a minimal unit of sound used in differentiating words. He goes into problems of broad significance such as the problem of showing how various languages differ in the ways in which they "encode" experience, and the problem of classifying languages as to type.

Finally, Mr. Carroll makes a plea for greater interdisciplinary cooperation and for the support of research and study that would bring about a satisfactory fusion of the various approaches to the study of language and contribute to the vigorous and fruitful development of linguistic studies. This book, amply documented and with an extensive bibliography, is written in the light of the most modern linguistic and psychological theories. It should appeal not only to specialists with a professional interest in the subject, but to educators in general, as well as to the general reader interested in language and communication.

Mr. Carroll, who received his professional training in psychology, has been a member of the Linguistic Society of America since 1936, and has conducted considerable research on various problems in the psychology of language. He is Associate Professor of Education at Harvard University.

HARVARD UNIVERSITY PRESS
CAMBRIDGE 38, MASSACHUSETTS

THE STUDY OF LANGUAGE

A Survey of Linguistics and
Related Disciplines in America

JOHN B. CARROLL
Harvard University

Harvard University Press

Cambridge

1953

Distributed in Great Britain by
GEOFFREY CUMBERLEGE
Oxford University Press
London

Library of Congress Catalog Card Number 53–5067
Printed in the United States of America

PREFACE

This book is an outcome of a report written originally at the request of the Carnegie Corporation of New York. That report, entitled "A Survey of Linguistics and Related Disciplines" and submitted to the Carnegie Corporation in December 1950, was circulated informally among a number of linguistic scientists and other professional workers concerned with the study of language. As a result, I was urged to revise and expand the material in the report and to make it available in published form. This book is addressed to all who are interested in the study of speech, language, and communication, and particularly to those who recognize that these studies require coöperative effort on the part of the various specialists concerned with particular aspects of language problems. It is intended in no way to supplant the general and technical references available in various areas of interest; rather, one of the purposes of this book is to serve as a study guide, by providing the reader with references to some of the more significant books and articles pertaining to each part of the presentation. The very wide scope of the present treatment has precluded, in many cases, a detailed discussion of technical issues. Instead, the intention has been to suggest the mutual relations of various approaches to problems of language study.

The assignment originally given me by the Carnegie Corporation was broad and contained few specifications. I was asked to survey the field of linguistics—its present status, its methodological problems, and its connections with neighboring disciplines. Considerable attention was to be given to possible implications of linguistic science for educational problems in our schools, from the kindergarten up through the postgraduate levels.

In approaching this task, I found it impossible to limit my attention to the field of linguistics as defined in the standard works on linguistics and language study. The breadth of interest in problems of language and communication which has been manifested in recent years made it necessary to go far afield, for example, into a brief study of communication engineering. The scope of this survey, therefore, can best be described as attempting to embrace the totality of present-day inquiry into various phases of human communication, as seen from the standpoint of modern linguistic science in America. To encompass such a scope without neglecting, slighting, or misinterpreting at least some of the more important developments in the field would be a truly staggering task, and it would be immodest to claim that this report fulfills such a mission even approximately. Nevertheless, to the extent that there is need of a work which would attempt to bring under one cover a review of the present status of the study of language in America, the effort represented here seems to be justified.

As an aid in the preparation of the original report, I was fortunate in having been enabled by the Carnegie Corporation of New York to visit a number of universities and other centers where linguistic studies are being pursued. Many hours were spent in stimulating discussions with linguists and other interested specialists. A special debt of gratitude is owed to the following persons, who welcomed me on my visits to their institutions and were most gracious in arranging conferences and discussions with members of their staffs: Professors Franklin Edgerton and Bernard Bloch, Yale University; Joseph Greenberg, Columbia University; J Milton Cowan, Cornell University; Zellig S. Harris, University of Pennsylvania; Henry L. Smith, Jr. and George L. Trager, Foreign Service Institute, Department of State; Hans Kurath and Charles C. Fries, University of Michigan; Charles F. Voegelin, Indiana University; William N. Locke, Massachusetts Institute of Technology; and Leon Dostert, Georgetown University; and Miss Mary Bray, Executive Secretary, International Auxiliary Language Association.

In addition, I wish to express appreciation to Professors Joshua Whatmough, Roman Jakobson, Ivor A. Richards, and Clyde Kluckhohn, and Dean Francis M. Rogers, all of Harvard University; Professor Irving Lorge of Columbia University; Professor Martin Joos of the University of Wisconsin; and Dr. George M. Cowan of the Summer Institute of Linguistics. These persons were particularly helpful in supplying information and suggestions for the preparation of the original report.

I am also much indebted to the following persons who offered comments which were helpful in preparing the present revised version:

Bernard Bloch, J Milton Cowan, Leon Dostert, Franklin Edgerton, Mortimer Graves, Eric Hamp, Archibald Hill, Roman Jakobson, Albert Marckwardt, R. I. McDavid, Norman McQuown, George A. Miller, I. A. Richards, Henry Lee Smith, Jr., and his associates at the Foreign Service Institute, and Charles F. Voegelin.

My colleagues in a seminar in psycholinguistics, held at Cornell University in the summer of 1951 under the sponsorship of the Social Science Research Council, were helpful in stimulating further clarification of the relation between psychology and linguistics: Frederick B. Agard, Cornell University; Stanley S. Newman, University of New Mexico; Charles E. Osgood, University of Illinois; Thomas A. Sebeok, Indiana University; and Richard L. Solomon, Harvard University.

For permissions to quote, the author makes grateful acknowledgment to the following sources: The American Psychological Association, for a quotation from the *Psychological Bulletin;* Columbia University Press, for a quotation from Linton's *Science of Man in the World Crisis* (copyright 1945); Ginn and Company, for quotations from Agard and Dunkel's *Investigation of Second-Language Teaching* (copyright 1948); Dr. Robert A. Hall, Jr., for quotations from his book *Leave Your Language Alone!* (copyright 1950); Harcourt, Brace and Company, for quotations from Sapir's *Language* (copyright 1921) and Ogden and Richards' *Meaning of Meaning* (1936); Harper and Brothers, for quotations from Wendell Johnson's *People in Quandaries* (copyright 1946); Harvard University Press, for quotations from Kluckhohn and Leighton's *The Navaho* (copyright 1946); Henry Holt and Company, for quotations from Bloomfield's *Language* (copyright 1933); The International Society of General Semantics, for quotations from its copyrighted journal *Etc., A Review of General Semantics;* Dr. Robert Lado, for a quotation from his doctoral thesis; the Linguistic Society of America, for numerous quotations from its copyrighted journal *Language,* and for quotations from Bloch and Trager's *Outline of Linguistic Analysis* (copyright 1942) and Joos's monograph *Acoustic Phonetics* (copyright 1948); the McGraw-Hill Book Company, for quotations from George Miller's *Language and Communication* (copyright 1951) and from Dollard and Miller's *Personality and Psychotherapy* (copyright 1950); the W. W. Norton Company, for quotations from Richards and Gibson's *Learning Basic English* (copyright 1945); Scott,

Foresman and Company, for quotations from W. S. Gray's *On Their Own in Reading* (copyright 1948); the *Southwestern Journal of Anthropology;* the George W. Stewart Co., for quotations from Lasswell and associates' *Language of Politics* (copyright 1949); *The Technology Review,* edited at the Massachusetts Institute of Technology, for quotations from articles by Benjamin Lee Whorf; Dr. George Trager, for quotations from his paper *The Field of Linguistics* (1949); the University of Illinois Press, for quotations from Shannon and Weaver's *Mathematical Theory of Communication* (copyright 1949); the University of Michigan Press, for a quotation from Fries's *Teaching and Learning English as a Foreign Language* (copyright 1945); and John Wiley and Sons, Inc., for an excerpt from E. C. Berkeley's *Giant Brains* (copyright 1949).

I am especially indebted to Dr. John W. Gardner of the Carnegie Corporation of New York, whose request that I make the survey on which this book is based again brought me into active contact with the field of linguistics after some years spent away from these pursuits. It is to be understood, of course, that by virtue of providing funds which made the original report possible, the Carnegie Corporation of New York does not necessarily endorse any of the statements made or the views expressed here. The opinions expressed in this book are, of course, made solely on my own responsibility; my informants are not to be held to account for any aberrant views or other deficiencies that may be found here.

As in all such enterprises, writing this book had both its pleasant and its tedious phases. For her encouragement and expressions of delight in the former, as well as her patient understanding in the latter, I am very grateful to my wife, Mary Searle Carroll, who had no small part in enabling me to bring the work to a conclusion.

JOHN B. CARROLL

Cambridge, Massachusetts
July, 1952

CONTENTS

CONTENTS

CONTENTS

THE STUDY OF LANGUAGE

Chapter 1 **INTRODUCTION**

This book is concerned with the whole range of phenomena to which we ordinarily refer when we use such terms as *language, speech,* and *communication.* More specifically, it is concerned with those particular problems or aspects of language, speech, and communication which by reason of either their theoretical or their practical significance have become the central points of interest for certain groups of scientists, scholars, and educators.

Phenomena of language, speech, and communication are so diverse and complex that it was perhaps almost inevitable that a number of separate, specialized disciplines devoted to the investigation and teaching of various aspects of this subject matter should have developed. The process of specialization has by now gone so far that the integration of the efforts of various disciplines is not as complete as might be desired. Each discipline has overlooked possible bases of coöperation with other disciplines, with the result that we can observe not only a wasteful duplication of effort but also the neglect or the mishandling of certain important problems.

The study of language thus cuts across the interests of many fields. We shall address our attention to each of these fields, examining their assumptions, problems, methodologies, and findings. We shall also attempt to suggest areas in which the interests of different fields intersect. While we shall be concerned primarily with scientific and scholarly activitiy, we shall not lose sight of the interests of the layman, who is often conscious of language problems, whether he may be conversing with a friend who speaks a different dialect, training his child in what he thinks is "good English usage," or simply having difficulties in making his arguments understood.

First of all we recognize a group of scientists, scholars, and teachers whose interest in language is central. Within this group, there is a relatively small number of individuals, located chiefly at higher academic institutions, who call themselves *linguistic scientists.* In this book, we shall frequently use the term "linguist" for convenience; nevertheless, a linguistic scientist would not want to be confused with a person who merely knows a variety of languages—a polyglot. Linguistic scientists are engaged in developing a sound body of scientific observations, facts, and systematic theory about language in general and about languages in particular. This body of scientific knowledge is properly referred to as *linguistics,* or *linguistic science.* But it must not be thought that linguistics is concerned with all phases of human communication. Instead, it narrows its attention to the study of languages conceived as what may be called "linguistic codes." A linguistic code may be regarded as a system of distinct sound symbols underlying the manifest speech behavior of the individuals comprising a speech community. While the existence of a linguistic code is obviously a necessary factor in any communication situation, it is only one factor. The linguist does not immediately concern himself with how linguistic codes are learned by speakers or with how they are used by these speakers in referring to whatever they are communicating about.

Language teachers are engaged in teaching people to use particular linguistic codes. Since they must presumably know the characteristics of these linguistic codes in order to teach them, one would think that they ought to be closely allied with linguistic scientists. The majority of language teachers, however, have little knowledge of the science of linguistics in its present state of development. For the most part, they have been brought up in a different tradition—either the tradition of literary and philological interest, or simply the tradition of teaching the "three R's." Perhaps the teacher of "foreign" languages is more likely to have some acquaintance with the results of linguistic studies in his own field than, say, the high-school English teacher. Nevertheless, most language teachers in the United States have been accustomed to use, in their teaching, concepts of language structure which are not completely scientific and which derive ultimately from a historical tradition that stems from the work of ancient Greek and Latin grammarians. Teachers of language have been prone to emphasize a normative rather than a descriptive point of view in talking about language.

The linguistic scientist, of course, is frequently a teacher of foreign languages, but in this role he is still primarily a linguistic scientist. A small number of language teachers have become sufficiently interested in linguistics to associate themselves with the Linguistic Society of America, an organization founded primarily in the interests of linguistic science.

To complete the list of specialties most closely associated with linguistics we must mention *philology*. In the sense of the term which is coming to be accepted in the United States, philology is the large middle ground between linguistic science, on the one hand, and the literary and humanistic studies, on the other. (In England, the term is more apt to refer to linguistic science as a whole, including philology in the American sense. It must also be noted that both in the United States and abroad the university department in which linguistics is pursued is often called a department of "comparative philology"; this is a reflection of the traditions of nineteenth-century scholarship out of which present-day linguistic science developed.) Philology is thus concerned with the linguistic aspects of literature and related art forms, as well as of cultural and social documents of various sorts. It attempts to interpret its materials in the light of linguistic history as well as in the light of the broader contexts of social and cultural history. The student of literature, the historian, or the archaeologist often finds it profitable to draw upon the results of linguistic science, especially in connection with the decipherment or interpretation of written documents from past ages. Philological studies also include those literary and cultural studies which are focused on major languages. For example, there is widespread interest in and study of the status of the English language and its dialects throughout the English-speaking world; these studies frequently pass beyond the purely structural interests of linguistic science, narrowly defined, and trace the development of the language in terms of cultural history. As another example of such studies, we may cite scholarly endeavors in the field of the Indic languages (for example, Sanskrit, Pali), where attention has been devoted to the interpretation of ancient religious documents.

The next broad group of pure and applied scientists who are concerned with language may be referred to as the *psychological* group. The *general* or *theoretical psychologist* is interested in describing and explaining human behavior in terms of broad theories and first principles. A major aspect of human behavior which cries out for such explanation is language behavior, and a majority of the great theoretical psychologists, from the time of Wundt, have given some account of speech and language in their theories. The *social psychologist* may become interested in language problems because of the importance he ascribes to communication in social interaction. The *child psychologist* finds the development of language and speech in the child one of his most interesting topics, and it is a curious fact that child psychologists have done much more with this problem than linguistic scientists. The *educational psychologist* is interested in language because of the overriding importance of language arts in contemporary education, from the teaching of reading and writing to the teaching of literary composition and foreign languages. The *psychometrician* is drawn into the picture when he tries to make tests of "verbal intelligence" or tests of achievement in various language arts. The *abnormal psychologist* and the *psychiatrist* meet problems of language in studying aphasia and the disordered speech of psychotics. For convenience, we shall classify the *speech pathologist* with the psychological group, because he is quite likely to have had considerable training in clinical psychology, neurology, etc. Similarly, we mention here those who are concerned with the education of the deaf and the blind, whose speech training involves peculiar difficulties. Recently, psychologists interested in acoustics and acoustic perception have become concerned with problems of language to a degree only equaled in the early history of modern psychology, when persons like E. W. Scripture were interested in experimental phonetics. Finally, it should be mentioned that there has existed in the psychological profession a group—a very small one at that—of individuals who are specifically interested in what they call the *psychology of language,* endeavoring to tie together a number of facts drawn from the various fields of psychology mentioned above. This group has recently been augmented by some of those who have been led to the study of language through their interests in acoustics, perception, and group communications; these latter have also been strongly influenced by the Wiener-Shannon theory of communication, and prefer to call their special interest the *psychology of communication.*

In general, psychological studies of language and communication have been marked by frequent failures to take proper account of the methods and results of linguistic science. But it is also true that few linguistic scientists are acquainted with the development of post-Watsonian psychology and have thus been somewhat handicapped in their attempts to discuss the psychological interpretation of linguistic phenomena. In the last two or three years, however, there have been a number of signs of increasing communication between linguists and psychologists.

4

A third broad group of specialists whose interests touch problems of linguistics is represented by what may be called the *social science* group. Strictly speaking, linguistic scientists belong in this group, for linguistics may be classed as a social science. Passing over linguistics, however, we would be inclined to mention anthropology as the social science most closely concerned with problems of language and communication. In fact, a major branch of present-day American linguistics developed primarily within anthropology. The anthropologist regards language as one of the cardinal aspects of culture—defining culture as a series of habits, customs, and attitudes of a particular tribal or national group. The anthropologist becomes interested in linguistic problems if only because it is frequently necessary for him to surmount the language barrier before being able to make an ethnographic description of a particular tribe, but having surmounted that barrier, he is likely to inquire into the possible interrelations between the language and other aspects of the culture pattern.

The sociologist, however, has thus far demonstrated surprisingly little interest in linguistic problems. He may pay lip service to the importance of communication in social interaction—in fact, a recently published textbook of social psychology (written by sociologists) lays considerable emphasis on language as a means of social control—but he seems to have shown, thus far, very little appreciation of the role of linguistic phenomena in the formation and differentiation of social groups.

The political scientist and the historian will occasionally meet problems of a linguistic nature, particularly when they are concerned with national origins and ethnic boundaries, or with the analysis of propaganda.

A fourth major group of specialists concerned with language problems, somewhat indirectly in this case, may be referred to as the *engineering group*. The history of this interest seems to have begun with the efforts of telephone and sound engineers to increase the suitability of various communications systems for the transmission of human speech. In the course of such efforts it became necessary to study the physical characteristics of speech sounds, and it was a natural development that sound engineers should attempt such projects as the synthesis of speech sounds by electronic means and the development of tests of speech intelligibility. It was only natural, also, that the engineer should have perceived the possibilities of developing various sorts of "linguistic machines," such as a machine for instantaneously converting human speech into a series of printed alphabetic symbols as the speech is emitted. Recently, communications engineers and mathematicians have developed a broad theory of communication, which is conceived to apply to any type of communication system whether organismic or mechanical. This theory of communication will be given considerable attention in later chapters of this book.

The last major group of individuals who are interested in language may be called the *philosophical* group. Some philosophers have addressed themselves to the metaphysical implications of language. Others have concerned themselves with symbolic logic as a kind of language. Still others are interested in linguistics as an exemplification of scientific method. Although the school of thought which was represented by Alfred Korzybski is not regarded as fully respectable in philosophical circles, we may note here, finally, that Korzybski's *general semantics* contains several attitudes and viewpoints which may have a place in linguistic theory, or if not that, at least a place in a general theory of communication.

Such is the varied assortment of specialists interested in the study of language and communication phenomena, a study which is beginning to emerge as one of the most fundamental disciplines in the psychological and social sciences—quite as important, for example, as the study of molecular physics in the natural and biological sciences.

Chapter 2 THE SCIENCE OF LINGUISTICS

LANGUAGE AND LINGUISTICS

Linguistics is the science of language; hence we had better start by trying to define language.

Suppose we go to some remote corner of the world and observe two persons conversing with one another. We ask ourselves whether these persons are speaking the same language. (This need not be the case; on a visit to the conclaves of the United Nations we happened to observe one delegate speaking in French and another replying in Russian.) We make a tape recording of the sounds we hear, and upon careful study of this recording it turns out that the sounds uttered by the two persons have at least some similarities. Though many of the sounds may seem strange to our ears, we can learn to recognize, fairly well, the vowels and consonants which occurred in the speech of our subjects. Suppose we find that the various vowels and consonants we recognize sound approximately the same no matter which one of our subjects is talking, and that they occur on the average with about the same frequencies. This would be partial evidence for concluding that the two persons are speaking the same language. But it is not enough: they might perchance be speaking two different languages with the same systems of elementary sounds (though this would be a rare case). We analyze our tape recording further and find that the sounds often occur in similar sequences; if we listen carefully to the breaks between these sequences we might conclude that our subjects use many "words" in common, and we would then have further evidence that they are speaking the same language. We could go on in this way, making increasingly detailed analyses. We should want to study how the longer sequences of sounds are put together; we would try to discover certain constancies or invariances in the structure of our subjects' utterances. We would probably have to go back to our subjects for further information. We might, for example, be able to get them to give us verbal responses to a number of common objects and situations, with a view to seeing whether their responses are similar. If we could find a high degree of similarity in their verbal responses, or at least a large number of common traits in their utterances, we would probably be justified in concluding that they are speaking the same language.

Let us consider several things about this observation.

First, the mere fact that our subjects seem to "understand one another" is no guarantee that they are speaking the same language. Mutual intelligibility is a necessary but not a sufficient condition for such a conclusion. We might have a situation in which the speakers are using two languages, but in which each speaker understands the language of the other. Our conclusion that the same language is being used must emerge from our finding that a high degree of similarity, in some sense, is manifested in the utterances of the two speakers.

Second, the utterances do not have to be similar in all respects. Even the elementary sounds which we ordinarily call vowels and consonants may vary slightly in their acoustical properties, and certainly the total utterances of the two speakers will rarely be found to be even approximately parallel. It is only when we find that these utterances are in most respects *structured* according to the same self-consistent *system* that we can conclude that they are in the same language.

Third, we might find that the utterances of one or both of our speakers occasionally depart from the self-consistent *system* we have discovered. We might suspect, in such a case, that our speakers are occasionally making "quotations" from still another language, just as we do when we use a French or Latin phrase in our English speech, or when we utter a foreign surname (like Turgenev, for example, particularly if we give it the Russian pronunciation) which does not pattern itself like English names. There would be enough self-consistency in the bulk of the utterances to enable us to spot such "quotations" from another language and lay them aside.

Fourth, let us notice that the discovery that two speakers are using the same language does not imply that we would necessarily find any other human beings using this language. Our two subjects might have developed this language themselves, or they might be the last remaining speakers of a moribund language. Whatever the case, the system we have discovered would still be a language. As a matter of fact, everyone knows of languages without speakers currently living, but ancient Greek or ancient Hittite can still be called languages.

Finally, we might ask ourselves whether our two subjects are merely uttering structured nonsense. The test of this would be to see whether they verbally respond in any similar and consistent way to certain objects and situations, whether their verbal responses represent discriminations between various aspects of their physical environment, and finally whether the speakers are in any sense able to control differentially each other's behavior in ways depending on their use of structured verbal responses. If these things are found to be the case, we can say that the language common to the two speakers has a symbolic, communicative function. A structured system of verbal responses would not be a language unless it has a symbolic, communicative function. Of course, there is hardly any reason for such a system to be structured unless it is to be used for communication.

One may rightly ask why we have introduced *two* speakers in our illustration. It is true that a language can be a system possessed by only one person. (He could have invented it for his own purposes, assigning his own arbitrary symbolic functions of the language.) Furthermore, it is possible to make an analysis of a language system solely on the basis of the utterances of a single informant; in fact, this has often been done. Nevertheless, there is much reason to believe that the symbolic function of a language arises only by social facilitation—that the elements of a language system come to have symbolic functions only by virtue of the discriminative verbal responses of two or more human beings who desire to influence each other's behavior in various ways. The users of a common language system constitute the *speech community* of that language. All the major languages of the world have, or have had at some time, a speech community of considerable extent. It is characteristic of a language system to correspond to a certain speech community, represented in the present illustration by our two speakers. There can of course be such a thing as a speech community consisting of one speaker, but this is usually a historical residue from a larger speech community. Even the man who invents a new artificial language does so by virtue of the verbal habits he has acquired in a larger speech community.

A language is never perfectly uniform throughout a speech community of two or more persons; as the speech community gets larger, there is likely to be less uniformity. Indeed, each member of a speech community may be said to possess his own *idiolect,* his own personal variety of the language system. A single individual will often possess several idiolects, to be used as the situation demands—for example, one for talking to contemporaries and one for talking to children. (Of course, such idiolects would have their parallels in other speakers.) Furthermore, the various members of the speech community will not possess *all* the linguistic items which properly belong to the language; for example, large numbers of people in the English speech community do not use or even recognize the meanings of many words which are used by the educated classes or by members of specialized trades and occupations. All these items, however, are structured according to the patterns which are characteristic of the English language. The learned word *psychoanalytic,* for example, contains sounds which are characteristic of other, more common English words; its syllabic structure and its accentuation follow usual patterns; and from the standpoint of word order it falls into sentence positions at least partially similar to those of numerous common words like *good, proper, lovely,* etc. The abstracted system of common traits in the idiolects of all members of a speech community, then, is what we call a language. If we find certain members of a speech community whose idiolects resemble each other rather more than they resemble those of other members of a speech community, we say that their system of common linguistic traits constitutes a *dialect.*

We are now ready to essay a formal definition of a language, if we bear in mind the various issues raised in the foregoing discussion.

A language is a structured system of arbitrary vocal sounds and sequences of sounds which is used, or can be used, in interpersonal communication by an aggregation of human beings, and which rather exhaustively catalogs the things, events, and processes in the human environment. The sounds and sequences of sounds are arbitrary only in the sense that they have no inherent or necessary connections with the things to which they are said to "refer," or to the situations or contexts in which they are used— these connections having been established only by specific processes of learning.

It will be observed that this definition of language excludes nonvocal acts such as gestures and pantomimic responses. Though such acts may

10

often be structured somewhat as vocal responses are, and though they may perform a communicative function which parallels or supplements that of verbal acts, they are as a matter of definition not included in language. (We may, however, speak of *gesture language* by a transferred meaning of the term language.) Our definition also excludes any system of written or printed symbols which may be used to represent the possible utterances of a language. (Here we must speak of *the system of writing language X;* particularly to be avoided is any suggestion that a language may be equated to a system of writing.)

We reserve the term language, as a general rule, to refer to a system which "rather exhaustively catalogs the things, events, and processes in the human environment." This restriction excludes such special "languages" as the "language" of chess—a system which permits one to communicate only in reference to the moves of pieces on a chessboard. In contrast, natural languages like English, French, Chinese, and even artificial languages like Esperanto, permit one to communicate with reference to nearly everything in one's environment and experience. The number of truly ineffable things is surely small; perhaps there is nothing that cannot be formulated in language in some manner.

If we define a *semeiotic system* as any system of signs which can be used in some communicative function—however broad or restricted that function may be—we see that a language, as we have defined it above, is merely one type of semeiotic system, but a most important type. Gesture and writing constitute other types of semeiotic systems, even though they may be, and usually are, connected intimately with language. Systems of mathematical notation and the "language" of chess constitute still other examples of semeiotic systems.

We can now say what is meant by *linguistics* by stating that it is the scientific enterprise of investigating the languages and dialects which are in use, or have been used, by various speech communities throughout the world. The analysis of a language system is possible only by examining and comparing actual manifestations of language as represented by samples of speech or text, but the end result is a description of the "linguistic code" which more or less uniformly manifests itself in all verbal communications or messages observable in the speech community. The distinction between the language system (*la langue*) and the manifestation of that system in

11

the speech of particular individuals (*la parole*) was emphasized by the Swiss linguist Ferdinand de Saussure (1916),* who pointed out that linguistics is concerned primarily with *la langue,* the language system.

The subject matter of linguistics, so defined, has far-reaching ramifications, but for several reasons the field has had to be kept within certain confines. And there are inevitably certain matters of emphasis within this field of investigation. It must be made clear that we are here describing the field of linguistics as it has actually developed. A number of linguistic scientists have indicated possible expansions of the field, many of these overlapping considerably with allied fields such as philosophy, psychology, and anthropology, but such expansions must be regarded as justified only if their development depends inherently upon the concept of structure which is central in scientific linguistics.

First of all, the linguist limits his field of inquiry by refusing to be concerned, except in a rather indirect way, with the content of the communication, that is, "what is being talked about." The linguist is not interested in *what* is communicated; he is interested primarily in the *vehicle* of communication, that is, the language system. If he became concerned with the content of communication, he would in effect be concerned with the totality of human knowledge.

Secondly, the linguist limits his field by refusing to inquire into the mechanisms, psychological or otherwise, whereby human beings are able to use linguistic symbols; nor does the linguist ask about their motivations in making any particular utterance. To put the matter in common-sense terms, the linguist is not interested in what an individual is talking about or why he wants to talk at all but only in the fact that what is said is cast in a certain culturally determined mold, that mold being the language of the individual's speech community.

A third limitation which the linguist usually imposes on himself arises from the way he defines language. Of the various types of communication which are observed in human societies—communication by sequences of speech sounds, by visual symbols, by signaling and gesturing, or by other means—the linguist has concluded that the most important for his purposes is communication by sequences of speech sounds. Other types of semeiotic systems have been regarded as either primitive, "nonstructured" sets of

*Dates in parentheses are used to refer to the References (pp. 246ff.).

signals, or as systems which have developed out of, and by virtue of, speech systems. Thus, the linguist is likely to become concerned with the written or orthographic accompaniments of a living language system, for example, only after the phonetic characteristics of the spoken language have been thoroughly investigated. Even when a linguist is investigating the structure of a "dead" language which can be studied only from written records, he tries to discover what the spoken form of the language must have been, and draws on principles and results developed in connection with the study of living languages.

Since the linguist is first of all a social *scientist,* he is not immediately concerned with normative aspects of communication. He does not try to evaluate how things *should* be said, what grammatical constructions *should* be used, or how words *should* be pronounced. He only observes the way people actually say things, the grammatical constructions which they actually use, and the way they actually pronounce words. His interest in prescribing norms extends only to suggesting how greater stability and efficiency of communication may be achieved in a linguistic system.

The narrowing of attention to language as a system of spoken communication may have been unfortunate, in that the study of gesture and other nonlinguistic semeiotic systems related to language has thus far been slighted. The study of spoken communication systems is in itself a tremendous task and linguists may perhaps be excused for not taking full account of other forms of communicative behavior.

Nevertheless, throughout the modern era of scholarship, writing systems have received considerable attention. It was early realized that systems of written symbols may have a status and structure of their own, in some ways dependent on the spoken language system, in other ways independent of it. It is only in recent years, however, that renewed emphasis has been placed on this notion; examination of a recent article by Bolinger (1946) will give some idea of the possibilities of investigating writing systems from this standpoint. While the study of vocal sounds plays a very large role in language investigations, the study of writing systems is therefore certainly not precluded in linguistics, if only because of the close parallels between writing and linguistic systems. This branch of linguistics has been termed *graphemics* by some linguists, and *graphonomy* by others (Hockett, 1951b). Gelb (1952) has written an important work on the genetic stages manifested by writing systems, and Diringer's (1948) study of the alphabet is already regarded as a classic.

Studies of gesture and other semeiotic systems are also not precluded in linguistics, particularly when their relations to spoken language responses are investigated. The methods of linguistics can be carried over to such studies in a surprisingly detailed manner, as has recently been shown by Birdwhistell (1952) in his studies of what he calls *kinesics,* which is equated to the study of all nonvocal bodily movements which may play a part in communication.[1]

Essentially, linguistics is a sort of logical calculus, although the analogy must not be pushed too far. It is concerned with the identification of linguistic symbols, with the discovery of the ways in which these symbols can be arranged in a temporal sequence, and to some extent with the conditions under which these symbols are used in communication. In some branches of linguistics, these symbols and their arrangements are also studied from a historical point of view.

The central concept in linguistic analysis is *structure,* by which is meant the ordered or patterned set of contrasts or oppositions which are presumed to be discoverable in a language, whether in the units of sound, the grammatical inflections, the syntactical arrangements, or even the meanings of linguistic forms.

Although the primary business of linguistics is to describe language structures and trace their development from a historical and comparative point of view, linguistics is also an explanatory science. Linguists wish to determine why sounds and meanings change and how linguistic structures develop. They are concerned also, to the extent that their data may be relevant, with some of the broader issues about language in general, such as the origin of language, the effects of language on behavior, and the relation between language and culture. They desire to arrive at a number of general statements about language as a phenomenon of human society, and to discover satisfactory means for classifying and typing language structures. Some of these broader issues will be discussed in this chapter; others will be treated in later chapters as the primary concerns of other disciplines.

Two classical treatments of linguistics from the standpoint of the American school (if we may speak of a number of loosely interrelated approaches as a "school") are Sapir's *Language* (1921) and the book with the same title by Bloomfield (1933). The chapter headings in Sapir's book are as follows: Introductory: Language Defined; The Elements of Speech; The Sounds of Language; Form in Language: Grammatical Processes; Form in Language: Grammatical Concepts; Types of Linguistic Structure; Language as a Historical Product: Drifts; Language as a Historical Product: Phonetic Laws; How Languages Influence Each Other; Language, Race, and Culture; Language and Literature. Bloomfield's book covers a similar scope but it is a more systematic and modern treatment. For the advanced student, Harris's *Methods in Structural Linguistics* (1951) provides the most comprehensive exposition of contemporary analytic techniques in America; there have, of course, been many striking methodological developments since the publication of Bloomfield's book. Other general works to which the reader may be referred are Sturtevant's *Introduction to Linguistic Science* (1947), Bloch and Trager's relatively brief *Outline of Linguistic Analysis* (1942), and R. A. Hall, Jr.'s popularized exposition *Leave Your Language Alone!* (1950). L. H. Gray's *Foundations of Language* (1939) is written primarily from the point of view of historical linguistics, with relatively little attention to descriptive linguistics. Among the important general works and texts which have appeared abroad are the following: Ferdinand de Saussure, *Cours de Linguistique Générale* (1916); Antoine Meillet, *Linguistique Historique et Linguistique Générale* (1921–1938); Jespersen, *Language, its Nature, Development and Origin* (1922); Firth, *The Tongues of Men* (1937); and Tagliavini, *Introduzione alla Glottologia* (1949). Ullmann's popularly written *Words and Their Use* (1951a) is a useful introduction to semantic problems of language; his *Principles of Semantics* (1951b) is a more comprehensive treatment. A generally sound, though brief, account of linguistics written by one who is not himself a technical linguist is McGalliard's essay in Foerster's *Literary Scholarship* (1941).

THE HISTORY OF LINGUISTICS

It is an often-stated truism that the history of almost any major intellectual development in Western culture can be traced back to the Greeks of classical times, and this is the case in linguistics.

Early Greek philosophers were concerned with the question of whether language exists in the very nature of things and therefore is fundamentally regular and logical, or whether it is simply an arbitrary set of symbols with frequent irregularities and logical faults. Despite Socrates' able discussion of the latter view, as recorded in Plato's *Cratylus,* the former view seemed to have prevailed. Several Greek grammarians, notably Dionysius Thrax, Apollonius Dyscolus, and Herodian, developed descriptive grammars of Greek. Unfortunately these works were sometimes colored by an undue emphasis on a philosophical interpretation of linguistic phenomena and a reverence for Greek as an ideal and fundamentally logical language. Latin grammarians, taught by the Greeks, took over, in the main, the models provided them by Greek grammar, sometimes describing Latin in the same categories even when these categories did not exist in Latin. This is the sort of traditional grammar which, incidentally, has come down to the present day and influenced present-day teaching. In English grammars used in our schools not so long ago, it is possible to find such a declension as the following:

Nominative	"the man"
Genitive	"of the man"
Dative	"(to) the man"
Accusative	"the man"
Ablative	"from the man, by the man, etc."

The categories represented by such a declension have little validity in English.

In about the third century B.C., or earlier, a remarkable development took place in India, quite independently of the work of the Greek grammarians. A Hindu grammarian, Pāṇini, performed the feat of writing a purely descriptive, nonphilosophical account of the Sanskrit language. How much scholarly work must have preceded this feat, we do not know, but Pāṇini's grammar is still regarded as one of the most comprehensive descriptive grammars of any language. It had only indirect influence on the development of Western linguistics until Sanskritist scholars raised it to a position of eminence in the nineteenth century (Bopp, 1816; Böhtlingk, 1887).

In Western culture the study of language proceeded in a relatively unscientific way through the Byzantine era, the period of medieval scholasticism, and even into the days of the Renaissance and the Reformation.

16

Latin replaced Greek as the ideal language, a thing God-given and to be revered. Language was an object of study by philosophers, who advanced what now seem fantastic theories of the origin of language such as the "bow-wow" and "pooh-pooh" theories.[2] The "bow-wow" theory, for example, proposed that language began in man's attempt to imitate animals. During this prescientific period, attempts were made to trace the origin of particular words. Word etymologies were proposed in a rather capricious fashion. When the study of Hebrew and Arabic came into vogue in the late Renaissance, a serious attempt was made to show that various words in modern languages were derived from Hebrew. Such an attempt may not have seemed unreasonable at that time, in view of the validity that was then attached to Biblical writings which said that Noah's sons peopled the world, but what the modern linguist objects to in these early efforts is their unscientific procedure. Such etymological fantasies have their parallels even in recent times; the writer recalls having seen a book, published in the early twentieth century, which proposed that the Maya language of Yucatan shows remarkable similarities to Hebrew, hence suggesting that the Maya people were descended from one of the lost tribes of Israel. Capricious and unscientific etymologizing seems to be a perennial habit of the human race. The most recent example of pseudo science in etymology is a book by Samuel Reiss, *The Rise of Words and Their Meanings* (1950), which purports to show that all words of all languages have an underlying kinship.

The era of discovery and exploration brought new knowledge about the languages of the world. Travelers and missionaries wrote grammars and dictionaries of languages they found in Africa, America, and other parts of the world. There was no science of linguistics, or even of articulatory phonetics, to aid them in recording and describing these strange languages. Some of these layman-linguists did remarkably well, considering the materials available to them. Jonathan Edwards's (1788) observations on the Indian languages of Massachusetts are still, *faute de mieux*, useful material for the present-day student of Algonkian linguistics. Around the turn of the nineteenth century there appeared several collections of oddly assorted linguistic materials from the four corners of the globe. As a linguistic curiosity, we may cite the treatise which appeared in the years 1806–1817 under the title *Mithridates*, by Adelung and Vater, which contained the Lord's Prayer in nearly 500 languages.

Despite the panoply of material which was now at hand, few scholars up to the end of the eighteenth century had begun to perceive the possibilities of making any careful scientific examination of these data. It remained for Sir William Jones, in an address delivered in 1786, to point out the possible existence of a great family of Indo-European languages, including Greek, Latin, Sanskrit, Germanic, and Celtic branches. This suggestion of Jones was soon followed by the scholarly work of Bopp, Rasmus Rask, Grimm, and Pott in the early nineteenth century. That century was the heyday of historical comparative linguistics, a period which began with the formulation of what are known as Grimm's laws and culminated in the publication of Brugmann and Delbrück's *Outline of the Comparative Grammar of the Indo-European Languages* (1886–1900). The latter work, at the time of its publication, may have seemed to have left few stones unturned in the domain of Indo-European comparative linguistics. Even today, however, Indo-European studies constitute a relatively fertile field, for at least two reasons: (*a*) recent developments in scientific methodology make it possible to clarify or revise earlier conclusions, and (*b*) recent archaeological and other discoveries have brought to light new materials bearing on the Indo-European languages, for example, materials in two varieties of Tocharian (Central Asia) and in Hittite and other early languages of Asia Minor.

Concurrently with nineteenth-century studies of the Indo-European language family, and not intimately related to them at all, a philosophical-descriptive stream of studies emerged. Western scholars were for the first time exposed to the descriptive methods of the Hindu grammarian Pāṇini, and, influenced either directly or indirectly by Pāṇini, began to produce descriptive and historical studies of a variety of non-Indo-European languages (Friedrich Müller, 1876–1888; Finck, 1910). Significant general treatises on language were written by von Humboldt (1836–1839), Steinthal (1860), and von der Gabelentz (1891). The psychological study of language was given an impetus by Wundt with the publication of his treatise on language, as the first part of a series of volumes on social psychology (1900–1909). Toward the middle of the nineteenth century, the first systematic treatments of articulatory phonetics appeared, and the physicist and psychologist von Helmholtz (1863) may be regarded as one of the founders of acoustic phonetics. Kempelen (1791) and Willis (1830) are two other men who deserve to be mentioned in connection with early phonetic studies.

The development of any area of study is a continuous process. In few instances do there occur any great spurts or marked turning points. It is certainly difficult to find such turning points in linguistics. Nevertheless, one gets the impression that the close of the nineteenth century marked the end of a long chapter of linguistic science and paved the way for the development of linguistic science in the twentieth century. This was true both in America and in Europe. Perhaps Bloomfield has best summarized the status of linguistics at the end of the nineteenth century: "The merging of these two streams of study, the historical-comparative and the philosophical-descriptive, has made clear some principles that were not apparent to the great Indo-Europeanists of the nineteenth century, as represented, say, by Hermann Paul. All historical study of language is based upon the comparison of two or more sets of descriptive data. It can be only as accurate and only as complete as these data permit it to be" (1933, p. 19). The European linguist who best formulated the methodology of descriptive linguistics as it had developed up to his time and who was most influential among later students was Ferdinand de Saussure, whose lectures were assembled by his students and published under the title *Cours de Linguistique Générale* (1916).

Toward the end of the nineteenth century, there was advanced and developed a principle of linguistic analysis which has made possible the refined descriptions of language which are now the rule. This concept was that of the *phoneme*. The two men primarily responsible for the original development of the concept were the Russian linguists Baudouin de Courtenay and his student Kruszewski (see Kruszewski, 1881); the subsequent developments took place largely among linguists of the so-called Prague circle (Jakobson, 1928; Trubetskoy, 1939a). We shall look at the concept of the phoneme later on, indicating its importance for linguistic analysis and attempting to demonstrate that it has an application which goes beyond the identification of the elementary distinctive sounds of a language—the sphere in which it was originally conceived.

The tradition of American linguistics may be said to have started with William Dwight Whitney, who lived from 1827 to 1894 and was professor of Sanskrit at Yale College. His principal works, *Language and the Study of Language* (1867) and *The Life and Growth of Language* (1874), have had wide influence both in America and in Europe, and are well worth reading even today.

It remained for European-trained Franz Boas of Columbia University to set the stage for the development of a modern linguistic science in America. From 1897 to 1908, Boas collected materials on American Indian languages for a revision of Powell's *Introduction to the Study of Indian Languages* (Powell, 1880); the resulting volumes, *Handbook of American Indian Languages* (Boas, 1911–1922) contained a magnificent introduction which is still regarded as a remarkably acute discussion of the problems of descriptive linguistics.[3]

The history of American linguistics since Boas's first works on language is the history of the influence of two great men, Edward Sapir and Leonard Bloomfield. These men were in a very real sense complementary to one another. Sapir, on the one hand, was blessed with great insight and breadth of interest. He could be rigorous where rigor was needed, but rigor and devotion to a theoretical framework were the hallmarks of Bloomfield's work, characterized also, particularly in his later years, by a stark refusal to consider broader problems as a part of linguistic science. Sapir exerted a tremendous influence through his teaching, having many students who are now to be found at nearly every major university in the United States which supports linguistic studies. Bloomfield exerted his influence chiefly through his writings. Sapir did work in a very wide variety of languages, especially in American Indian languages. Bloomfield's practical work was confined largely to his studies of Algonkian and Tagalog, though he had a specialist's knowledge of problems in Indo-European linguistics.

Most of Sapir's principal writings, covering a broad territory which ranged from technical linguistic problems to musical criticism, have been conveniently assembled in one volume (Mandelbaum, 1949). Bloomfield's chief works were two general treatises on language (1914, 1933) and several shorter monographs, such as *Linguistic Aspects of Science* (1939).

In the recent history of American linguistics, there has been a marked efflorescence, not only in the volume of work accomplished and in the number of personnel added to the field, but also in the refinement of method. These developments have been partly due to various circumstances associated with World War II, such as government-sponsored language-teaching programs, but they have also come about owing to the continued influence of the sound methodological foundations laid down by Sapir and Bloom-field.

Although the present work is concerned primarily with American linguistics, something should be said about the similarities and contrasts between American schools of linguistics, on the one hand, and European schools of thought, on the other. American linguistics in the traditions of Sapir, Bloomfield, and now Harris, is characterized by an outlook which emphasizes the rigorous application of basic concepts, both in descriptive and in historical work. Such concepts include the phoneme, the morpheme, and other units of linguistic analysis which Bloomfield utilized to build a general theory of linguistic structure. Linguistic analysis is regarded as a logical calculus which involves the discovery of the basic units of a language and their formal arrangements, a procedure which can in principle be pursued without any reference to the external meanings of linguistic forms. There often seems to be a compulsion to carry such a procedure to its logical conclusion, even when the results may seem somewhat absurd from a common-sense point of view. (Usually, the absurdities clear up in further theoretical developments.)

When an American linguist sets out to publish a description of a language, the first half dozen pages are occupied by a systematic exposition of the phonemes of the language, the phonetic alternants or allophones, and the morphophonemics. This is followed by a treatment of the morphology and the syntax of the language. All of this looks quite formidable. One American linguist told the writer that though this manner of presentation is good in principle, it tends to frustrate the reader. At the end of the first dozen pages or so one feels like saying, "Just show me a sentence or two in this language!"

It is impossible to characterize European schools of linguistics in any neat phrase. There are, of course, a number of diverse trends, as in America. The influence of the Prague circle is still felt in many quarters, even though the Prague circle itself no longer exists as such. Descriptive linguistics is strongly emphasized in a number of European countries, notably Holland and the Scandinavian countries; historical and comparative linguistics, particularly as applied to the Indo-European family, continues to receive much attention. But it may be said, perhaps, that European linguists have devoted even more attention to theoretical questions than have American linguists. The Danish linguist Hjelmslev, for example, has developed a new theory of linguistics called *glossematics* (Hjelmslev, 1943; see also Martinet, 1946). In any case, European linguistics covers a vast territory. It is increasingly active, and if anything, the interests of European linguists are broader than those of American linguists. There are perhaps ten or more periodicals in Europe devoted primarily to general linguistics, as compared to only three or four in America.[4]

In the last year or two, there have been signs of a necessary and well-justified rapprochement, after a temporary lapse beginning in the thirties, between American and European linguistics. With the end of World War II and the consequent return of international communications to a nearly normal status, it became evident that recent developments in European linguistics in some ways paralleled those in America. In his 1950 presidential address before the Linguistic Society of America, Einar Haugen (1951) gently chided American linguists for their provincialism in thinking of linguistics in the tradition of Sapir and Bloomfield as the only sound linguistics. He pointed out that few American linguists had taken the trouble to compare the terminology of European linguists like Hjelmslev with their own, and that they had consequently failed to appreciate fully the extent to which the systems of discourse were similar. Hockett (1951a), at least, has pointed the way to a more balanced stock-taking of developments on both sides of the Atlantic. In a review of some published lectures by Martinet, Hockett gave credit to the advantages of Trubetskoy's system of phonology and defended it from the trivial criticisms leveled at it by certain American detractors. Whereas there had been considerable suspicion, on the part of American linguists, of the hypothesis of binary opposition, it is reported that at least some measure of agreement was achieved as the outcome of a series of lectures given by Roman Jakobson at the University of Michigan in the summer of 1951. American linguistics, for all that it has accomplished independently, should certainly seize any opportunity to achieve a broader synthesis of approaches; such an opportunity seems now to be afforded by the presence of a number of European scholars in America and by the increased availability of European publications.

A useful source of information on the history of linguistic science before the twentieth century is Pedersen's treatise (1931). Iordan's *Introduction to Romance Linguistics* (1937), which has a broader scope than its title might indicate, contains illuminating discussions of general linguistic theory in the nineteenth century. One other treatise on the history of linguistics (Milewski, 1947) is unfortunately in Polish, making it relatively inaccessible to most American students; it does, however, contain French summaries. As yet, there is no formal history of American linguistics. Some impression of recent trends and events can be gained from the obituaries of such men as Sapir (Swadesh, 1939) and Bloomfield (Bloch, 1949). Other valuable references are Bloomfield's article "Twenty-one Years of the Linguistic Society" (1946), the previously cited article by Haugen (1951), and a recent article by Hall (1951) on "American linguistics 1925-1950."

BRANCHES OF LINGUISTICS

The whole field of linguistics can be divided in a number of ways, depending upon one's vantage point. For example, it can be divided into branches corresponding to the major language families or areas of the world, so that we have Indo-European linguistics, American Indian linguistics, etc., or even into smaller subdivisions, such as Germanic linguistics, Algonkian linguistics, etc. But such a division of the field of linguistics merely reflects the fact that many linguists tend to specialize in the languages of one or two fairly restricted groups. Our concern here is with a subdivision of linguistics into a number of branches and subbranches corresponding to the types of content and method which are involved. All branches are related, however, and in many cases overlapping, so that the branches described below can be characterized only as foci of interest.

As we have already stated, the primary business of linguistics is to study the living and the recorded language systems of the world. This enterprise is usually considered under two major headings, *descriptive* linguistics and *historical,* or *comparative,* linguistics. Descriptive linguistics studies the characteristics of language systems or dialects at given points in their histories, while historical and comparative linguistics describes changes in language systems over periods of time and considers the familial and genealogical relationships of languages. A special branch of linguistics which often involves both descriptive (synchronic) and historical (diachronic) considerations is *linguistic geography,* which studies the characteristics and the geographic diffusion patterns of the various dialects of a language system.

Whether one is concerned with descriptive, historical-comparative, or geographical problems, one operates with a body of analytical methodology which may be considered under several headings, corresponding to the levels of analysis which may be undertaken:

(1) *Phonetics* is the science of the vocal sounds used in language systems; as applied in linguistic analysis, it usually takes the form of a description of the sounds of a language (vowels, semivowels, consonants, pitches or tones, stresses, and junctures) in terms of certain more or less standardized classificatory schemes which appeal to articulatory or to acoustic principles.

(2) *Phonemics,* as applied in linguistic analysis, pertains to the classification of the sounds of a language into those units of sound, called phonemes, which operate in making the essential perceptual distinctions between the possible utterances of a language.

(3) *Morphology* is the study of the manner in which words are constructed. More precisely, it is concerned with the identification of *morphemes,* their arrangements in words, and the changes in morphemes and their arrangements which take place in various grammatical constructions. Morphemes, composed of phonemes, may be roughly defined as the smallest units of structure which embody grammatical or lexical meanings. The study of morphology necessitates the discovery of form classes, that is, classes of morphemes or words which can serve in similar positions in utterances. These form classes will often correspond roughly to what are ordinarily called parts of speech.

(4) *Morphophonemics* is a branch of morphology which consists of statements about the ways in which the morphemes of a language are constituted from a phonemic point of view and about the phonemic variations in morphemes which are observed in different grammatical constructions.

(5) *Syntax* studies the manner in which sentences are constructed from words; it bears an intimate relation to morphology, however, because the morphological constructions of a language are usually greatly conditioned by syntactical arrangements, and because the building blocks of a sentence consist of words as members of form classes. Thus, the morphology and the syntax of a language are often treated together, or even as a single class of phenomena.

(6) *Lexicography,* in linguistic analysis, is the listing of all meaningful elements in the language system, with statements of their meanings or ver-

bal equivalences. It should be realized that the meaningful elements of a language include not only its words, such as are ordinarily listed in dictionaries, but also all morphemes which are not words, and in fact all other elements or grammatical features which carry some kind of meaning (such as gender, tense, case, aspect, etc.). A truly adequate lexicon of a language would have to list even the stress and intonation patterns of a language, together with an account of their meanings or (if the meanings depend on other structural features) their conditional meanings. It is also proper to state, in lists of morphemes and words, the form classes to which these belong.[5]

All that there is to do in studying language systems and their changes can in principle be done by the application of methodology in phonetics, phonemics, morphophonemics, morphology, syntax, and lexicography. The methodology used in historical and comparative studies is often called the *comparative method,* but this can be said to consist of a special aggregation of procedures from the basic methodological disciplines in linguistics, with the addition of temporal and spatial dimensions.

Beyond the study of particular language systems, linguistic scientists are also concerned with developing valid generalizations about all language systems. For example, the phonemic, morphological, or syntactical features of languages can be studied comparatively, whether these languages are familially related or not. This general comparison of the features of language systems has been called *general contrastive linguistics* by Trager (1949), but it might as well be thought of as the subject matter of *general linguistics,* divided into *general phonemics, general morphology,* etc. When one's interest centers in the classification of linguistic structures, one speaks of *linguistic typology.*

General phonetics, in fact, is virtually a science in its own right, with two chief branches, *motor phonetics* (or *articulatory phonetics*) and *acoustic phonetics.* The former is concerned with the physiological, articulatory aspects of speech-sound production; the latter studies the physical attributes of speech sounds. A third branch of phonetics, which might be called *perceptual phonetics,* is concerned with the characteristics of speech sounds as perceived by the hearer; this branch, however, has received less attention than the others. *Instrumental phonetics* is a term often used to denote those aspects of phonetics which are studied by means of physical instruments, such as the sound spectrograph or the x-ray camera. The term *experimental phonetics* is also sometimes used in this connection, but in some ways it is a misnomer, for many studies in instrumental phonetics utilize observational rather than truly experimental methods. (By an experimental method, we would understand a method which seeks to determine the effects of certain operations under controlled conditions.)

Until now, we have considered those branches of linguistics which are concerned with phenomena intrinsic to language systems as such. It may be presumed, however, that language systems bear relations to other cultural and social institutions and in general to the behavior of the human beings who use language systems. As we shall see, there has for many years been a persistent interest in such relations. Trager, in the paper cited above (1949), has proposed to term the study of these relations *metalinguistics*. To quote from Trager's own words:

Language has been indicated as being only one of the systematic arrangements of cultural items that societies possess. A culture consists of many such systems—language, social organization, religion, technology, law, etc. Each of these cultural systems other than language is dependent on language for its organization and existence, but otherwise constitutes an independent system whose patterning may be described. In theory, when one has arrived at the separate statements of each such cultural system, one can then proceed to a comparison with the linguistic system. The full statement of the point-by-point and pattern-by-pattern relations between the language and any of the other cultural systems will contain all the "meanings" of the linguistic forms, and will constitute the metalinguistics of that culture.

From this point of view all the special fields of social science, and of the so-called humanities, are special problems in metalinguistics. But this is not to say that they are not perfectly proper and independent fields of study in themselves. It is simply that certain of their fundamental statements and approaches can only be properly delimited in terms of a formulation based on the linguistic system. On the other hand, the statement of the meanings of linguistic forms is dependent on the formulations of other cultural systems than language, and the technical applications of linguistic analysis—such as language teaching and language learning, are largely metalinguistic.

The psychologist concerned with the learning process must necessarily be aware of that part of metalinguistics dealing with the relation of the linguistic system and its parts to the entities—material or nonmaterial—presented for learning. The political scientist deals constantly with metalinguistic data. The analyst of style or of art trends is doing metalinguistics, though badly and pre-scientifically. The logician and mathematician must be aware of certain metalinguistic data about linguistic systems to avoid being carried away into nonsense.

Metalinguistics is then a greatly expandable field of science which can come to serve as the means whereby linguistics, and language, can become the tool for the scientific description (= measurement) of all phenomena in the universe. Its data will serve to connect the physical and biological sciences on the one side with linguistics, and the latter with the other social sciences (and humanities) on the other side.

One may not agree with Trager in every respect, but the central ideas which he seems to stress are the following:

(a) Language embodies a way of describing, or talking with reference to, all aspects of the environment in which the speaker may find himself. The description of the meanings of linguistic forms must therefore involve reference to that environment, including the cultural environment. Since, in Trager's view, the study of language systems as such cannot embrace all problems of linguistic meaning (except in so far as differences in linguistic form correspond with differences in meaning), the making of statements about meaning properly falls within the province of metalinguistics.

(b) The very act of using language, whether in day-to-day routine behavior or in the pursuits of the physical, biological, and social sciences, depends in some way upon the structure of the linguistic code which is being used. The study of communicative behavior in general, and in particular the critique of scientific activities, must therefore take account of the linguistic codes which are inevitably involved in these behaviors. Perhaps linguistic codes have an effect in such kinds of activities as art, mathematics, logic, or religion.

Several questions may be raised about this definition of metalinguistics. First, does it go too far, and does it include too much territory? Let us agree that Trager's statement was intended as merely a description of an area of study, *not* as an arrogation of subject matter for linguistics, nor as a specification of the division of labor in science. For in that respect, metalinguistics would necessarily be an interdisciplinary field. From this point of view, metalinguistics does not seem too broadly defined. From another point of view, however, the definition is debatable. Trager seems to have fallen into the Bloomfieldian error of supposing that one cannot talk about meaning unless one has a complete scientific description of the objects, events, and relations to which linguistic forms refer (see Bloomfield, 1933, pp. 74–75, 139). While it may be true that to define the word *apple* we would like some comprehension of the scientific classification of the things to which the word refers, we do not have to know all about apples to state the meaning of the word. The fact that the words *pineapple* and *love apple* do not refer to kinds of apples can properly be commented on in metalinguistics, but it has no bearing on the scientific classification of plant forms. Meanings of linguistic forms can be stated by rephrasing in terms of other linguistic forms (as is done in a dictionary), or in various other ways which would not necessarily appeal to scientific description.

An even more basic assumption made by Trager is that the specification of linguistic meanings is not the proper business of descriptive linguistics, and that semantic considerations should be treated only in metalinguistics, where the relevant cultural and ethnological information can be brought to bear. The idea of such a division of labor is seductive, but completely fallacious and at all events unnecessary. A system of meanings, as we have previously stated, is intrinsic to the notion of a language system; therefore, to describe a language system is, among other things, to state its system of meanings, and this is always possible by the usual lexicographical procedures (translation into other words of the same language or into words of another language). As a matter of methodology, it is preferable to attempt the isolation of linguistic elements purely by reference to their distributional characteristics, that is, without reference to their meanings, but to describe a language without at some point stating its meanings is to set up a code book without a key.

There remains the question of whether it is dangerous to specify meanings before cultural and ethnological data have been considered. Actually, the large majority of high-frequency linguistic forms in the languages of the world refer to experiences which are common to the whole human race; for the remainder, the special cultural denotations are readily translatable into the common experiences of other peoples. Meanings can and should be stated in descriptive linguistics; as a matter of fact, they usually are—witness almost any descriptive grammar of a foreign language. It may even be postulated that meanings (in the sense of verbal equivalences) could be determined by distributional analysis, perhaps by methods of what Harris (1952) calls *discourse analysis.*

It cannot be denied, however, that the further study and analysis of meanings with reference to cultural systems can be fruitful; such study and analysis can be regarded, if one chooses, as in the province of metalinguistics.

One may also take exception to Trager's statement that "all the special fields of social science, and of the so-called humanities, are special problems in metalinguistics." It is true that the social sciences and the humanities all involve linguistic problems to an extent which has not been fully appreciated; nevertheless, not all statements in these disciplines concern behaviors or phenomena which are necessarily dependent on language structure or language meanings. While the statements themselves may be verbal, they are rather freely convertible into equivalent, but different, verbal statements; they are usually translatable into other languages, or sometimes into statistical, graphic, or other nonverbal representations. Any fair-minded social scientist or humanist will be able to perceive the relevance of linguistics for his own pursuits, but he should not be pushed to admit that his work is merely a special variety of metalinguistics. (The writer, as a psychologist, will vouch for the soundness of this judgment in the case of social psychology.)

Let us therefore agree to restrict "metalinguistics" to studies of cultural systems or behavior patterns which show special correspondences with language structure and language meanings. For such studies there is a great need, and it is well that Trager has proposed a term to cover them. In this sense, metalinguistics represents a return to the kinds of interests which Sapir so fruitfully explored.[6]

Several linguists (for example, Haugen, 1951, p. 212) have pointed out the need for replacing the term "metalinguistics" with a term which would not lead to confusion with its present use by philosophers in referring to "a theory of languages about languages." One term which has been proposed is *exolinguistics,* the prefix suggesting that one is dealing with something which stems out of linguistics but which is not identical with linguistics.[7] I shall use this term, rather than metalinguistics, throughout the remainder of this book.

CURRENT TRENDS IN THE METHODOLOGY OF DESCRIPTIVE LINGUISTICS

General Remarks

It is safe to say that the science of linguistics is in a well-developed stage, so far as methodology is concerned. The methodology of descriptive linguistics evolved slowly but surely in the nineteenth century; with the wide acceptance of the concept of the phoneme in the early twentieth century and the publication of Bloomfield's general treatise *Language* (1933), descriptive linguistics in America entered its mature phase. Bloomfield's book is in many ways a remarkable work. By 1933, a sufficient variety of data and observations had accumulated to enable Bloomfield to construct, almost singlehanded, a comprehensive and systematic theory for the methodology of linguistic analysis. True, the concept of phoneme had been well explored by others, but it was primarily Bloomfield who elaborated techniques of analyzing higher linguistic units such as the morpheme, the tagmeme, and so forth. Even now, Bloomfield's work is regarded by many linguists as far in advance of the times. At one sweep, he set forth conclusions as to the details of linguistic methodology which are even now being finally verified. There may be certain detailed questions on which linguists have not yet reached agreement, but the essential framework for settling these arguments is to be found in Bloomfield's procedures.

Since the publication of Bloomfield's work in 1933, theoretical discussions among linguists have been largely on matters of refinement, for example, on terminological questions, or on problems of the classification of certain theoretical concepts. A very recent authoritative treatment of the methodology of linguistic analysis, with numerous expansions and modifications of Bloomfield's techniques, is that by Harris (1951).

One test of a scientific methodology is the extent to which it achieves consistent results in the hands of different scientists. Let us look at linguistic methodology from this point of view.

It can be confidently stated that linguistic methodology is so well advanced today that if we took two fairly bright graduate students, trained them in linguistic analysis at two different universities, and sent them out to make descriptions of a new and unanalyzed language at two different times and using two different informants (assuming the informants spoke the same dialect), the resulting analyses would be highly similar, differing only in matters of emphasis and minor detail.[8] Objective tests of this assertion have probably never been made, because trained linguists are too much in demand and there are too many languages which remain to be recorded and analyzed, but the evidence points strongly to such a conclusion. The Navaho language has been independently studied by a number of linguists, for example, but no startling discrepancies in their analyses have turned up.

The methodology of descriptive linguistics has been developed in such a way that it is no longer an art in any sense, but simply a matter of intelligently following a number of definite operational procedures.

What happens when linguistic analysis is attempted by untrained persons, without the aid of a rigorous methodology, can be seen in the often divergent and unsatisfactory accounts of American Indian languages made by travelers and missionaries in the eighteenth and nineteenth centuries. Their phonetic and grammatical descriptions were too often colored by unconscious biases and false preconceptions stemming from the characteristics of their native tongues or from their training in traditional grammar. The misguided analyses which even today are occasionally undertaken by untrained persons are usually of little use to linguistic scientists. We make this point only because of the common belief that any educated person can make a study of a language; after all, in a field like chemistry few nonspecialists would claim competence in making a chemical analysis.

We would not wish to imply that methodology is a finished chapter of linguistics. The basic procedures for describing the sounds of a language, and for identifying the phonemes and morphemes, have been fairly well worked out, but there still remain questions of detail, and even some questions of basic theory. When we get to the study of some of the higher units of a language, by which we mean the units involved in the systematic arrangement of forms, theory has advanced more slowly. There are a number of reasons for this. It has been thought necessary to develop the methodology for the study of the smaller units first; once the smaller units have been identified, the way is open to the study of the higher units. A second reason is that the data which have to be collected for the study of the larger units of a language are more unwieldy. A page or two of running phonetic text would provide illustrations of practically all the phonemics and a considerable portion of the morphology of a language, but it would yield only a moderate sample of the possible variety of syntactical constructions characteristic of the language. A third reason for lack of progress is the relatively great complexity of the higher units of linguistic structure.

A general characteristic of the methodology of descriptive linguistics, as practiced by many American linguists today, is the effort to analyze linguistic structure without reference to meaning. It is thought possible in theory that one could identify the phonemes and morphemes of a language purely on the basis of their distribution, that is, by noting the linguistic environments in which they occur. Such a type of analysis would be desirable, it is thought, because unconscious biases might lead one to prejudge the analysis if one makes references to meanings. Harris offers procedures which place "stress on distribution rather than meaning in setting up the morphemes" (1951, p. 3); he presumes that "any two morphemes A and B having different meanings also differ somewhere in distribution: there are some environments in which one occurs and the other does not" (p. 7 fn.). Thus, to Harris, the use of meaning in linguistic analysis is only a hit-or-miss, intuitive short cut which can always be replaced, if rigor is desired, by distributional procedures. Nevertheless, for Harris, distributional analysis is used only up to the point of identifying linguistic entities and features. After they are identified, their linguistic meanings can be sought. This is indeed what Fries (1952) has tried to do in his analysis of English structure; he has identified English form classes primarily on distributional grounds, but he has then attempted to specify the "structural meanings" which are conveyed by these form classes.

In practical linguistic work, it is recognized by most linguists that the meanings of linguistic forms need to be taken account of in building up the structural analysis of a language. Voegelin (1948), for example, points out that *differences* of meaning help us to designate the phonemes of a language, and that *equivalences* of meaning help us to determine the morphemes. In field work, the linguist often asks his informant whether two forms are the same or different, either in sound or in meaning. He will also ask the informant about the circumstances in which the forms are used, and he may listen to the informant holding a conversation. For all the emphasis that some linguists have put, as a matter of theory, upon the analysis of linguistic structure apart from its meanings, these same linguists have put at least an equal emphasis on getting meanings and behavioral and cultural correlates, when studying a language in the field. It is a natural step for a linguistic fieldworker to concern himself with lexicography.

Methodology in Phonetics

Motor phonetics was well established in the nineteenth century by the time Sievers's *Grundzüge der Lautphysiologie* (1876) and Sweet's *Handbook of Phonetics* (1877) were published. The major achievements since then are represented by further standardization of phonetic alphabets and by refinements in the description of sounds. Progress has been stimulated by the discovery of a very wide variety of speech sounds in the various languages of the world. Pike's *Phonetics* (1943) is widely regarded as one of the best contemporary treatments of this subject; a recent handbook appearing in Europe is Dieth's *Vademekum der Phonetik* (1950).

Acoustic phonetics was also fairly well established in the nineteenth century. Major advances in acoustic phonetics have been made only recently, however, attendant upon the availability of electronic means of sound analysis and sound production. Joos's monograph, *Acoustic Phonetics* (1948), reports the first attempt by a linguist to use in acoustic phonetics a recently developed instrument known as the sound spectrograph. The sound spectrograph, in its commercial form, is an instrument which makes it readily possible to display on a time base the distribution of energy over the sound-frequency spectrum (up to, say, 4000 cycles per second) in an utterance lasting 2.4 seconds. Sound spectrography promises to yield important results for linguistic analysis. As will be shown in Chapter 7, communications engineers are making significant contributions to this presently very active field.

Methodology in Phonemics

If we examine a series of utterances by the speakers of a language, we note that some segments of these utterances are similar. If we carry our analysis down to the smallest units which can be recognized as similar, we may be able to identify a *class* of sounds all of which are similar. It is held that no two sounds heard in an utterance are ever exactly similar. Nevertheless, the sounds which may be put together in a class may under certain conditions be regarded as constituting a phoneme. These conditions are embodied in the principles of *complementary distribution* and of *patterned congruence*. The principle of complementary distribution requires that no two of the phonetically similar sounds ever contrast with each other, that is, operate in such a way as to produce distinctions of meaning between two utterances. For an English example, *t* in *tone* and *t* in *stone* are phonetically different, the former being aspirated and latter being unaspirated. Nevertheless, in English there are no situations where the contrast between an aspirated and an unaspirated *t* makes any difference in the meanings of

words; therefore they may be assigned to the same phoneme. The two
t-sounds are then regarded as different *allophones* of the same phoneme,
but in describing their difference one appeals to phonetics rather than to
phonemics. The principle of patterned congruence involves grouping the
sounds of a language with respect to the kinds of environments (that is, the
preceding and following sounds) in which they occur and noting certain
congruences in the behavior of partially similar sounds. Application of these
principles enables linguistic workers to arrive at reasonably consistent and
replicable descriptions of the phonemes of a language. The phonemic systems of a fair number of languages have been worked out, at least with
respect to their segmental phonemes; phenomena of pitch, stress, and juncture have received less attention.

Interest has lately been manifested in a more refined linguistic analysis
of the phoneme, for both theoretical and practical purposes. Trubetskoy
(1939a) and Roman Jakobson (1928, 1949) have defined the phoneme as a
bundle of simultaneous distinctive features. These distinctive features consist of binary, two-valued oppositions or contrasts, such as *voiced/unvoiced,
high/low,* or *rounded/unrounded.* Examples of the application of this
theory may be found in papers by Jakobson and Lotz (1949), Soffietti
(1949), and Garvin (1948). Lotz (1950) points out that there are usually
only six to eight distinctive features to be found in any given language, as
contrasted with an average of 25 to 30 segmental phonemes. Jakobson's important work on child language (1941) attempts to show that the distinctive
features come into a child's phonemic equipment in a definite ontogenetic
sequence, which also reflects a possible phylogenetic classification of languages.

The formulation of the theory of the phoneme takes its place as one
of the more significant intellectual achievements in the social sciences. Essentially, a phoneme exemplifies a unit of a culturally determined system which
arouses a differential response in a member of the culture. It represents,
within that system, a class of possible events (in this case, *allophones,* that
is, physically or phonetically different sounds) which are equipollent with
respect to the behavioral discriminations which can be observed in the
users of the system. The discriminations involved in the case of the phoneme
happen to be those having to do with differences in meaning of the forms in
which the phonemes appear. By analogy with the phoneme, higher-order

linguistic units are identified in terms of equivalences or differences of response which they evoke, or in terms of the substitution groups within which they are equipollent in respect to structural arrangement. The general methodology of phonemics has been employed by Birdwhistell (1952) in identifying what he calls "kinemes," that is, units of gestural expression.

It has been suggested that methods of linguistics which have been developed for the purpose of discovering units can be applied to other cultural systems, for example, folklore, songs, and dances. Such a suggestion has thus far been very little explored; however, the methods used by the anthropologist Rouse (1939) in connection with identifying what he calls "types" and "modes" in Haitian pottery relics bear some similarity to linguistic methods for identifying phonemes. We may also mention, in this connection, the work of Lévi-Strauss (1949, 1951) on kinship systems and of Bogatyrev (1937) on folk costumes.

Methodology in Morphology and Syntax

The traditional procedure in morphology and syntax was to identify the various "parts of speech" (nouns, pronouns, adjectives, verbs, and so on), to notice their changes in form under various grammatical conditions, and to describe the arrangements of these forms in complete sentences in accordance with the "meanings" of these sentences. Parts of speech were identified with reference to their assumed functions: for examples, nouns were held to be words which refer to "things" or sometimes to "persons," verbs to "actions," and adjectives to "qualities." Such a procedure has worked reasonably well for languages in the Indo-European family, but it demands fundamental modifications when applied to certain languages which are structured differently from those of the general Indo-European pattern. Even when applied to familiar languages like English, however, it is likely to lead to confusing or inconsistent results. For example, the concept of the verb must be taken differently depending on whether we are dealing with so-called copulative verbs like *be* or *seem,* or with various other types of verbs like *make, hit,* or *happen,* since not all of these verbs can be regarded as referring to "actions," and they do not always occur in similar positions in sentence constructions. The basic fault of traditional procedures in morphology and syntax has been that the principles on which they have operated, along with their strong emphasis on a logical analysis of categories of meaning, have tended to prejudge the results of the analysis.

Modern linguistics has been remarkably successful in overcoming the mental hazards which traditional procedures have created for anyone desirous of making objective analyses of language. Linguists will admit the inherent difficulties of making such analyses, pointing to the relative complexity of morphological and syntactical phenomena, but the basic rules of proper procedure are now reasonably well established.

If there is to be a perfectly objective procedure in linguistic analysis, it must be thought of as a process of decipherment. It is as if the linguist were a cryptanalyst trying to "crack" a code whose units he does not know. In such a process, the linguist who has identified, at least tentatively, the phonemes of a language would next seek ways of segmenting utterances into valid units of *form*. Each form would consist of an aggregation of phonemes. The linguist would look for and find a considerable number of phoneme aggregations occurring with relatively high frequency in the corpus being analyzed, but he would not know whether all of these aggregations constituted real units in the language. Some of them might, for example, be aggregations composed of the end of one unit and the beginning of the following unit. Fortunately, in all languages there are at least some *constructive features* which serve to guide the linguist in finding the boundaries between units. In English, for example, units are marked off by features of stress, pitch, and juncture, and by certain characteristics of sound sequences. By use of constructive features and other phenomena, the linguist is eventually able to identify what are called the *morphemes* of a language. The first step in morphological analysis is, in fact, the tentative identification of morphemes. The procedures are relatively complicated and cannot be discussed here in detail.

Bloch and Trager (1942, p. 54) define the morpheme in the following way: "Any form, whether free or bound, which cannot be divided into smaller parts [that is, smaller forms] is a morpheme. Thus, *man, play, person* are words consisting of a single morpheme each; *manly, played, personal* are complex words, since each of them contains a bound morpheme (*-ly, -ed, -al*)."

Having identified the morphemes of a language, the linguist proceeds to study the ways in which morphemes are put together in words, and the ways in which morphemes change in various grammatical constructions.

This study is properly called *morphology*. Just as phonemes have allophones (positional variants), morphemes have *allomorphs*. The allomorphs may be sometimes quite different phonemically; for example, the allomorphs of the morpheme { *be* } include *am, are,* and *is,* the occurrence of these allomorphs being conditioned by their environments—*am,* for instance, normally occurring only in the environment of *I.*

Another step in morphology is to assign forms to form classes on the basis of their differential positioning in utterances. This can be done for either free or bound morphemes, or even for complete words. For example, we might determine the class of morphemes which can be substituted for *good* in *goodness,* comparing it, perhaps, with the class of morphemes which can be substituted for *good* in *goodly.* Fries (1952) has given a particularly vivid demonstration of this procedure as applied to complete words. For example, by setting up the "frame"

$$\textit{The} \text{ --- } \textit{was good}$$

and listing words found in the position denoted by the blank, he tentatively sets up a form class consisting of *concert, food, coffee, taste, container, difference, privacy, family,* and *company.* In addition to the procedure of determining substitution classes, one must also study the modifications which take place in morphemes, or the additional elements which may be affixed to them, when they are used in different classes.

It is only after form classes of morphemes and words have been (at least tentatively) established that one proceeds to syntactical problems. Syntax is concerned primarily, of course, with the arrangements of words in sentences. A sentence may be roughly defined as an utterance consisting of one or more form classes arranged in any of certain sequence patterns found in a given language. The study of syntax is essentially a problem of determining the regularities in the arrangements of form classes.

One other concept which is important in morphology and syntax is that of the *immediate constituent.* An immediate constituent is a group of linguistic elements which functions as a unit in some larger whole. The phrase *old men and women* could be divided into immediate constituents in either of two ways, depending on whether *old* is to refer to both the men and the women or just the men (in speech, the difference would normally be conveyed by features of stress and juncture):

37

Old | men and women
Old men | and | women

The study of syntax is greatly facilitated by studying the types of immediate constituents which occur. (The reader may note certain similarities with the traditional procedure of "parsing" a sentence; however, the fact that the end results are frequently, but not always, the same should not be allowed to obscure the basic differences in fundamental approach.)

It will have been evident from the above discussion that modern practice in identifying the morphological and syntactical features of a language appeals largely to the arrangements of various types of linguistic forms and very little to the "meanings" expressed by these arrangements. Once the features have been identified, however, their meanings deserve to be determined. Fries (1952, p. 56) states that "the grammar of a language consists of the devices that signal structural meanings." Structural meanings are those which are conveyed by patterns of arrangement and the selection of form classes, as contrasted with lexical meanings, the meanings of the forms themselves. For example, among the structural meanings signaled by the construction of a sentence are those which have to do with whether it is a statement, a question, or a request. Other structural meanings may have to do with the roles played by the various items referred to (for example, who or what was the "performer" of an action, what is being identified, etc.), and the relative time at which something is said to be true. Statements as to the structural meanings of such grammatical features as gender, tense, aspect, case, etc., all have a place in the description of a language system. It must be realized, nevertheless, that these meanings are solely formal and structural and may have only accidental bearing on anything in the world of experience. To illustrate: in languages which have the grammatical feature of gender, the "meaning" of gender implies only a linguistic contrast between several classes of forms. The fact that truly male beings are *usually* assigned to one of these classes and that truly female beings are usually assigned to another of these classes needs to be stated, if it happens to be the case, but it should not be understood to imply that the "meaning" of the former class is "male" and of the latter class "female."

Among recent works on morphology and syntax, we may cite, first of all, Harris's *Methods in Structural Linguistics* (1951), a major part of which is devoted to procedures in this field. Nida's *Morphology* (1946) and several articles on immediate constituents (Wells, 1947; Nida, 1948) are also significant. A somewhat older work of interest is Jespersen's *Analytic Syntax* (1937). Two somewhat different approaches to the analysis of English structure are Trager and Smith's *Outline of English Structure* (1951), distinguished by its use of a much greater range of linguistic phenomena than had been taken account of previously, and Fries's *The Structure of English* (1952), concerned chiefly with syntactical problems. Pike's *The Intonation of American English* (1946) shows how the intonation of English is an intrinsic part of its grammar.

In the remainder of this section, I wish to discuss several problems relating to the possible implications of results in morphology and syntax for psychology.

Many students of language have remarked that there appears to be considerable psychological validity in the *word* as a unit of language. "Linguistic experience," writes Sapir (1921, p. 34), "both as expressed in standardized written form and as tested in daily usage, indicates overwhelmingly that there is not, as a rule, the slightest difficulty in bringing the word to consciousness as a psychological reality. No more convincing test could be desired than this, that the naïve Indian, quite unaccustomed to the concept of the written word, has nevertheless no serious difficulty in dictating a text to a linguistic student word by word." The *word,* then, appears to have some sort of psychological validity, but there is no way of being sure of this. On the other hand, linguistic scientists have had not a little difficulty in specifying rigorous operational procedures in identifying words.[9] Bloomfield, for example, defined a word as a minimal free form, that is, a free form which cannot be divided entirely into smaller free forms (1933, p. 178). Nevertheless, Bloomfield himself had difficulty in making this criterion work for him.

Of course, the division of speech into "words" which is provided by conventional systems of writing would never be accepted as anything more than a rough guide. For example, the fact that French *je* ("I") is written as a single word is no guarantee that it is a minimal free form, for actually it seems not to be "free"—it is always used with a verb, and there are a limited number of ways in which it may be separated from the verb (only by such particles as *me, ne, y,* and the like). From a structural point of view, *je* is almost as closely bound to the verb as the suffix *-o* in Latin *amo.* Linguists thus regard *je* and *-o* as morphemes, but do not regard them necessarily as words.

Linguists would also stoutly reject any suggestion that words be identified by reference to the concepts they are said to express. The word is *not* necessarily a counterpart of a single concept, as so many nonlinguists seem to feel. Sapir (1921, p. 33) mentions a Nootka "word" which denotes "I have been accustomed to eat twenty round objects [for example, apples] while engaged in [doing so and so]." Any attempt to equate words with concepts can lead to erroneous conclusions. Let us consider, for example, a statement made by the educational psychologist Judd in his book *Education as the Cultivation of the Higher Mental Processes* (1936, p. 24). On the basis of his finding that there are many more nouns, verbs, and adjectives in dictionaries than there are relational words such as prepositions and conjunctions, Judd concludes that there is "a limited number of ways in which the mind is capable of combining and relating substantive experience." At least two fallacies are involved here. First, Judd assumes that prepositions and conjunctions have to do with relations, while nouns, verbs, and adjectives do not. This is highly questionable: many nouns, verbs, and adjectives clearly have to do with "relations." Secondly, there is the assumption that words have a one-to-one correspondence to concepts. The number of different conceptual relations which can be expressed by a single preposition in English (for instance, *of*) is quite large, even if we rely only on the number of distinctions recognized by an unabridged dictionary.

It is clear, then, that the analysis of a language system must be made not on the basis of intuitive psychological analysis but on the basis of rigorous operational procedures. Suppose linguistic analysis were able to show that there is no such thing as a *word;* we would then be forced to accept that fact, regardless of any psychological intuitions we might have to the contrary. Before we can talk usefully about the psychological or exolinguistic interpretations of linguistic structure, we must have adequate descriptions of that structure, prepared by linguistic scientists using their own methods of analysis. We must know with confidence that the true signaling units have been identified. Before Fries's analysis of English sentence construction became available, one would have been somewhat hesitant in setting forth upon any program for experimentation into the psychological process involved in the perception of the structural meanings in sentences.

GRAMMATICAL CATEGORIES

Many parts of descriptive linguistics are exacting, difficult, and tedious for the nonspecialist, and even for the specialist. There is, however, one area of descriptive linguistics which will perhaps seems especially fascinating to the nonspecialist. This is the problem of grammatical categories; actually it grows out of the study of form classes and morphology.

Let us start with some examples, suggested by Sapir (1921, Chap. 5). In Chinese, it is permissible to utter a sentence of three morphemes standing for "man kill duck," which in English would have to be translated in a more specific way, depending upon the circumstances under which this sentence was uttered. One would have to select a translation such as "the man killed the duck," or "the man will kill the ducklings." The English sentence "The farmer killed the duckling" says a great deal more than it appears to say. It is specific as to the number of farmers, the time of the action, the number of ducklings involved, and which farmer and which duckling one refers to. On the other hand, there is a great deal that it does not say. It says nothing about the degree of certainty in the statement, or about who vouches for its truth. Thus, English has selected certain concepts which almost necessarily must be present in certain kinds of statements, but it has left out of account other kinds of concepts. It is easy enough to find languages which leave out of account some of the mandatory categories of English, but introduce others which English brings in by circumlocution only when they are necessary. In an Indian language known as Yana, one mandatory concept has to do with whether a statement is known to be true and vouched for by the speaker, or simply made on another's authority. Thus, it would be impossible to say "the farmer killed the duckling" without at the same time specifying whether this statement is made on the speaker's, or someone else's, authority. In Kwakiutl, a language of British Columbia, one could not say "the farmer killed the duckling" without saying something about the place relations of the farmer, the duckling, etc., with respect to the speaker and the listener.

In other words, to paraphrase awkwardly certain latent "demonstrative" ideas, does this farmer (invisible to us but standing behind a door not far away from me, you being seated yonder well out of reach) kill that duckling (which belongs to you)? or does that farmer (who lives in your neighborhood and whom we see over there) kill that duckling (that belongs to him)? This type of demonstrative elaboration is foreign to our way of thinking, but it would seem very natural, indeed unavoidable, to a Kwakiutl Indian. (Sapir, 1921, pp. 97–98.)

An important step in descriptive linguistics, therefore, is to delineate the grammatical categories which are mandatory in a given language. Ever since linguists started to analyze languages which varied from the Indo-European pattern, they have been more keenly aware of the importance of such grammatical categories and of their possible relevance to some psychological interpretation of linguistic events.

Thus far, linguists have not had occasion to prepare a systematic display of the variety of such grammatical categories to be found in the languages of the world, usually confining their studies to selected languages. This is a task which urgently needs to be done. A considerable portion of the raw data is available, but it needs collation and assembly.

LINGUISTIC TYPOLOGY

It has long been thought that it should be possible to classify languages or language families in terms of their structures. In the nineteenth century it was proposed that languages might be classified in three groups: isolating, agglutinative, and inflective. Later, a polysynthetic group was added. Sapir (1921, Chap. 6) pointed out the difficulties in such oversimplified schemes and tentatively suggested a considerably more complex classification based on the manner in which various languages treated various kinds of concepts. Until very recently, other American linguists have paid little attention to the problem; one looks in vain for any detailed studies in this country. At the present time, however, a renascence of interest in linguistic typology is setting in, though from a different point of view from that adopted by Sapir. At the December 1949 meeting of the Linguistic Society of America, C. F. Hockett of Cornell University read a paper which presented a statistical approach to linguistic typology. One measure, for example, had to do with the ratio of the number of morphemes to the number of words in a representative sample of speech. Independently of Hockett, Joseph Greenberg of Columbia University has been making parallel studies using measures similar to Hockett's.

It is worth quoting part of a footnote in Sapir's chapter on types of linguistic structures:

In spite of my reluctance to emphasize the difference between a prefixing and a suffixing language, I feel that there is more involved in this difference than linguists have generally recognized. It seems to me that there is a rather important psychological distinction between a language that settles the formal status of a radical element before announcing it—and this, in effect, is what such languages as Tlingit and Chinook and Bantu are in the habit of doing—and one which begins with the concrete nucleus of a word and defines the status of this nucleus by successive limitations, each curtailing in some degree the generality of all that precedes. The spirit of the former method has something diagrammatic or architectural about it, the latter is a method of pruning afterthoughts." (Sapir, 1921, p. 135; this and the preceding extracts are reprinted by permission from *Language,* by Edward Sapir, published by Harcourt, Brace and Company.)

It is supererogatory to comment on the implications of this statement.

One problem in linguistic typology which could be investigated quite readily has to do with the comparison of the phonemic systems of languages. Some languages have only a limited number of phonemes, while some others appear to possess extremely complex phonologies, offering a large number of finely differentiated phonemes. A comparative analysis of these systems would be of great intrinsic interest; the results, incidentally, might be of value to sound engineers. Lotz (1950) has presented a discussion of the kind of analysis of phonemic systems which needs to be made, and a statistical approach to phonemic typology is represented by the work of Menzerath (1950).

THE LINGUISTIC *WELTANSCHAUUNG* PROBLEM

There exists in linguistic science, though as yet in a poorly defined way, a topic or a possible area of study which for want of a better term may be called the *linguistic Weltanschauung* ("world-view") problem. Some linguists have described the problem as one of "metalinguistics," but if we accept Trager's definition of metalinguistics (1949), this problem is only a part of that branch of linguistics, which is here referred to as exolinguistics (see p. 29).

The linguistic *Weltanschauung* problem concerns the way in which a language system organizes human experience. To give a simple and somewhat trite example, the normal human organism is sensitive to a certain band of wavelengths of electromagnetic energy, that band of wavelengths which we refer to as *light*. In English, we have a certain series of terms applied to various parts of that spectrum, normally *red, orange, yellow, green, blue,* and *violet.* (Textile manufacturers find it necessary to concoct all sorts of other words for special shades and tints, but these terms often change from year to year and may have no fundamental significance in our language.) Our language thus provides certain verbal symbols in terms of which we habitually classify colors. It is quite possible to conceive other languages (and there are such languages[10]) which break the spectrum into different groupings of wavelengths. For example, instead of there being a special word for the color of orange, that color might be grouped with yellow and qualified as reddish. Now, the reader may say that this has little to do with one's world view or *Weltanschauung,* and I would agree. This example is only a paradigm.

The admirable articles written by the late Benjamin Lee Whorf (1939, 1940a, 1940b, 1941) will provide us with somewhat more convincing demonstrations.

In English we divide most of our words into two classes, which have different grammatical and logical properties. Class 1 we call nouns, e.g., "house," "man"; Class 2, verbs, e.g., "hit," "run." . . . Our language thus gives us a bipolar division of nature. But nature herself is not thus polarized. If it be said that strike, turn, run, are verbs because they denote temporary or short-lasting events, i.e., actions, why then is fist a noun? It also is a temporary event. Why are lightning, spark, wave, eddy, pulsation, flame, storm, phase, cycle, spasm, noise, emotion, nouns? They are temporary events. . . It will be found that an "event" to *us* means "what our language classes as a verb" or something analogized therefrom. And it will be found that it is not possible to define event, thing, object, relationship, and so on, from nature, but that to define them always involves a circuitous return to the grammatical categories of the definer's language.

In the Hopi language, lightning, wave, flame, meteor, puff of smoke, pulsation, are verbs—events of necessarily brief duration cannot be anything but verbs. Cloud and storm are at about the lower limit of duration for nouns. Hopi, you see, actually has a classification of events (or linguistic isolates) by duration of type, something strange to our modes of thought. On the other hand, in Nootka, a language of Vancouver Island, all words seem to us to be verbs, but really there are no classes 1 and 2; we have, as it were, a monistic view of nature that gives us only one class of word for all kinds of events.

Linguistics must imply a sort of Copernican revolution if what Whorf writes has any validity:

When linguists became able to examine critically and scientifically a large number of languages of widely different patterns, their base of reference was expanded; they experienced an interruption of phenomena hitherto held universal, and a whole new order of significances came into their ken. It was found that the background linguistic system (in other words, the grammar) of each language is not merely a reproducing instrument for voicing ideas but rather is itself the shaper of ideas, the program and guide for the individual's mental activity, for his analysis of impressions, for his synthesis of his mental stock in trade. Formulation of ideas is not an independent process, strictly rational in the old sense, but is part of a particular grammar and differs, from slightly to greatly, as between different grammars. We dissect nature along lines laid down by our native languages. The categories and types that we isolate from the world of phenomena we do not find there because they stare every observer in the face; on the contrary, the world is presented in a kaleidoscopic flux of impressions which has to be organized by our minds—and this means largely by the linguistic systems in our minds. We cut nature up, organize it into concepts, and ascribe significances as we do, largely because we are parties to an agreement to organize it in this way—an agreement that holds throughout our speech community and is codified in the patterns of our language. The agreement is, of course, an implicit and unstated one, *but its terms are absolutely obligatory;* we cannot talk at all except by subscribing to the organization and classification of data which the agreement decrees. (Whorf, 1939, p. 231; reprinted from *The Technology Review,* edited at the Massachusetts Institute of Technology.)

In the words of Edward Sapir (1921, p. 105):

It is almost as though at some period in the past the unconscious mind of the race had made a hasty inventory of experience, committed itself to a premature classification that allowed of no revision, and saddled the inheritors of its language with a science that they no longer quite believed in nor had the strength to overthrow. Dogma, rigidly prescribed by tradition, stiffens into formalism. Linguistic categories make up a system of surviving dogma—dogma of the unconscious. They are often but half real as concepts; their life tends ever to languish away into form for form's sake.

In principle, the idea that linguistic structure and categories in some way influence our modes of thought is an attractive one. Whorf was by no means the first to call attention to it; such eminent scholars of older generations as W. von Humboldt (1836–1839) and Baudouin de Courtenay (1929) have also written on the subject. For various reasons, however, this notion has never become one of the generally accepted doctrines of general linguistic theory. In the writer's talks with a number of contemporary American linguists, he encountered a considerable skepticism. One individual characterized Whorf's propositions as "untested generalizations." Many linguists think Whorf's ideas represent too much of an extrapolation from available data. Nevertheless, one can find everywhere an interest in these questions. Their possible contemporary importance is attested by the fact that the linguistic staff of the Foreign Service Institute in the Department of State has had several of Whorf's papers reprinted for use in its training program for foreign-service officers (Whorf, 1949).

In order to put the linguistic *Weltanschauung* problem to empirical test, we must follow, as a preliminary step, two lines of analysis. First, we must assemble more information on a variety of linguistic structures, with particular reference to grammatical categories, inflectional systems, and form classes; in addition, we must know more about the manner in which various languages express different kinds of abstract relations, for example, relations having to do with causality, quantity, quality, time, and space. It might be convenient to draw up a standard list of about a hundred concepts to be investigated in an equal number of languages. Such a job, obviously, is one for a well-trained linguist. The results would be helpful in the second line of analysis, namely, the formulation of hypotheses about the influence of linguistic structure on behavior. These hypotheses must be stated in a way which will make them amenable to experimental test. An extremely liberal interpretation of the *Weltanschauung* problem would lead to the hypothesis that linguistic categories actually influence what the user of a language *can* perceive—to the extent that he can perceive some things and *cannot* perceive others. It seems improbable that such a hypothesis would be sustained. A more conservative hypothesis is that linguistic structure predisposes the individual to pay attention to some things more than others, or to perceive things in one mode rather than in others, even though with respect to his general perceptual capacities he is no different, on the average, from users of other languages. For example, by virtue of the fact that English uses the adjective *hot* in referring to pepper, the native speaker of English may perceive more readily a relation between the sensation of heat and a peppery taste, but his actual sensations probably differ in no way from those of a speaker of one of the many languages which do not apply a word for "hot" to pepper. Experiments on the *Weltanschauung* problem must be designed in such a way as to control the effect of individual differences and of cultural differences which may be incidentally correlated with linguistic differences. It goes without saying that at least some of the experiments must be *cross-linguistic,* that is, they must involve the comparison of the responses of native speakers of different languages.

One reservation that we may have about the *Weltanschauung* problem, particularly in the positive form in which Whorf states it, is that although language provides a mold in which statements are made by a speaker, it does not necessarily have any bearing on the "truth" of those statements, nor on the logical "correctness" of the speaker's thought processes. One world-view is as good as another, for all we know, and for that matter different world-views and logics *can* be expressed in the same language, as is demonstrated by the very fact that English permits us to speak about the varying ways in which Hopi, Nootka, and other linguistic systems describe experience. In general (that is, aside from differences arising from culture and technology), contrary to the popularly held misconception, anything that can be said in one language can be said in any other language. There is no guarantee that our thought habits would be improved by the use of an improved language, or of a different language. It is probably not true that the speakers of some languages (for example, Japanese, we are sometimes told) must necessarily think illogically because their language forces them to do so. In the face of these facts, it is nevertheless true that the study of what is termed here the linguistic *Weltanschauung* problem may in the long run help us to improve our thinking by drawing our attention to the linguistic foundations of our perceptions and thought processes.

Many writers have pointed out the need to examine the relation of language to reality. General semantics, as developed by Korzybski (1933) and his students, claims to be concerned with this problem and its implications. Korzybski emphasized his conviction that language is a finite system of abstractions from the infinitely differentiated sense impressions of reality. The word *chair,* for example, is an abstraction from a manifold set of immediate experiences related to objects with certain characteristics. We can in no way avoid the fact that from this point of view "there is a fundamental lack of correspondence between the structure of our language and the structure of reality" (Wendell Johnson, 1946, p. 115). General semanticists declare that lack of full awareness of the ways in which language abstracts reality can lead to errors in thinking (Hayakawa, 1949) and even to personal maladjustments and speech disorders (Johnson, 1946). Now, language structure as conceived by general semanticists is something quite different from linguistic structure as defined in linguistic science, but it would certainly include the kinds of phenomena noted by Sapir and Whorf. General semantics has recognized the existence of problems relating to the effect of formal linguistic categories,[11] but to my knowledge it has not developed any detailed investigations of these problems.

The linguistic *Weltanschauung* problem, therefore, has thus far received very little attention in America. Among the few papers which reflect a preoccupation with this problem we may cite those of Dorothy Lee (1943, 1950a, 1950b) and Thompson (1950). Basson and O'Connor (1947), in England, have attempted to investigate the influences of linguistic structure upon logic and philosophy. Kluckhohn and Leighton (1946) have described possible relations between Navaho language and Navaho culture, and in a careful study the linguist Hoijer (1951) adduces evidence of these relations in at least two important respects: (*a*) The verb system emphasizes the reporting of "eventings" which are very concretely linked to the motions and resting states of objects; this seems associated with the nomadic character of the culture and the thematic "restlessness" found in the mythology. (*b*) The linguistic structure divides objective reality "into a number of sharply defined object classes in motion or at rest"; thus, "both movement and position . . . are inherent in and specific to an object class; they are not extraneously produced by an actor, nor imposed as a force on a goal." One is tempted to think, from this evidence, that the Navaho views his world as something which is not subject to manipulation by human beings, and in which human actions get somehow involved as an almost incidental function of Nature, which is regarded as being more powerful than Man. But one may rightly remain skeptical as to whether this evidence truly demonstrates any fundamental relation between linguistic structure and world-view.

HISTORICAL AND COMPARATIVE LINGUISTICS

Developed during the nineteenth century primarily in connection with studies of the Indo-European languages, comparative linguistics is generally regarded as possessing a most rigorous methodology. It is concerned with showing the historical development of languages and in some cases with showing the common genetic origins of groups of languages, by means of such procedures as the identification of uniformly operating changes in the sounds of a language. These uniformly operating sound changes are sometimes known as "phonetic laws," though it is probable that they have no status which can be generalized beyond the history of a given group of languages. Thus, a linguist who studies the comparative linguistics of American Indian languages does not postulate for them phonetic laws taken bodily from the phonetic laws known to operate in the Indo-European languages; what he draws upon from Indo-European comparative linguistics is a method, and nothing else.

The comparative linguist can attempt to trace back the forms of a given language to the forms of another, older language, or he may try to show that the forms of two related and known languages can be traced back to a postulated form in a putative parent language. Historical linguists have prepared lists of "reconstructed" forms (that is, forms of words or morphemes, usually) of a postulated parent language of the Indo-European family. In this case, the scientist is considerably aided by the fact that various ancient languages are recorded in written form—Latin, Greek, Sanskrit, and Hittite, for example. Even in American Indian linguistics, however, the methods of comparative linguistics are sufficiently powerful to have enabled Bloomfield to reconstruct some of the forms of what is known as Proto-Algonkian (see Hockett, 1948b) and Whorf (1935) to delineate the outlines of Uto-Aztecan, a supposed parent language for certain languages in the American Southwest and in Mexico.

In fact, the term "comparative linguistics" implies a rigorous method to such a degree that it was necessary for Voegelin (1942b) to point out that Sapir used the methods of comparative linguistics *only* when he was studying rather narrowly restricted language families, and that he used mainly *intuitive* procedures in his attempt to group widely scattered language families in America into a rather small handful of broad families.

While the methodology of comparative linguistics may be regarded as being highly advanced, comparative studies present vexing problems when the linguist is faced with a tremendous variety of languages which are known to be related, but which have no early recorded forms. As an example we may cite the work of Isidore Dyen at Yale University on the Malayo-Polynesian group of languages. It is comparatively easy to show that the 500 or more languages and dialects in this group are related, by the methods of conventional comparative linguistics. But if Mr. Dyen's work promises to show any wide significance, it is that he hopes to show by comparative linguistics the detailed relations and historical origins of these languages in order to make inferences concerning the migration paths of the Pacific Islanders from the mainlands of Asia. Currently available methods of comparative linguistics may not be entirely adequate for such a purpose. For one thing, the mass of data, much of it scanty or poorly recorded from a descriptive point of view, requires a quasi-statistical approach. Furthermore, the relative roles played by chance similarities and by linguistic borrowings have to be evaluated. On the face of it, the problem looks nearly insoluble, but the linguistic approach offers almost the only hope for untangling the prehistory of Polynesia; the ethnographic approach does not offer much because nonlinguistic cultural materials are too easily borrowed from one culture to another.

Similar tasks are faced by linguists attempting to set forth the comparative linguistics of the native languages of North America, South America, Africa, Asia, and Australia.

In the highly advanced comparative linguistics of Indo-European, interesting relations have recently been demonstrated as a result of the study of Hittite (an ancient language of Asia Minor) and Tocharian (a language of central Asia known to us from manuscript fragments of the sixth century A.D.). The characteristics of primitive Indo-European are by now fairly well known. Studies of language relations in the Indo-European family may, with cautious interpretations, give evidence as to the prehistory of our culture.

One of the most intriguing problems connected with historical linguistics is that of phonetic change, as embodied in what are called phonetic laws. The status and validity of phonetic laws has been the subject of much polemic discussion in linguistics. Leskien (1876) was apparently the first to formulate the principle that sound changes follow laws which admit of no exceptions, and Osthoff and Brugmann (1878–1890) further developed this principle in extensive comparative studies. In opposition to the neogrammarians (*Junggrammatiker*), as Leskien, Osthoff, and Brugmann came to be called, Schuchardt (1885), Curtius, and Ascoli pointed to what seemed to be exceptions to phonetic laws and in general refused to ascribe to phonetic laws the positive validity of physical laws, as suggested by the neogrammarians. Even in recent years the neogrammarian position has been attacked, but from a different slant. The "neolinguists," as represented by Bertoni and Bartoli (1925) and later by Bonfante (1947), have wished to reject or at least to qualify the idea of regular sound change because they see linguistic development as a result of complex geographical and chronological factors which cannot be summarized in phonetic laws. They tend to support, in some instances, the so-called "substratum" theory, at least that variety of the theory which attempts to explain phonetic change by appealing to the idea that a community which finds itself in the position of adopting a new language will speak it imperfectly and with many traces of the mother tongue.[12] Hall (1946) takes the position, however, that neolinguistics has nothing to offer to contemporary comparativists beyond what they have already known.

American linguists have taken over from the neogrammarian school the idea of regular sound change, but chiefly as a working hypothesis rather than as an article of faith. The comparativist tries to assemble as much of his material as possible in accordance with a consistent system of phonetic changes and correspondences, but he would be willing to explain any irreducible residue of "exceptions" in any way that stands inspection; in fact, he accepts responsibility for seeking such explanations wherever possible.

Whatever the ultimate status of phonetic law may prove to be, the mechanics of phonetic change have never been satisfactorily explained.[13] Linguists know that phonetic change has occurred in the past, and assume that it is also taking place at the present time, despite the tremendous pressures toward uniformity represented by mass media of communication. They have also assumed that any changes now taking place are not detectable and therefore are not available for study. Professors Bloch and Wells of Yale University doubt this, however, and have suggested to the writer that this problem might be attacked by a team of linguists and psychologists, possibly with the help of sound engineers, who would develop experimental techniques for detecting whether any sound changes are taking place at present, and, if so, for discovering the factors which produce these changes. They suggest that the results of such an investigation might have important implications for our knowledge of factors determining cultural continuity and cultural change.

Though it does not play as large a part in the methodology of comparative linguistics as does the study of phonetic change, the study of semantic change can be a fascinating one. A number of general principles of semantic change have been postulated. This topic furnishes interesting studies in this history of cultures, and deserves to be further explored. Stern's classic work (1931) on this subject is the fullest treatment available to date. Any good etymological dictionary is an inexhaustible source of interesting material for study; Buck's recent dictionary (1949) is particularly useful for its arrangement of Indo-European materials according to semantic categories. It is significant, incidentally, that Buck subtitled his work "a contribution to the history of ideas."

These and other problems in comparative linguistics sometimes have an exolinguistic flavor. Sounds, forms, meanings, and syntactical arrangements show changes along a historical dimension. Languages "borrow" forms and meanings from other languages, or adapt their own linguistic forms to the designation of items borrowed from other cultures, as the Navaho language does in describing a watch as "a round thin object goes around." The description of such phenomena lies within linguistics proper, but their deeper explanation and interpretation must come, no doubt, from psychology and other social sciences.

A general remark on the implications of present-day descriptive linguistics for comparative linguistics is in order at this point. We have already cited Bloomfield's comment to the effect that the merging of the historical-comparative and the philosophical-descriptive streams of study at the end of the nineteenth century shows that the historical study of language can be only as accurate and only as complete as the descriptive data allow it to be. Every new methodological advance in descriptive linguistics reinforces this conclusion. In the late 1930's, for example, the interest of descriptive linguists began to be focused on the description of what are called "suprasegmental" phonemes such as pitch, stress, and juncture, which had not been adequately described previously. These interests culminated, as several linguists remarked to the writer, in the realization that much of the historical linguistics of English needs to be revised in the light of these recent methodological advances, and, indeed, in the light of modern phonemic theory as a whole.[14] In effect, the history of a language must be developed by comparing descriptive studies of the language as it existed at various chronological stages.

52

THE TERRITORY OF LINGUISTICS

Thus far we have been talking about linguistics in highly general terms, addressing our remarks primarily to methodological questions. But linguistic scientists busy themselves not only with general questions of theory but also with the study of actual languages, their description, analysis, and historical delineation. Therefore, something should be said about the progress which linguists have made in the coverage of their subject matter.

We can look at the territory of linguistic science in three dimensions.

The first dimension is represented by the fact that there are a large number of languages and dialects to be covered. The figures often given in encyclopedias and other references as to the number of languages in the world (the number usually given is around 2000) are probably serious underestimates. Linguistic scientists refuse to estimate the number of languages which now exist or have existed; the question is largely meaningless because in many cases there is no clear demarcation between a language and a dialect. Suffice it to say that with respect to the number of languages to be covered the territory of linguistics is huge.

A second dimension is represented by the extent to which the identifiable languages and dialects have been described and analyzed, in particular, the extent to which each language or dialect has been subjected to the most advanced methods of linguistic analysis. Bloomfield (1933, p. 57) wrote, "Among the languages that are spoken today, only a few are even tolerably well known to science." This statement is still true. Linguists are fond of stating that common languages like English, French, German, Russian, and Chinese, for example, have been less well described than some exotic and unusual languages like Navaho. By this, they mean that Navaho and some other languages has been more adequately studied from a structural point of view, *not* that more effort has been expended on Navaho. Of course, it remains true that the materials available for the study of the commoner languages—dictionaries, grammars, historical studies, and the like—are much more extensive than those available for exotic and unusual languages.

A third dimension of the territory of linguistic science is the historical dimension. One is concerned here with the extent to which languages have been described in historical terms and grouped into language families by the methods of comparative linguistics.

Obviously, it would require a huge amount of labor to discover in detail how much linguistic territory, in the three dimensions described here, has been covered in relation to the territory that could be covered. It would probably take a staff of a score of linguistic bibliographers a period of several months to compile even a tentative report. Even then, many details would remain to be filled in by field work. In any case, one gets the impression that the territory of linguistic science has thus far received only a very incomplete coverage, despite the mass of work that has already been done.

The Indo-European Languages

As is well known, the Indo-European languages now command a predominant position in the world today, comprising such widely spoken languages as English, French, German, Spanish, Italian, and Russian. The subfamilies of Indo-European, with some of their principal languages, may be listed as follows: Germanic (English, German, the Scandinavian languages); Italic and Romance (Latin, French, Spanish, Portuguese, Italian, Rumanian); Celtic (Irish, Welsh, Breton); Baltic (Lithuanian, Lettish); Slavic (Russian, Czech, Serbo-Croatian); Albanian; Greek; and Indo-Iranian (Sanskrit, Hindustani, Persian).

The study of the Indo-European languages is a traditional part of Western culture. As we have seen, comparative linguistics in the nineteenth century was primarily founded in the study of the Indo-European languages. With the concentrated efforts of Western scholarship expended on the more widely known Western languages and literatures, with the widespread emphasis given to some of these languages in our schools, colleges, and universities, and with the natural interest of Western scholars in their own languages, the study of the Indo-European languages now proceeds largely on its own momentum. The principal languages of every subfamily have been given much attention, not only for themselves but also for the determination of their positions in the general scheme of the family as a whole. There are, of course, many questions of detail which remain to be worked out, and there are a number of relatively less well known languages and dialects which have not been adequately studied. For example, in the Indo-Iranian group, much is known about Sanskrit and some of its direct descendants, but there has been less coverage of certain of the numerous modern languages of India, Iran, and neighboring territories. Studies of Hittite, which shows certain relationships to Indo-European, are reserved to a handful of scholars, as are also investigations of various obscure ancient languages and dialects to be found scattered throughout the Indo-European family.

It is still true, however, that there is a paucity of systematic analyses of modern languages in the Indo-European group, made with the apparatus of modern descriptive linguistics. Among recent American attempts in this direction are the highly condensed monographic studies of French and Italian by R. A. Hall, Jr. (1948a, 1948b), and Trager and Smith's *Outline of English Structure* (1951).

Other Well-Studied Language Families

A considerable amount of effort has been expended on various languages of the Semitic-Hamitic group, comprising such languages as Hebrew, Arabic, Ethiopian, and Berber, along with such ancient languages as Babylonian, Phoenician, and Egyptian. There remain, however, many minor languages of this group to be investigated, and their precise familial relationships have not been firmly established. The many forms and dialects of Arabic, ranging geographically from the northwest coast of Africa to Iraq, present a particularly vexing problem.

The Finno-Ugrian group includes at least three languages with a significant literary tradition: Finnish, Estonian, and Hungarian. These languages have been well investigated by European scholars.

Beyond the groups which we have mentioned thus far, it is hard to find any language families which could be said to have been "well investigated." At most, only the more widely spoken languages of the various families have been investigated. For example, the Turkish language is fairly well known, but several related languages in the so-called Altaic family of languages have not been adequately investigated. Soviet linguists, of course, have studied a large number of languages lying within the territory of the U.S.S.R.

Major Language Families of Asia

When we get beyond the pale of languages of Europe, the Near East, and the U.S.S.R., we begin to find a regrettable lack of coverage. Linguists have confined their attention to the languages spoken by a large number of people or to those of particular political or commercial importance.

One large family of languages which has been postulated is the Sino-Tibetan family, including Chinese, Siamese, Tibetan, and Burmese. In recent years, some doubts have arisen as to the validity of this classification. In any case, only the major languages of this broad grouping have been investigated. The many languages and dialects of China present an enormous problem, particularly since linguists have not had adequate opportunity to study the spoken dialects of Chinese. It must be remembered that written Chinese is of such a nature as to obscure dialect differences; a single Chinese character may stand for two entirely different linguistic forms from different sections of China.

Likewise, only the major languages of the Dravidian family (chiefly occurring in India) are known. Even less known are languages of the Munda and Mon-Khmer families of Southeastern Asia.

The Languages of the Pacific

We have already mentioned the tremendous Malayo-Polynesian family, which extends from the Malay peninsula across the Pacific to Easter Island. Some languages of this group are of considerable importance, such as Tagalog (by recent decree the "national language" of the Philippines) and Javanese (the dominant language of Indonesia). In the first volume of his monumental work, von Humboldt (1836–1839) more than a century ago laid the foundations of the comparative grammar of the Malayo-Polynesian languages, but there is still a paucity of adequate scientific studies of these languages.

Turning to the South Pacific, we find that relatively little of any scientific value is known about the languages of the Papuan family, on New Guinea and adjacent islands, and the native languages of Australia.

The Languages of Africa

The languages of the northern portion of Africa belong primarily to the Semitic-Hamitic group, and have received a fair share of attention. Despite a considerable amount of work by untrained linguists, few detailed and scientific accounts of the native languages of the southern portion of Africa are available. British and German scholars have contributed most of the better studies. An American linguist working on these African languages is Joseph Greenberg of Columbia University. On the basis of a more refined analysis, he has postulated an entirely new classification of these languages, and doubts very much the validity of certain early theories that such languages of South Africa as Bantu and Hottentot are in any way related to the Semitic-Hamitic group (or as he calls it, the Afroasiatic group). There seem to be important implications of this work for the pre-history of Africa, since the earlier theorists had inferred from their classificatory schemes that some South African tribes were herdsmen driven south by the Egyptians and Arabs. The scope of African linguistics is tremendous, much of it relatively untapped.

The Native Languages of North America

The variety of languages which existed in North America at the coming of the white man can hardly be estimated except in terms of the probable number of language families represented. The figure is conservatively put somewhere between 25 and 50. Many of these languages have already become extinct; many of them will become extinct in the very near future. In some areas, notably along the west coast, a great number of unrelated languages are tightly packed in relatively small geographical areas.

Linguistic scientists in America have naturally been much interested in the American Indian languages. A mere handful of individuals have done wonders in studying a number of American Indian languages from both descriptive and historical points of view. It is frequently said that the particular methodological and theoretical direction taken by American linguistics has been signally influenced by the problems encountered in American Indian linguistics. Boas, Sapir, and Bloomfield all devoted a major part of their efforts to the study of American Indian languages. Some of the best descriptive grammars are those of such languages as Navaho, Nootka, Yokuts, Hopi, and Siouan. Nevertheless, there remains much work to be done. Our knowledge of some languages is represented only by mere sketches made after a couple of weeks of field work; there are many languages about which we know next to nothing, except that they exist.

Linguists believe it is urgently necessary to complete the investigation of American Indian languages for two primary reasons: First, American Indian languages are unusually rich in features which would appear strange and out of the ordinary to anyone familiar only with the European languages. The study of American Indian languages will therefore contribute to the advancement of linguistic science in a general way. Secondly, as in other areas of the world, comparative linguistics provides a major key to the prehistory of the region. The geographical distribution of languages and language families may provide evidence on culture areas and their movements.

The languages of central America are of particular interest, since at least two of them, Nahuatl (or Aztecan) and Maya, were languages of early American civilizations. The Mayans had a highly developed written language, but little of it has been deciphered, aside from numerical and astronomical portions of the texts found on the stelae of Yucatan. Several preconquest codices have also come down to us. Whorf (1933) did some remarkably clever work in showing how they might be deciphered; his work ought to be followed up.

Voegelin's (1949) description of recent work on American Indian languages is a useful source of information for one wishing to pursue this field further. There are a number of compilations of language descriptions (Boas, 1911–1922, 1933–1938; Hoijer, 1947), and one of the major linguistic journals in this country, the *International Journal of American Linguistics,* is devoted chiefly to American Indian languages.

The Native Languages of South America

The situation in the linguistic analysis of the native languages of South America presents a great void, filled only with sporadic attempts to record a few selected languages. It is known, however, that a tremendous variety of languages exists, and some tentative hypotheses have been made with respect to the grouping of these languages. Some of them have been studied by missionaries or by linguists whose techniques were not particularly well advanced. Linguists in the United States feel a sense of obligation in pursuing studies of South American languages.

A small amount of work has been done on the languages of the Caribbean area. Some of these languages present interesting problems in terms of the influence of the African languages of slaves brought to those areas in the seventeenth and eighteenth centuries. In Haiti, we have an interesting example of a Creole language, largely based on French, and created as a result of the association of African slaves with their French masters.

Studies in Linguistic Geography

In the foregoing sketchy survey of the extent to which linguistics has covered its subject matter, we have not mentioned studies of linguistic geography, sometimes also called dialect geography or dialectology. The purpose of linguistic geography is to make a detailed analysis of local linguistic variations within a broad speech area, usually displaying the results in a series of maps assembled into a linguistic atlas. Variations in phonology, morphology, syntax, or meanings can be studied, depending on the thoroughness with which one desires to make the study. Efforts are made to establish isoglosses, which may be described as cartographic lines separating the geographical localities which show a difference with respect to a specific linguistic item. Isoglosses for any given group of items do not always coincide, though they tend to bunch; on a time dimension they probably show gradual shifts. Linguistic geography furnishes important data for the interpretation of linguistic change and cultural history. One of the foremost students of the subject was the French linguist Gilliéron (see, for example, Gilliéron and Edmont, 1902–1910). A critical survey of dialect geography has recently been published by Pop (1950).

The preparation of even a reasonably satisfactory linguistic atlas of a broad speech area is a major undertaking. Atlases of varying thoroughness have been prepared, or are being prepared, for many regions in Europe, including France, Germany, Italy, Denmark, and Rumania. Renewed efforts are now being made to survey the complex dialect geography of the British Isles. In the United States, the work of Kurath and his associates is notable. A definitive study of the New England area has been published (Kurath *et al.,* 1939), and the work for the remaining portions of the eastern United States is nearing completion, some interpretations of the material having been published already (Kurath, 1949). There are, in fact, a number of other linguistic atlas projects under way, to provide coverage of the western United States.

General Remarks

It can readily be seen that except for the case of the Indo-European language family, and possibly one or two other families, the scope of the territory of linguistic science has been covered only in a highly restricted way. If we measure progress in terms of the three dimensions set forth above, the amount of coverage is extremely scanty with respect to the total territory. The historical dimension cannot be attacked with any propriety until the descriptive studies have been partially completed, and there is a crying need for more descriptive studies of more languages.

This situation is so vexing to some linguists that they have begun to reëxamine their operational procedures in order to find more efficient ways of collecting and analyzing data. There is an extreme scarcity of trained linguists in America. Linguists are not being trained fast enough to keep up with the pace with which languages change or become extinct. A quotation from a book review by Voegelin may give some further insight into this problem:

> In no case which I know has missionary material been restated by a linguist without returning to the field. In practice, missionary efforts are simply neglected by Americanists. But even if studied, such work provides the returning field worker with little more than memoranda of what to look for.
>
> The incomplete report of the trained linguist has too often had the following effect: X is now described, we must now turn to language Y; and if two students are interested in language Y, the second must be sent to language Z. After a generation of such work, languages X, Y, Z, if they are American Indian languages, are not only incompletely described, but extinct (Voegelin, 1942a).

Several linguists have been exploring the feasibility of using modern recording equipment in collecting data more efficiently than is possible when the field worker attempts to transcribe the utterances of his informant directly on paper. Professor Lounsbury of the Yale University Department of Anthropology made a trip to the Matto Grosso area of Brazil in the summer of 1950, carrying with him a wire recorder and other recording machines. His plan was to spend no more than two weeks on a particular language. The first week was to be spent in developing the phonemics and some of the morphology of the language by the usual techniques, that is, by face-to-face contact with the informant and phonetic transcription of the utterances. The second week was to be spent wholly in obtaining lengthy continuous texts in the native language by means of wire recordings. Simultaneously, translations into a "contact language" would be interpolated and recorded on an auxiliary recording machine. At the end of two weeks' study, enough material would be gained, it was estimated, to make it possible for a linguist to do at least a moderately satisfactory descriptive study of the language. If this procedure proved feasible, Lounsbury looked forward to the establishment of an extensive project to obtain data on a wide variety of languages as speedily as possible. Upon returning from South America in October 1950, Lounsbury reported to me that the experiment seemed to have been successful. Certain troubles were encountered with the recording equipment, but no grave difficulties arose which could not be remedied in further expeditions.

It is to be noted that Lounsbury's plan depends upon the use of modern recording equipment which was not available twenty years ago, when studies of American Indian languages first began to intensify under the sponsorship of Sapir and Boas. It would seem that this scheme represents a most realistic and sensible proposal for at least one solution to the problem of data collection in linguistics. It would make efficient use of the scarce manpower in linguistic science, and at the same time provide a training ground for future linguistic workers.

THE STATISTICAL STUDY OF LANGUAGE

It has already been suggested that a statistical or quantitative approach to language study may be desirable for the following reasons: (*a*) since linguistic data are massive, a statistical approach may be necessary to reduce these data to a usable form, not only to yield statistical summaries but to make possible the application of tests of the adequacy of sampling; (*b*) since a language structure may be viewed in terms of a sort of logical calculus, the analytic models provided by symbolic logic and by the theory of stochastic processes may be useful; and (*c*) as soon as one becomes interested in the actual frequency of occurrence of various linguistic forms in a large sample of texts or of spoken discourse, a quantitative approach must be adopted both because of the inherent nature of the problem and because of the extensiveness of the data.

The strength of contemporary interest in a quantitative approach to linguistics is attested by the establishment of a "Committee on Quantitative Linguistics" by the Sixth International Congress of Linguists in Paris, 1948.[15] One of the members of the original committee was the late George Kingsley Zipf of Harvard University. The objectives of this committee, as set forth in a published statement, are as follows:

1. To set up concrete empiric principles for a systematic quantitative research into linguistic systems;

2. To establish quantitative characteristics of languages on a comparative basis (e.g., comparative cultural-chronological data, comparative meaning-frequency distributions, etc.);

3. To disclose the underlying principles that govern the frequency distributions of linguistic elements;

4. To disclose by means of extensive scientific methodology the relationships between these observed frequency distributions and the "qualitative" aspects of individual and social human behavior.

A course in statistical linguistics was offered, for the first time, at the summer 1951 session of the Linguistic Institute (see p. 214).

With regard to the statistical approach to linguistic systems, several linguists discussed with the writer the possibility of using punched-card techniques. It is rather clear, however, that the approach of the American linguist in this connection would be to use punched-card techniques chiefly in order to arrange linguistic data to facilitate descriptive analyses of the usual sort. Few linguists are aware of the full possibilities of punched-card techniques of analysis.

There have been some attempts by linguists to adopt statistical approaches to linguistic typology and to certain aspects of comparative and historical linguistics. For example, Hockett (at Cornell) and Greenberg (at Columbia) have studied linguistic typology by the use of certain statistical measures and ratios, like the number of morphemes per 100 words. D. W. Reed (1949) has been exploiting the theory of statistical inference in connection with linguistic geography. Kroeber and Chrétien published two papers (1937, 1939) in which they desired to show the relations among various languages in the Indo-European family by the use of statistical correlations between these languages with respect to the presence or absence of common elements. These studies yielded interesting results, but a more refined and promising technique was proposed by Morris Swadesh at the summer 1950 meeting of the Linguistic Society of America. Swadesh is interested in what he terms glottochronology, a technique for inferring, from statistical comparisons of language systems, estimates not only of their probable familial relationships but also of the dates when the branches of a language family broke off from one another or from the parent language. The estimates are made on the basis of empirically determined parameters of the rates at which languages change, and from preliminary experiments the estimates appear to have considerable accuracy. For linguistics, glotto-chronology may prove to be as valuable as the carbon-14 dating technique, recently developed by the University of Chicago physicist W. F. Libby, is for archaeology and geology.

Various sorts of frequency counts have engaged the attention of linguists and others for many years. For example, the American linguist William Dwight Whitney (1874, Chap. VII) studied the relative frequency of sounds in English. Around the turn of the twentieth century, we find a number of frequency counts made for such purposes as assisting the development of reading materials for children or of stenographic systems. Kaeding (1897–1898) studied relative frequencies of words in German and Dewey (1923) made a somewhat similar analysis for English sounds and syllables. The work of the psychologist Thorndike (1932) in counting relative frequencies of words in English texts is known to every educator interested in grading the reading difficulty of children's school materials. Further investigations by Thorndike and his student Lorge have resulted in the recent publication of a part of what is known as *The English Semantic Count* (Lorge, 1937, 1949), which gives relative frequencies of words classified according to their dictionary meanings. Fries and Traver (1940) have published an able review and critique of English frequency lists and their uses. Frequency lists have also been made for other languages, such as French, German, and Spanish, in most cases utilizing the word as the unit of analysis. Eaton (1940) prepared a list of the common-est concepts in four modern languages. Bull (1948) published a provocative critique of frequency counts made for pedagogical purposes.

Frequency counts, while they may have some uses in the analysis of linguistic structure, have been primarily studied in an effort to identify in them evidences of inherent mathematical lawfulness. Among those who first pointed out such mathematical regularities was the physical scientist E. U. Condon (1928). The chief exponent of a mathematical approach to linguistic frequency counts has been the late G. K. Zipf, who in a series of books and articles (see chiefly Zipf, 1935, 1949) has used word counts as a basis on which to build a generalized theory of psychobiology, cul-minating in his "principle of least effort." Word-frequency phenomena are viewed by Zipf as only one manifestation of a general principle, ap-plicable also to such items as the relative sizes of cities in a nation or the optimal placement of tools at a workbench, which states that the organism attempts to "minimize the average rate of work-expenditure over time." A mathematical formulation of the relation between the frequency of individual items and their relative rank of frequency plays a central part in this theory. Specifically, it is held that an empirical relation which is approximated in the normal case is that the product of frequency and rank is constant. Zipf's work has had many critics, including Joos (1936) and Carroll (1938), who point out that the relation with Zipf postulates cannot possibly hold in samples larger than a certain size, and that the plot of rank against frequency is bound to have the appearance of regularity because of its monotonic character and the logical dependence of rank upon frequency. Many linguists are of the belief that Zipf has not established proper units of analysis. Nevertheless, the data assembled by Zipf are sufficiently striking to cause one to think that his general technique is highly suggestive. A considerably more satisfying approach to the analysis of frequency counts is that of the British statistician Yule (1944), based on the mathematics of probability; the work of Thomson and Thompson (1915) is also valuable in this connection. A further study based on mathematical statistics has been contributed by Ross (1950).

It must be noted that these mathematical studies of frequency counts inevitably concern themselves not with *language* (a linguistic code, or *la langue* in Saussurean terms), but rather with *speech* as the manifestation of the linguistic code. Though it is possible to conceive a code which in itself contains specifications of probability, it does not seem likely that any of the natural languages of the world contain such a code; nevertheless, it is remarkable that on the whole the linguistic codes of languages as diverse as English and Chinese, together with the environmental circumstances which condition the emission of speech, work in such a way as to produce verbal materials characterized by the apparent regularities studied by Zipf and others. It is therefore tempting to think that frequency studies have some implications for the study of linguistic structure, but the present writer, for one, is by no means convinced of this.

Other types of statistical studies of language are those concerned with differentiating samples of verbal materials from different speakers or writers, but these studies properly fall in the domain of psychology and will be discussed in the next chapter.

PHILOLOGICAL STUDIES

It would be amiss not to mention in this chapter the long tradition of philological study which has always been closely tied with the study of language and languages. In Chapter 1, I have described philology (at least in the American use of the term) as the large middle ground between linguistic science and the literary and humanistic studies. Philological scholarship results in such diverse products as studies of the cultural history of a language, dictionaries of slang and dialectal forms, editions and exegeses of literary works, and studies of folklore, fairy tales, and myths. Foerster (1941, p. 3) divides the field into linguistic philology and literary philology: in linguistic philology the focus of attention is upon linguistic phenomena as responding to historical and cultural forces, while in literary philology the emphasis is upon the interpretation of literature in the light of linguistic structure and its history. Foerster and his colleagues recommend that younger scholars preparing for either type of study get a thorough grounding in linguistic science in order to acquire valuable techniques of research and a proper perspective on the nature of language. At the same time, noting that preoccupation with the mere collection of philological facts has led to a decline in the prestige of literary and humane scholarship, they urge a return to the striving toward synthesis and interpretation which was characteristic of Renaissance humanism.

The spirit of contemporary linguistic philology is embodied in such works (to speak only of studies of the English language) as Baugh's *History of the English Language* (1935), Krapp's *The English Language in America* (1925), and Mencken's monumental study *The American Language* (4th edition, 1938, and supplements, 1945, 1948). The authors of these works would not be regarded as technical linguists in the tradition of Sapir and Bloomfield. When Mencken treats British and American variations in word usage, he has little need of technical linguistics; however, in his chapter on the pronunciation of American English one might be happier if he had used the scientific approach to phonetics and phonemics which is now customary in technical studies. But aside from points of technical accuracy which might be raised by caviling critics, Mencken has done what linguistic science as such would never propose to do, namely, to portray the growth of the English language in America, in most of its important details, as a resultant of the vicissitudes of history and the attitudes of the people who used the language.

Linguistic philology has other important areas of preoccupation, one of the most important being the preparation of dictionaries. Such works as the *New English Dictionary,* Mathews' *Dictionary of Americanisms* (1951), or the Middle English dictionary now in progress under the supervision of Hans Kurath[16] involve not only the careful examination of usage in all forms of verbal expression but also the scholarly evaluation of the materials from the point of view of linguistic history.

Literary philology can be traced back to the Hebraic and Alexandrine exegetic traditions. In the editing, interpretation, and criticism of literary works, one must draw extensively on a knowledge of the structure and history of the language in which they are written. For example, the reading of Chaucer requires a knowledge of the fact that the double negative was an approved syntactical construction in his day. It would be more than futile to give here any listing of representative studies in literary philology, for this pursuit ranges over the whole gamut of classical and modern literature. One development of note, however, is represented by Leo Spitzer's application of linguistic methods to literary works with the purpose of inferring an author's state of mind in the act of composition (Spitzer, 1948b). Such studies in stylistics verge upon psychological studies in nonconventional, individual variations in language usage, to which we shall allude in the next chapter. For a general evaluation of the implications of linguistics for the study of literature, one may refer to Wellek and Warren's *Theory of Literature* (1949; see, however, Malone's review in *Language,* 1950, 26, 311–313).

SUMMARY

There is considerable basis for conceiving of linguistics as one of the most advanced of the social sciences. Its methodology is sound and highly developed. Its data are highly concrete and manageable through appropriate techniques. It is rapidly approaching the status of a self-contained system of facts and principles which will embrace the totality of its possible subject matter. In this respect it resembles most closely the natural sciences such as physics and chemistry. There is no other social science which can claim to be so rapidly approaching such a status; linguistics is far in advance of psychology, for example, with respect to the development of its methodology and its relative comprehensiveness. When we speak of comprehensiveness, we mean that linguistics is becoming a complete theory to cover *language* as it is defined by linguists—the study of the "systems of arbitrary vocal symbols used by the members of a speech community in social interaction," to use the definition offered by Bloch and Trager (1942). We do *not* mean, however, that linguistics bids fair to become the general science of the communicative process; in fact, linguistics as it is ordinarily conceived does not propose to do so. Nevertheless, the body of knowledge which is developing in linguistic science is prerequisite for any more general communication science.

The major forward-looking tasks of present-day American linguistics are as follows:

1. The further refinement of linguistic methodology, with special attention to the identification of the larger units in language structure and the development of more rigorous procedures for studying syntax.

2. The collection of large amounts of field data from relatively unknown languages, as well as more intensive efforts in the descriptive analysis of the well-known languages.

3. The further development of methodology in comparative linguistics, partly by inference from principles known from Indo-European comparative linguistics, in order to make possible more rigorous comparative studies on language families whose early origins are not known through written documents.

4. After the collection and analysis of further data, more intensive efforts to make generalized statements about languages, with special reference to linguistic typology and the general classification of languages from a structural point of view.

5. Extension of the borders of linguistics to include such problems as linguistic psychology and the discovery of relations between linguistic systems and culture patterns. Special attention needs to be given to the role of linguistic systems in habitual patterns of thought (the *"Weltanschauung"* problem as it was discussed above).

Like scientists in many other fields, linguists regard their activities as valuable in their own right. They do not believe that their activities need to be immediately justified by reference to some "practical" applications which may emerge. They recognize, however, that long-range support of their pursuits by society at large rests upon the value which society puts on them, and in some measure upon the extent to which practical applications are foreseen. The remainder of this book will discuss numerous practical applications of linguistic studies. The ultimate justification for the science of linguistics, however, is possibly seen in the fact that linguists study the phenomenon *language* by virtue of which society is able to exist.

Chapter 3 LINGUISTICS AND PSYCHOLOGY

INTRODUCTION

Despite the fact that linguistics is most closely allied with the social sciences, it is not illogical to begin the consideration of its relations to other disciplines by devoting our attention to its connections with psychology. If we follow the principle of reductionism in our view of the organization of scientific endeavor, we may want to look first to psychology for explanations of certain linguistic phenomena. But even aside from this, the study of verbal behavior is an important field in its own right. We must therefore examine the implications of linguistic science for such a study.

It must be assumed at the outset that the reader knows something of the scope, methods, and results of psychology. Nevertheless, it is necessary to draw his attention to certain facts.

Textbooks of psychology usually introduce the student to psychology as the "science of human behavior." It is not always emphasized that this is a broader definition of psychology than is warranted by what psychologists actually do. Psychologists do not study *all* human behavior; if they did, their subject matter would overlap with that of all other scientists. In the division of scientific labor, psychology addresses its attention to the attempt to discover general laws of human behavior. Among the major categories of the psychologist's subject matter are learning, motivation, perception, and individual differences in ability. In studying any one of these problems, psychologists pay relatively less attention to the specific content of the behavior being studied than to the general laws presumably underlying that behavior. In studying learning, for example, the psychologist may care little whether he studies the responses of rats pressing levers or the responses of human organisms learning a series of nonsense syllables. It is natural, therefore, to expect that the psychologist is not going to be immediately interested in linguistics, because linguistics is the study of the structure of certain learned responses as determined largely by the social environment of the individual. The verbal responses studied by the linguist constitute only *one* class of responses that could be studied by the psychologist, and the psychologist need not necessarily ascribe special merit to these responses as objects of investigation, as compared with others.

Actually, the statements of the last paragraph present a much oversimplified view. They are made only to highlight the contrast between the respective subject matters of linguists and psychologists. In point of fact, there is ample evidence that psychologists have been impelled, by the nature of the case, to mark off verbal behavior as a special class of behavior. The study of verbal behavior is apparently of central importance in the study of complex response systems like thinking, imagination, reasoning, and judgment, and it plays some part even in the study of perception, motivation, and emotion. Skinner (1938, p. 442) hazards the guess that the only differences (aside from enormous differences in complexity) between the behavior of rats and that of human beings will be found to lie in verbal behavior. G. A. Miller (1951a, p. 173), in a recent book on the psychology of language and communication, explains phenomena of meaning by saying that "a special area of behavior is marked off because it depends entirely on the intervention of another person for its reinforcement."

It seems quite proper, therefore, to think of the study of verbal behavior as a major field or branch of psychology. This field, which has variously been called the *psychology of language, linguistic psychology,* or *psycholinguistics,* has been sometimes classed as a branch of social psychology,[1] but it seems to have broad implications for the whole field of psychology. It is even possible that the study of verbal responses may make a fundamental contribution to the general theory of behavior.

A complete theory of verbal behavior would have to take into account the manifold influences which come to bear upon any particular linguistic response, or upon the perception of and response to any particular language response. The number of such influences is undoubtedly very large, including organismic factors, factors associated with the structure of the language system, and specific environmental and situational factors. We may regard linguistic psychology as the study of all these influences. But our study need not stop with the description, explanation, and prediction of verbal responses; we may also be concerned with the effects of verbal behavior on other activities of the person. In this sense, as well as in others, linguistic psychology has implications for other fields of psychology.

A BIBLIOGRAPHICAL NOTE

In this chapter one could hardly hope to cover even a small fraction of what has been written on the subject of linguistic psychology. We must limit our attention to certain major problems, attempting to evaluate some of the more significant approaches and to sketch those aspects of linguistic psychology in which there seem to be important mutual implications of psychology and linguistics for one another. The reader interested in gaining a more detailed knowledge of achievement in linguistic psychology, both in America and abroad, may be referred to books and reviews by G. H. Mead (1904), Esper (1921, 1935), Adams and Powers (1929), McGranahan (1936), Pronko (1946), and G. A. Miller (1951a). European studies have been emphasized in Kainz's surveys (1941–1943, 1946). The citation of these references will perhaps serve to excuse the apparent neglect of many things which only lack of space forbids mentioning.

TREATMENTS OF LINGUISTIC PROBLEMS IN PSYCHOLOGY

One can readily see that the major theoretical questions in linguistic psychology would in many instances be also those of general psychology, in its historical development. Boring (1950) has traced the lines of thinking about such problems as the nature of mind, thought, idea, and consciousness through the history of psychology from the time of Aristotle up to the present. Since these are delicate problems, it may be advisable to stop here long enough to examine them from a modern standpoint and to state the position which will provide the orientation for later discussions.

Philosophical dualism—the notion that mind and body are distinct entities—was a predominant theme in the prescientific era of psychology. It is widely recognized today that psychology as a science must be independent of metaphysical philosophical questions, but perhaps the most pernicious heritage from the days of philosophical psychology is a confusion, still current in some quarters, between the *philosophical* problem of dualism and the uniquely *psychological* problem of subjective, implicit behavior as distinguished from overt, directly observable behavior. The confusion seems to have arisen specifically in the form of an erroneous notion that to attempt to study subjective behavior is to attempt to study the activities of mind, viewed as a separate, noncorporeal entity. There have been psychologists who have been either so overimbued with the notion that scientific psychology must deal only with immediately observable "public" behavior, or so fearful of being labeled "mentalists" in the philosophical sense of the term, that they have wanted to rule out any consideration of subjective events in psychological discussions. I take the initial position that subjective events can be regarded as behavioral, that they play an important role in many behavior sequences, and that appeal to them in a psychological context bears no necessary trace of philosophical dualism. I further take the position that there are publicly observable indices of subjective events (not the least of which is verbal behavior) and that subjective events may be assumed to follow much the same laws as those events observable as neurological, motor, and glandular responses. It may be granted that under certain conditions (for example, when the individual is deliberately lying) indices of subjective events may appear to be untrustworthy if taken at face value, but this fact is not a sound basis for ruling out all indices of subjective events.

This "neobehavioristic" position, which I espouse, is in fact widely current in psychology. Psychologists constantly behave on the assumption that subjective events occur; they are willing to talk about "thought," "images," "dreams," and "percepts," though they prefer to speak of these things as events and processes rather than states. Even in planning experiments of the most objective character they are likely to draw hypotheses from self-observations of subjective behavior. The problem of subjective behavior becomes critical only when one speaks of consciousness, for there is a danger that one may lapse into philosophical dualism again by stating that something happens in consciousness which independently guides or directs overt behavior. We can regard the problem of consciousness as a spurious one, however, for if we think of subjective behavior as a series of responses, the notion of consciousness need not enter our discussions. Wherever the term *consciousness* is used here, it can be equated with subjective behavior.

What is properly objectionable in some psychological discussions which appeal to subjective behavior is a naïve faith in the validity and generalizability of one's own introspections which fails to consider alternative interpretations, to check with the self-observations of others, or to attend to the publicly observable indices of behavior which are often available. This is a lesson well learned by those who have been interested in studying imagery, "imageless thought," and similar problems, and it is from this standpoint that we may have occasion to criticize a number of views which may be found in writings on the psychology of language.

To return now to the history of linguistic psychology, we may cite first the views of the British empiricist school. James Mill and his son, John Stuart Mill, proposed that simple ideas and perceptions get combined by a sort of "mental chemistry" to produce more complex thoughts. Such a proposal seems to reflect its authors' observations of language phenomena, for complex thoughts might be represented by combinations of words in syntactical constructions showing the relations between the lower-order notions expressed by those words. Indeed, J. S. Mill's treatise on a system of logic (1843) starts with a chapter urging the necessity of making an analysis of language in studying intellectual activities, and proceeds to make a division of "namable things" into feelings and states of consciousness, minds, bodies, and "successions and coexistences." The school of psychology represented by the British associationists was centrally concerned with the explanation of mental processes by association of ideas. Nevertheless, these interpretations could hardly be said to rest on any sophisticated knowledge of language beyond the notions of subject, object, attribute, etc., popularized by grammarians, and one may take exception to the unbridled introspective analysis on which they were based.

Wilhelm Wundt, a German who is often identified as the founder of the first laboratory of experimental psychology, was probably also the first psychologist to write major treatises (1900–1909, 1901) devoted specifically to the psychology of language. These treatises, particularly *Die Sprache,* deserve more attention than they have usually been accorded, for, despite their somewhat antiquated theoretical orientation, they contain a number of provocative discussions and interpretations of certain detailed aspects of language behavior, such as sentence construction, word compounding, and speech perception. Wundt was an alert observer, even if his observations were frequently of an introspective character. Wundt's work on language does not seem to have been influential in America, despite the impact on American psychology of some of his other work, at least in the early years of the present century. Titchener (1909), one of Wundt's chief American students, was responsible for setting the tone of the psychology of that day—

a "structuralism" which hoped to analyze the contents of the mind by precise and carefully controlled introspective methods.

One outcome of Wundt's work and the experiments which were stimulated by his teachings was the discovery, around 1900, of "imageless thought" —a kind of subjective behavior, noted in the process of thinking, which could not be described as falling into such familiar categories as sensation and perception. There was, indeed, an acrimonious debate over whether any such thing existed, as claimed by Marbe, Külpe, and others at the University of Würzburg, but at any rate the aspects of their work which may be of use for linguistic psychology are those which indicate the existence of "determining tendencies," "conscious attitudes," or "sets" which play a part in thinking, controlled association, and perhaps all verbal behavior. This phase of the history of experimental psychology has been well described by Woodworth (1938, Chap. 30), who incidentally had been one of the active investigators in this field.

Functionalism, as a reaction to structuralism, was shaped by Carr and others at the University of Chicago; it sought to emphasize the dynamic phases of behavior and mental life, as revealed by the new data on learning and conditioning which was starting to accumulate. This was the matrix in which there developed what is known as Watsonian behaviorism. Watson, however, declared that the mind is not a proper object of study in psychology because any observations on the mind are subjective and therefore cannot form a part of public, verifiable knowledge. Watson proposed instead to study only overt behavior and the stimulus-response relations revealed thereby. "Consciousness" and the contents of consciousness such as concepts, thoughts, and ideas were regarded as mere epiphenomena. "Thinking" was conceived as merely the action of laryngeal mechanisms or subvocal muscular movements.[2] These views were fully discussed by Watson in his *Psychology from the Standpoint of a Behaviorist* (1919) and in an article replying to critics (1920).

The advent of behaviorism had two effects on studies in the psychology of language. First, it explained language in too easy a fashion, language behavior being dismissed merely as a set of conditioned responses. Secondly, it turned the attention of theoretical psychology away from the study of language and toward other problems which seemed at the time to be of a more fundamental character, such as the nature of the learning process. The study of linguistic psychology subsequently played only a small part in psychological experimentation. Kantor (1922), Esper (1921), F. H. Allport (1924), and Weiss (1925, 1929) were among the few psychologists to continue a theoretical interest in language behavior, but they were concerned not with the analysis of languages but rather with ways in which linguistic responses are learned and with the part that they play in the total behavior of the organism. Esper (1925, 1933) and Wolfle (1932) performed interesting experiments bearing on the psychological interpretation of linguistic change. In May 1929, a whole issue of the *Psychological Bulletin* was devoted to reviews of various problems in the psychology and philosophy of language and speech; it included, incidentally, a short article by the linguist E. H. Sturtevant on the Linguistic Society of America, in which Sturtevant speaks of a "recent rapprochement" of linguistics and psychology. This rapprochement was short-lived, apparently, for linguists and theoretical psychologists, at least, soon went their separate ways.

One of the most provocative treatments of linguistic problems by a psychologist is Kantor's *Objective Psychology of Grammar* (1936), which is an attempt to carry through the implications of a variety of behaviorism for the study of verbal behavior. It contains an exhaustive and scholarly history of the psychology of language, with an examination of the views of such writers as Schleicher, Steinthal, Paul, Wundt, Delbrück, Vendryes, Hocart, Stout, Gardiner, Bühler, Sapir, and Bloomfield. Kantor has two major complaints about linguistics. First, he accuses many linguists (especially those of the nineteenth century) of misconceptions stemming from a mentalistic bias, chiefly the mistaken acceptance of a symbolic or expression theory according to which language is a tool for expressing or communicating thoughts, ideas, feelings, and images. Such a theory, Kantor declares, has no place in objective psychology. He proposes that the study of linguistic meaning should be regarded as the study of the speaker's adjustments to situations. Kantor's second complaint is that linguistics has in the past dealt "exclusively with the crystallized materials of thing-language," and that it has failed to study language as the adjustmental behavior of people talking to one another. One of Kantor's students, N. H. Pronko, expanded this point of view in a review, "Language and Psycholinguistics" (1946). For example, he criticized Sebeok (1943) for constructing a phonetic system of the language Santali from data secured *"in toto* from a grammar and folk tales." "Sebeok's study," he continued, "serves as an excellent illustration of the divergent interests between students of *linguistic behavior* and those of *phonemes*. The latter handle, arrange, and systematize textual materials; the former describe the action of an organism typically talking *to someone about something*." Several other representative studies in linguistic analysis were summed up as involving mere textual and transcriptional analysis, that is, the study of what Kantor calls "thing-language." Pronko finally admits, "This is not to criticize interest in such specialized portions of the linguistic event, but only to distinguish again the behavioral datum from other aspects of language phenomena."

The linguist may justifiably enter a mild protest at this point. It is misleading, he would say, to characterize linguistics as the "handling, arranging, and systematizing of textual materials." The textual materials used by the linguist are, at least in the ideal situation, merely the records of his observations of actual speech behavior, and are therefore quite comparable to the protocols which a psychologist makes during the course of an experiment. Even the "textual materials" represented by a papyrus fragment dug up from the sands of Egypt are inevitably the result of somebody's behavior. Fundamentally, the criticism that linguistics deals with "textual materials" misses the point entirely. As we have attempted to show in the previous chapter, linguistics is concerned with the analysis of the system of linguistic responses current in a given speech community. It does not in principle matter, therefore, whether a linguist uses textual materials, phonograph records, or his own speech patterns in making the types of analysis in which he is interested. In point of fact, the *system* which the linguist studies is tantamount to what Kantor (1936, p. 87) introduces as a "linguistic institution" as a factor conditioning language behavior. Finally, such a linguistic theorist as Trager (1949) would undoubtedly reply to Kantor and Pronko's objections by saying that in *metalinguistics*[3] the linguist would certainly be concerned with how an organism "talks to someone about something."

The bulk of Kantor's treatment is concerned with a careful evaluation, from his "interbehavioristic" point of view, of various problems in linguistics, such as phonology, morphology, syntax, semantics, parts of speech, person, gender, case, tense, voice, mood, and negation. His major achievement is to have cleared the ground of the many dubious, mentalistically toned, and purely speculative statements which have been offered by students of language as psychological "explanations" of linguistic phenomena. At the same time he proposes numerous interesting hypotheses as to an interbehavioral interpretation of grammar. He consistently maintains the point of view that "psychological grammar . . . is the study of how language adaptations are actually carried out." But Kantor seems to have little feeling for the importance of the linguistic system as a system of learned responses. On the theoretical side, Kantor protests too much about mentalism in language study. When he derides the symbol-expression theories of Ogden and Richards (1936) or of Gardiner (1932), for example, he is criticizing the words and phraseology of these writers as much as he is criticizing their concepts. Words such as "idea," "thought," "meaning" can after all be regarded as shorthand expressions for the prelinguistic situational factors which Kantor himself emphasizes. There is evidence that there are actually prelinguistic organismic events (sets, attitudes, etc.) which can be identified with what expression theorists regard as "thoughts" and "ideas," and Kantor even permits himself to speak of "attitudes" and "feelings." Kantor's treatment also suffers from a number of forced distinctions and unconventional definitions. For example, the nearest thing to what he conceives to be *language* is the spontaneous and creative communicative behavior of a speaker in a conversational situation. But he regards formulaic utterances like "Good morning" and "Thanks" as nonlinguistic, because they are "not linguistic adjustments" and are not likely "to constitute referential adaptations to speaker and thing spoken of" (Kantor, 1936, p. 21).

On the whole, Kantor is criticizing varieties of linguistic theory which are not widely held today; he overlooks the fundamental objectives of linguistic science, which in this context may be described as the study of the conventionalized aspects of adjustmental verbal responses. Perhaps we should not even use the term *adjustment,* for the concept of adjustment is in contemporary psychological theory being replaced by the concept of *reinforcement* (referring to the rewarding and punishing of responses). Thus, we do not have to be concerned with whether responses are "adjustmental," but only with whether they have been rewarded or punished. Furthermore, it is useless to require that linguistic responses be "referential adaptations to speaker and thing spoken of," for in reinforcement theory the speaker and thing spoken of are regarded as reinforcing agencies, and one may operate without the other.

The theoretical approach to verbal behavior adopted by Skinner (1936, 1947), Carroll (1944), and G. A. Miller (1951a) is notably different from Kantor's. It was Skinner (1938) who introduced the concepts of operant behavior and instrumental learning and who first pointed out that verbal behavior, par excellence, exemplifies operant behavior. Operant behavior may be defined as spontaneous behavior which can be, or has been, differentially reinforced by "instrumental conditioning." For example, a characteristic spontaneous behavior in the pigeon is the pecking response; this response can be rewarded so that it is established as an operant or instrumental response conditioned to some particular rewarding stimulus, say food. The pigeon can then "use" this response as a "sign" that it is hungry. Skinner points out that spontaneous verbal behavior in the child undergoes a somewhat similar process of reinforcement, but in this case the reinforcement is social. The child hence learns to say "milk" when it wants milk, and the rewarding situation can be said to be the "meaning" of the word *milk*. This account of verbal behavior, when supplied with the requisite detail, can presumably be extended to all linguistic phenomena. Carroll (1944) suggested that the results of linguistic science may be useful in identifying the units of many kinds of verbal behavior. Both Skinner and Carroll have emphasized that the problem of describing verbal behavior, as well as the problem of meaning, reduces to the problem of describing the strengths (or "latencies") of verbal responses under various stimulus conditions; this applies not only to the speaker but also to the hearer. Miller (1951b) has been particularly concerned with the effect of verbal context, that is, with the interdependencies between the responses in the speech flow.

There have been sporadic evidences of interest in linguistic psychology elsewhere. F. H. Sanford made an extensive study of possible relations between speech behavior and personality (1942a). Soon afterward, he published a review entitled "Speech and Personality" (1942b). The first two paragraphs of this review deserve to be quoted:

Language, traditionally, has been regarded the "vehicle of thought," with the thought attracting far more attention than the vehicle. But there are those who object to the traditional distribution of attention on the ground that the vehicle as well as the freight it carries should be given systematic scrutiny. We will pave the way for a nomothetic science of language, they insist, only when we stop worrying exclusively about the thoughts expressed and lay hold on the linguistic reactions themselves.

The psychologist whose curiosity is chronically skewed toward problems of personality finds considerable promise in this new "objective-descriptive" approach to language. He senses that precise linguistic data may lead not only to the formulation of general linguistic laws but also to a greater understanding of the individual who uses language.

One gets a curious sense of indirection on reading the foregoing statement. One is tempted to say that, instead of "the thought attracting far more attention than the vehicle," quite the opposite is true. Linguistic science, above all, has given attention to language as a *vehicle,* and could even be said to be a nomothetic science of language. It is regrettable, therefore, that in the remainder of Sanford's review there is not a single reference to the results of linguistic science. Nevertheless, Sanford's summary statement is valid and suggestive:

There are many indications that language is a vehicle of personality as well as of thought, for when the person speaks, he tells not only about the world but also, through both form and content, about himself (p. 840).

It is unfortunate that Sanford does not seem to realize that linguistic science may have something to say about this problem in so far as it may help to draw the line between what is purely formal and culturally determined in an individual's utterances, on the one hand, and the personal, stylistic elements which are peculiar to the individual, on the other.

There has been a considerable interest in the psychology of language on the part of a group of specialists concerned with speech education. Since this is primarily a field of application rather than of basic research, it will be more fully described in Chapter 6. While some textbooks in this field (for example, Gray and Wise, 1934; Eisenson, 1938) have drawn heavily, and sometimes rather uncritically, upon research and theory construction more strictly in the fields of linguistics and psychology, a number of speech educators have been active in performing research on certain special problems. Gilkinson (1943) has published a research-oriented bibliography of work in this area, much of which has been reported in such journals as the *Quarterly Journal of Speech* and *Speech Monographs.* There have been valuable studies of the relation between public-speaking ability and personality (Knower, 1938; Gilkinson and Knower, 1940), on speech training and intelligibility (J. W. Black, 1946), and on voice characteristics in emotion

(Fairbanks and Pronovost, 1939). Speech educators have devoted attention to dialectal variations in speech characteristics. The study reported by Byers (1947), while it is based on a pitifully small number of cases, suggests that men in military service during World War II tended to lose some dialectal speech characteristics. This study is one of the very few that have investigated linguistic change *in cursu*.[4]

One other development quite peripheral to the field of psychology as such may be mentioned. For a number of years, C. L. Meader and J. H. Muyskens[5] have been developing a theory of what they term *biolinguistics*. They have recently published the first volume of a major work on biolinguistics (Meader and Muyskens, 1950); from this it would appear that they treat language and communicative behavior as a biologically determined activity of the organism. The emphasis is neurophysiological, with a strong appeal to embryological and genetic data.

TREATMENTS OF PSYCHOLOGICAL PROBLEMS IN LINGUISTICS

It is probably safe to say that linguistics developed more rapidly as a science than did psychology. By 1879, the date of the founding of the first psychological laboratory by Wundt, linguistics, especially comparative linguistics, had matured as a fairly well-developed science. Psychology, on the other hand, was still just beginning to throw off its connection with philosophy. As a consequence, psychological linguistics in the nineteenth century was largely speculative. In *Prinzipien der Sprachgeschichte* (1880), Hermann Paul attempted to make psychological interpretations of various statements about the characteristics of languages and their development and growth. Bloomfield (1933, p. 17) asserts that Paul's insistence on psychological interpretations is one of the great weaknesses of his work. Writes Bloomfield, "He [Paul] accompanies his statements about language with a paraphrase in terms of mental processes which the speakers are supposed to have undergone. The only evidence for these mental processes is the linguistic process; they add nothing to the discussion, but only obscure it." Bloomfield himself had earlier been guilty of just such psychological interpretations, for in his *Introduction to the Study of Language* (1914) that part of his exposition which concerned psychological problems was based explicitly on Wundt's view of language as an outgrowth of emotional expression.

Franz Boas, who was something of a psychologist as well as an anthropologist and linguist, speculated about the relations of linguistics and psychology in his classic introduction to the *Handbook of American Indian Languages* (1911-1922, Part I). He rejected the idea that a nation's "psychic traits" may be reflected in its language; he believed that "obstacles to generalized thought inherent in the form of a language are of minor importance only." However, he discussed the importance of "the question of the relation of the unconscious character of language phenomena to the more conscious ethnological phenomena." He also stated his opinion that "the occurrence of the most fundamental grammatical concepts in all languages must be considered as proof of the unity of fundamental psychological processes."

By 1920, the upheaval in psychology which culminated in Watson's publication of *Psychology from the Standpoint of a Behaviorist* (1919) was already apparent. Behaviorism was in the air, and the first evidence that this upheaval influenced linguistics is to be found in Sapir's remark, in the introduction to his book *Language* (1921, p. iii), that he "had little to say of the ultimate psychological basis of speech." He preferred to "handle the subject of speech without constant and explicit reference" to a psychological basis (p. 9). Reaction to mentalistic psychology was full-blown by the time of Bloomfield's revised text, published in 1933, in which he wrote, "There has been much upheaval in psychology; we have learned, at any rate, what one of our masters suspected thirty years ago, namely, that we can pursue the study of language without reference to any one psychological doctrine, and that to do so safeguards our results and makes them more significant to workers in related fields" (1933, p. vii). "The findings of the linguist, who studies the speech-signal, will be all the more valuable for the psychologist if they are not distorted by any prepossessions about psychology. We have seen that many of the older linguists ignored this; they vitiated or skimped their reports by trying to state everything in terms of some psychological theory" (p. 32). None the less, at many places in his exposition, Bloomfield showed his inclination to support, if pressed to state a preference, a mechanistic theory of behavior. Bloomfield had been influenced, in this respect, chiefly by the behaviorist A. P. Weiss, author of *A Theoretical Basis of Human Behavior* (1929).

Nevertheless, Bloomfield's essential view, to the effect that linguistics should proceed without psychological interpretation, still stands as a guiding principle of contemporary linguistic analysis. While this view has indubitable merits, some linguists seem to have interpreted Bloomfield's position as ruling out all consideration of meaning in any context. Swadesh, a student of Sapir, views the "mechanical materialist" trends initiated by Bloomfield as "evidences of a struggle between realistic fact and mechanistic fetishism: particularly between the fact that meaning is an inseparable aspect of language, and the fetish that anything related to the mind must be ruled out of science" (Swadesh, 1948, p. 254). To be sure, Bloomfield's position on the meaning of meaning was extreme: to study meanings, in Bloomfield's view, is to study the sum total of human knowledge (Bloomfield, 1933, p. 139). If we reject this part of his doctrine, however, there remains his essentially correct, though incomplete, description of meaning in behavioristic stimulus-response terms.

Even today, however, linguists cannot avoid occasionally making appeals to psychological problems, particularly when they enter fields outside of strict descriptive linguistics. In his recent monograph on acoustic phonetics (1948), Martin Joos finds it interesting to make a number of hypotheses as to the way in which speech sounds are perceived, referring his readers to recent work on auditory perception by various psychologists.

It would be hard to ignore the psychological problems with which Whorf is concerned in his series of papers on broader implications of linguistics (1939, 1940a, 1940b, 1941) which have been discussed in Chapter 2. Whorf postulates, in effect, that the structure of an individual's language is a determining factor in the way he perceives and responds to the environment. Up to this point no psychologist has had occasion to cast this hypothesis in a form such that it could be subjected to experimental test, except in the case of the exploratory work reported by Cofer and his associates (Cofer, 1951).

It is not hard to draw the conclusion, from the foregoing summary of the history of linguistic psychology, that at least until recently there has been little common understanding or interest, at least in America, between the main streams of linguistics and of psychology. There is perhaps a perfectly good reason for this, namely that each field has had to solve some of its own problems before expanding its interests elsewhere.

CURRENT STUDIES IN THE PSYCHOLOGY
OF COMMUNICATION

There is a rapidly growing interest and activity today in what might be called the *psychology of communication.* During World War II, the military services sponsored a considerable amount of research on the psychology of audition; the results of this research were needed in connection with the design of communications systems on ships, planes, and tanks. It was almost inevitable that this research should concern itself in large measure with the variables affecting the intelligibility of speech when transmitted over a communication channel. In the main, the variables associated with the communications systems themselves were studied. For example, the effects of frequency distortion, variation in intensity level, the signal-to-noise ratio, phase distortion, wave clipping, and time selectivity were studied. A number of practical applications concerning the design and use of communications systems and components were discovered. In general, it was found that speech intelligibility is highly resistant to the various types of distortion that can be introduced, and that no single dimension of distortion is critical. A given type of distortion, or the combination of several types of distortion, does not reduce intelligibility unless the basic *pattern* of energy distribution over the basic dimensions of intensity, frequency, and time is impaired. An excellent summary of this work, by J. C. R. Licklider and G. A. Miller, has been published as Chapter 26, "The Perception of Speech," in the recent *Handbook of Experimental Psychology,* edited by S. S. Stevens (Licklider and Miller, 1951).

At the same time, it was discovered that there were variations in speech intelligibility which were independent of the mechanical features and variations of communications systems as such. Instead, these variations were dependent on characteristics of the speaker and the listener. It was found that not only were there considerable differences in the ability of talkers to utter a message which could be understood under difficult conditions of distortion in the communication system, but also that talkers could be trained to speak more intelligibly. Likewise, it was found that listeners showed wide individual differences in the ability to perceive distorted speech, and that to some extent they could be trained in this respect. The most important variations in speech which affect its intelligibility were found to be its intensity, its "noise-penetrating quality," the crispness of the consonants, and its deviation from "General American" dialect.[6] One implication of these findings for linguistic analysis would seem to be that a fieldworker studying a language must be careful to select as informants those speakers who talk most intelligibly, as determined by the intelligibility of their speech to other speakers of the language. If such a precaution is not taken, the linguistic analysis could easily miss certain features of the language which enable speakers to talk with maximal intelligibility under adverse conditions. Some linguists have recognized this possibility and have taken the care to distinguish between "slow speech" and "fast speech." Of course, it may be a mistake to draw a line of demarcation between slow and fast speech, for the rate of speech is a continuous variable; nevertheless, some recognition of variations in the intelligibility of speakers is mandatory in linguistic field work.

It will be noticed that the emphasis in these studies of speech intelligibility is upon the *reception* of speech in its acoustic aspects. The approach is initially a global or molar one: how much of a given stretch of speech can be understood? A molecular approach to the same problem has been essayed by the linguist Martin Joos in his monograph *Acoustic Phonetics* (1948). Joos is concerned with the question of what characteristics of individual speech sounds—the various vowels and consonants—make them intelligible.

The interest in problems connected with the reception of speech has naturally led several psychologists to consider the implications of Shannon's communication theory (Shannon and Weaver, 1949) for their results. As we point out in Chapter 7, communication theory as developed by communications engineers is concerned primarily with the efficiency of communication channels; in this theory the necessity arises of measuring the amount of information in a message in order to find out how much of the information gets through to the receiving end of the channel. Why not, ask Licklider and Miller, attempt to measure the amount of information in speech? First, what is the maximum amount of information that could be transmitted in speech? For an ideal system utilizing the same bandwidth as normal speech, Licklider and Miller (1951, p. 1070) suggest that 50,000 decisions, or bits of information, per second is a good estimate of this amount. Next, how much information is actually transmitted by speech? This question can be approached on different levels of analysis. One may consider the amount of information conveyed in the choice of a given phoneme, or in the choice of a given syllable, or in the choice of a given word, etc. In any case, these writers conclude that somewhat less than 50 units of information per second are transmitted in normal speech.[7]

Communication theory can also be applied, as G. A. Miller (1951b) points out, to the study of the way in which a speaker constructs his message. It is assumed that the "verbal context," defined as consisting of "the communicative acts that precede and follow the verbal response under consideration," is an important factor in the selection of the units of a message. Miller therefore focuses attention upon the statistical dependencies among the units of a connected sample of speech. The mathematical model is that of a "discrete Markoff process." (A Markoff process has to do with the different "states" into which a phenomenon can get, and the statistical probabilities which govern the transition of the phenomenon from one state to another.) With the aid of this theory, Miller computes the amount of information likely to be contained in typical samples of speech, as well as the average amount of redundancy in English.

Miller (1950) reports several interesting psychological experiments based on communication theory. In one experiment, he showed that the intelligibility of words in a test list is dependent on the size of the list. A subject who knows that only *two* words are going to be used in the test can identify these words even under severe conditions of distortion or interference. A subject who knows that the test list contains 256 different words has difficulty in identifying words unless the communication channel is relatively free of noise. The detailed results of this experiment were in good agreement with predictions made on the basis of communication theory. In another experiment, "sentences" were constructed in various degrees of approximation to English. The zero-order approximation consisted of a sequence of words picked at random from a dictionary without regard to their frequencies in actual speech. A first-order approximation contained words drawn at random from continuous text, so that each word had a chance to occur proportional to its relative frequency in normal English. A second-order approximation was constructed by considering the statistical dependencies between pairs of words in English, and so forth for the higher-order approximations. These sentences were read once to groups of subjects who were required to copy down immediately as much as they could remember.

It was shown that their accuracy in recall increased as the order of approximation to English increased. Thus, concluded Miller, meaningful material is easy to remember simply "because it preserves the short-term dependencies of English."[8]

Another application of Shannon's communication theory has to do with determining the range, in a typical sample of connected speech, over which statistical dependencies can be observed. For example, in a sample of speech, it is obvious that there is a high degree of dependence between one phoneme and the next (for example, in English the phoneme /ð/ is very likely to be followed by the phoneme /ə/,[9] but it is unlikely that a phoneme at one position would show statistical dependence with a phoneme ten positions farther on in the sequence. This problem is known as the *autocorrelation* problem and it can be studied through an application of the physical theory of damped vibrations. E. B. Newman (1951) reported a comparative study of the autocorrelation functions of a number of languages, including English, French, Italian, and German. He studied only the autocorrelation of vowels in contrast to consonants, and based his analysis on written texts in these languages. This statistical study of language structure would have been considerably more valuable if the analysis had been based on phonemic transcriptions; however, even an approach so modified would appear to ignore the morphophonemics of a language. Whorf (1940a) and Harris (1951, p. 153) have given schematic descriptions of the English monosyllabic word in terms of its permissible and nonpermissible sequences of phonemes. The autocorrelation function of a language would depend upon its structural features; therefore, one might argue that it would be preferable to study the structural features directly, by a method such as Whorf's, rather than to use a statistical artifact such as the autocorrelation function— an index which at best might be useful only for purposes of rough comparison.[10]

Bavelas (1950) has reported research on the behavior of task-oriented groups of people arranged in various types of communication nets. One group might be arranged so that each member can communicate directly only with one "key" man, while another group is arranged like a chain, each member being able to communicate only with his immediate neighbors. The variable studied in these experiments is the speed with which such groups can solve certain assigned problems. These studies appear very promising as an approach to the dynamics of social groups, but they seem to have no immediate bearing, at least thus far, on problems of individual verbal behavior. Nevertheless, the experimental setting might lend itself to studies of variables in individual language behavior. A similar remark may be made in connection with the work of Bales (1950), who is also studying the communicative behavior of small groups.

The practical importance of studies in the psychology of communication is attested to by a section of a report on human factors in submarine warfare (Panel on Psychology and Physiology, 1949). M. H. Abrams considers problems of selecting communications personnel and establishing approved phraseology. G. A. Miller reviews studies of the effects of masking and distortion on speech intelligibility, and W. S. Verplanck concludes the section by a discussion of visual communication systems, in which he considers, among other things, such systems as gesture language, sign language, lip reading, and manual signals (semaphore, blinker lights, etc.). Another report illustrating the relevance of the psychology of communication to practical problems is Fitts's (1951) study of communication problems in air navigation and airport traffic control.

An extensive project devoted to the study of the administrative conference and its techniques has been under way at the University of Michigan (Marquis et al., 1951). The major emphasis in this study is the attempt to understand the conference group in terms of group dynamics and the effects of individual personalities on the group process. One class of variables which are believed to be relevant to the success of the decision-making conference, however, is concerned with the communicative processes among members of the group. At least one preliminary study of communication in the group conference has been conducted by Roger Heyns and E. Miller of the project staff. According to their report, four types of communication measures were used: (1) verbal characteristics of the speakers, such as audibility, quality of speaking voice, and rate of speech; (2) measures of physical behavior accompanying speech, such as gestures; (3) measures of the amount of difficulty the participant had in understanding what was said; and (4) the understandability of the participant from the standpoint of his colleagues. These variables were found to have few significant correlations with each other, and it was difficult to find any relevance for them in connection with such measures as whether the participants were satisfied with the group decision. The investigators concluded that in normal situations the process of communication defined in this way does not vary sufficiently to affect the outcome of a conference to any significant extent.

Many of the studies described here bank heavily on the "information theory" of Shannon; in this respect the approach tends to be molecular in the sense that the smallest units and events in the communicative process are taken into account. On the other hand, in the studies of Bavelas and of the University of Michigan investigators of conference processes, the approach is one of investigating gross phenomena in the interplay of individuals. In none of these studies is there much concern with the role of linguistic structure; this structure is either ignored or taken for granted.

THE NATURE OF LANGUAGE BEHAVIOR

Anyone who reads deeply in the discussions of verbal behavior which we have reviewed will, I think, be struck with the exasperating way in which some of these discussions have made something complicated out of something which ought to be fairly simple, at least in its essence. Children learn language behavior quite early in life, and verbal behavior is, of all behavior, probably the most resistant to the effects of senility, drugs, and abnormal mental states. To be sure, language behavior has its complexities, but this is mostly because it is an aggregation of numerous simple things. Why, then, have linguists and psychologists not been able to agree on the nature of language behavior? Paradoxically, the answer to this question is not simple, but a part of the answer is surely rooted in semantic difficulties, as we have suggested previously. People have not agreed upon what they mean by such terms as speech, language, and thought. The very utterance of a term like "thought" or "idea" or "meaning" is anathema to many behavioristic psychologists, and taboo among many linguists. If psychologists and linguists will take the trouble to translate these terms into more objective phraseologies, an enormous amount of needless discussion can be avoided.

Let us see whether we can state, in the form of a simple model, what happens in any organismic communication situation. This model may be depicted in the form of a diagram:

Intentive behavior of speaker	Encoding behavior of speaker	Message	Decoding behavior of hearer	Interpretive behavior of hearer
→	→	→	→	

The diagram[11] may be interpreted as follows:

1. *The intentive behavior of the speaker.*—Presumably the speaker has some information to transmit, and he has some excitatory tendency to transmit it. From his own subjective point of view, his "information" may consist of sensations, perceptions, memories, thoughts, concepts, or even images, but if we desire to rule out subjective events as evidence for our description, we can infer the existence of some kind of "information," prior to its being linguistically coded, from the overt behavior—usually verbal behavior—that ensues, basing our inference on our knowledge of the general properties of stimulus-response systems. The events which take place prior to coding are summarized in the phrase "intentive behavior," which connotes at once that these events are behavioral (that is, they are responses) and that they are in some sense goal-directed or adjustmental at least with respect to the reinforcing conditions of behavior. No "mentalistic" flavor is intended in this description; it is no more mentalistic than such concepts as "attitude," "set," and "trace" in behavioristic psychology, and I think it would be consistent with, say, the position on mind and mechanism stated by Boring (1946).

2. *Encoding behavior of the speaker.*—Encoding behavior can be conceived of as a series of simultaneous and sequential "choices" or "decisions," made by the speaker, among one or more alternative learned responses in his repertoire, together with the behavior of the motor systems (speech, gesture, etc.) which each choice may entail. Even though we speak of "choices" here, the responses involved are conceived to be automatic but very complexly determined—not only by the nature of the "information" before it is coded, but also by associated responses, previous choices which have been made, the feedback from previous overt responses, situational factors, the nature of the audience, and so on. The learned responses involved are, in general, responses which have been reinforced by previous listeners, and most of them will be found to play some part in a particular language system. In many cases, the responses may constitute units of the language system. Two very important choices in all encoding behavior are (1) the choice of whether to make an overt response, and (2) the decision to use a particular dialectal language system—English instead of French, say. (If perchance the speaker is unilingual *and* unidialectal—if he has no coexistent "levels" or varieties of speech—then the latter decision is single-valued, but this would be a rare case except in beginning learners of the

language.) A further characteristic of encoding behavior is that it may be only partially run off, depending on situational factors. If the speaker is subvocally "talking to himself," many of the decisions made will be in the direction of a zero value of the response. On demand, a speaker can report such partially coded responses, either in speech or in writing, as, for example, when the subject is asked for a chain of free associations, or when he is asked to finish an incomplete sentence.

3. *The message.*—When it has come about that an individual manifests his encoding behavior overtly, we are presented with some kind of physical event which we, as observers, perceive to have emanated from the speaker. This event, whether it be a succession of sound waves, a series of marks on a page, or a pattern of bodily movements, may be regarded as composed of a message plus random, nondistinctive variations or "noise." By suitable techniques of analysis—by the comparison of events emanating from the speaker at different times or from different speakers—we can determine what is message and what is noise. Further, we can determine the recurrent regularities of messages. Linguistic scientists have fixed their attention on the recurrent regularities of sound-wave messages, and, as we have seen in Chapter 2, they have been able to determine the system of regularities constituting the linguistic code observable in a given speech community. At the same time, lexicographers have listed those regularities called words. Thus, in effect, lexicographers have pursued the task of listing, at a certain level of analysis, socially reinforced verbal responses found in certain speech communities, and in their "definitions" of words they have suggested the general nature and distinctive features of the reinforcing stimuli in each case.[12] Linguists, in the meantime, have described the socially reinforced structure of utterances (composed of sequences of responses) found in certain speech communities, with respect to their distinctive phonetic, morphological, and syntactical features. Now the question may be raised: can we infer from lexicographic and linguistic materials anything about the responses involved in encoding behavior? This is an empirical question which has been scarcely investigated at all, but in a general sense it can probably be answered affirmatively. In the aggregate, linguistic units probably represent *potential* response types in the individual members of a speech community. But they do not necessarily correspond to the units of response selection for any *particular* utterance. An utterance which consists

of the recitation of a poem would appear to involve a different set of encoding or response selection units from the set involved in the original creation of the poem, and, even in that original creation, the encoding units would not necessarily be identical in every case to the units obtained by a linguistic analysis of the utterance.

4. *Decoding behavior in the hearer.*—With the understanding that the "hearer" may sometimes be identical with the "speaker," we may proceed to describe decoding behavior as a sequence of events which consists of the perception of the message by the hearer and a series of discriminatory responses to the elements of the message as contrasted with the "noise" in the communication channel. To a certain extent, even an illiterate subject can report what these discriminatory responses are. As a working hypothesis, we postulate that the discriminatory responses correspond to the linguistically defined units of the language—that is, phonemes, morphemes, and syntactical patterns. Indeed, these discriminatory responses in the hearer are thought more likely to correspond to linguistically defined units than is the case for the selection units in the speaker. Discriminatory responses, are, of course, socially reinforced learned responses. Furthermore, just as the selection of encoding responses in the speaker is multiply determined, the discriminations made by the hearer are determined not only by the immediately perceived elements of the message but also by more remote elements of the message, by previously made discriminations, and by perceptions arising from the general environment. That is to say, the hearer is aided in his decoding of the message by the total context of the message. Now, the hearer's decoding of the message may not always be "correct"— that is, it will not correspond perfectly with the message as transmitted, and the discriminatory responses may not correspond at all well with the responses selected by the speaker. Perhaps the hearer has not learned all the responses which the speaker has learned, or perhaps the hearer's set or attitude is quite different from that of the speaker. The study of any given communication situation must analyze the discrepancies between the speaker's encoding behavior and the hearer's decoding behavior.

5. *Interpretive behavior in the hearer.*—Upon the decoding of the message into some set of units, the hearer usually makes a further response to at least some of those units. In other words, upon "understanding" the message, he acts upon it. Interpretive behavior can therefore be described

in much the same way as intentive behavior—it consists of "information" which is not linguistically coded. The hearer may at this point become a speaker, in which case his interpretive behavior is a factor in the formation of his intentive behavior and the ensuing encoding into speech. Indeed, in this case there is often a short-circuiting in which the responses involved in decoding immediately enter into the encoding behavior, that is, become stimuli for it. Such a response may be a mere echoic response, or it may take the form of linguistically coded "thinking." The hearer may also become an actor—he may, if he has been told to do so, get up and close the window, or he may, if so instructed, remember to get some groceries on his way home from the office. In all such cases, interpretive behavior consists of what may be called "sets to respond."

We may now suggest a division of scientific labor in studying the whole communication process. First, the study of intentive behavior and, what is much the same thing, of interpretive behavior is a part of the domain of general psychology. Second, the study of recurrent regularities in messages is indubitably the task of linguistic science, including lexicography. Third, the study of encoding and decoding behavior is the domain of linguistic psychology, or of what is beginning to be known more widely as psycholinguistics. Psycholinguistics, however, must take account of data from both psychology and linguistics. On the side of psychology, it must analyze the general nonlinguistic responses of individuals in terms of their stimulus conditions and how they are learned. Learning theory, in fact, plays a major role in the study of the linguistic responses themselves. From linguistics, psycholinguistics draws data concerning the units into which utterances can be analyzed and compares such data with whatever can be learned about the selection units in encoding and the discriminative responses in decoding.

The foregoing description of language behavior is a return to what Kantor (1936) calls "expression theories" only in the sense that it recognizes that prior to an utterance there must be "information" in various states of codedness. If one calls such information "thought" or "idea" or "concept," it is understood that one is simply using these terms as convenient expressions for the implicit behavior of the individual which immediately precedes an utterance or which immediately follows upon the perception of an utterance. Perhaps it would be better to use such terms as "set" or "attitudinal disposition." What has not been generally recognized is that the units of language behavior constitute evidence for such sets or dispositions. For example, a major unit of language behavior (in English, at least) is that which is involved in the choice of a question sentence-type in contrast to a statement sentence-type. (There are other units involved here, such as that concerned with the choice of intonation pattern, but we will avoid complexity in this discussion. At any rate, these structures can be distinguished in formal linguistics.) The stimulus for the choice of these types resides, we think, in some sort of set, disposition, or attitude: for a question, this set might possibly be described as a perception or feeling of incompleteness or inconsistency in some stimulus context, while for a statement, it might be possibly described as a sense of fulfillment, consistency, or even of need satisfaction. (These descriptions are highly tentative.) What is needed is an experimental technique for isolating the sets or dispositions antecedent to various types of linguistic responses.

Structural Units of Language Behavior

A striking feature of the linguistic analysis of messages is the appearance of a hierarchy of units, from the smallest units (distinctive features of phonemes) to the larger units in complete utterances (sentence-types). A large unit like the clause or sentence pattern can be analyzed into smaller units, phrase-types and words; these in turn can be analyzed into morphemes and ultimately into phonemes and distinctive features. In the analysis of speech—that is, of particular utterances—these linguistic units must play some part in encoding behavior, if the foregoing description of language behavior is correct. The encoding behavior involved in creating any sentence must then consist of a hierarchy of selection units. Hence, as I suggested in a previous publication (Carroll, 1944), we cannot speak of one kind of behavioral unit; instead, we must speak of several. Some psychological theorists have written as if there were only *one* kind of behavioral unit, but such a notion now seems to be controverted by an analysis of language behavior. At any rate, we may be able to determine by experimental techniques and by analysis of utterances the order in which units on various levels are selected. It is a reasonable guess that in general the larger units are selected before the smaller units. For example, the selection

93

of a word would seem to imply the selection of its phonemes; only in less frequent cases, best exemplified in the use of rhyming and alliteration in poetry, is the selection of a word influenced by the selection of phonemes.

SOME MAJOR PROBLEMS OF PSYCHOLINGUISTICS

Writers on the psychology of language have listed the various issues on which interest has centered. One is at a loss to arrange these issues in any logical order, but if the description of language behavior offered above has any validity it should suggest some integrated way of dealing with them. The following paragraphs represent an attempt to give a unified account of psycholinguistic problems. The most important of these problems is the determination of units of encoding and decoding behavior and the description of their stimulus-response relations, but since this problem has already been discussed we may turn to certain other problems.

The Acquisition of Linguistic Responses

It has been emphasized everywhere in the previous discussion that linguistic responses are learned rather than innate responses.[13] The conditions under which conventional linguistic responses are learned and modified should completely account for the "meanings" attached to them by a particular individual, and to the extent that these conditions are similar in the members of a speech community (that is, in that the reinforcements are similar or have common elements), they should account also for the "meaning" assigned to them by lexicography or linguistic analysis. The apparent difficulties in the concept of meaning stem from two sources: (1) the term "meaning" itself has a variety of denotations (Ogden and Richards, 1936), and (2) the conditions responsible for the learning of a single linguistic response by a single individual are so numerous, buried as they are in his life history, that it would be hard to recover them except in unusual cases. Nevertheless, the development of a "meaning" can be easily demonstrated in simple experimental situations. For example, consider Hull's (1920) experiment on concept formation. Hull presented to his subjects a series of Chinese characters, each containing one of a small number of radical signs. On presenting each character, a nonsense syllable (depending on which radical sign it contained) was uttered by the experimenter and repeated by the subject. As the experiment progressed, the subjects gradually acquired associations between the radical signs and the nonsense syllables and became able to anticipate the correct nonsense syllable for a completely new character. In this experiment, then, a radical sign became the "meaning" for a nonsense syllable, and, in fact, the conditions under which the association was learned and reinforced completely account for that "meaning." A similar interpretation can be advanced for the acquisition of a "meaning" through verbal context, as shown by the experiment of Werner and Kaplan (1950).

As Miller (1951a, Chap. 8) has suggested, this interpretation of meaning can presumably be extended to all linguistic responses, whether they are simple nouns (like "apple," "dog") with easily identifiable referents, or complex syntactical structures (like "if . . . then" clauses), although this notion has not been experimentally demonstrated. In fact, the question of what is meant by meaning seems to be so simple, theoretically, that Humphrey (1951a), in an article entitled "There is No Problem of Meaning," went so far as to say that the problem is wholly artificial, whether in talking about perception, "mental images," "general ideas," thinking, or language. The task of psychology, according to Humphrey, is to state the relations between the organism and the environment, and to observe what the organism *does,* not to erect useless intervening variables like "meanings." As Humphrey would have it, then, the problem of meaning in language is a problem of learning.

Granted the theoretical simplicity of the behavioral problem of meaning, there is no reason to discourage detailed observational and experimental studies of processes of language learning, particularly as applied to language learning in the child and the learning of second languages. Likewise, we need experimental and theoretical studies of the precise behavioral mechanisms of symbolic learning. Osgood's (1952b) work on a central mediation theory of meaning is of considerable promise in this respect.

The meaning of a linguistic form is often treated under two headings: its denotative meaning and its connotative meaning. The denotative meaning is described as the "actual" meaning of the form, while the connotative meaning refers to other meanings which the form may suggest. For example, the form "moon" usually denotes a certain object known to be a satellite of the earth (and, by transferred meaning, a satellite of any planet or a representation of such a satellite), but it may connote "meanings" such as "night," "shimmering," "cool," "pleasant," etc. In a general way, the distinction between these two types of meaning can be supported by learning theory. (1) Denotative meaning refers to the common elements in the reinforcing situations which have been associated with a given form, particularly as established by conditioned discriminations. In the case of the word "moon," the reinforcing situations have in common the fact that a certain kind of perceived object is present, or is represented, or is talked about. The stimulus-generalization gradient has a range such that full moons, crescent moons, moons in the daytime, pictures of moons, and so on, are responded to in an equivalent manner (*so far as the linguistic response* "moon" *is concerned*). Responses like "night," "shimmering," "cool," "pleasant," do not have a comparable range on the stimulus-generalization gradient. (2) Connotative meaning refers to reinforcing situations which have been associated with a given linguistic form with at least moderate probability (up to a probability of unity in some cases), but not in such a way as to produce a conditioned discrimination. That is, the reinforcing situations for "moon," "night," "shimmering," etc., are often similar, yet sufficiently different from each other to produce discriminated responses, that is, the stimulus-generalization ranges are not identical, even though they may in some cases overlap.

It should be noted that many kinds of things or events may become reinforcing situations—including concrete objects, temporal relations, complex social situations, verbal contexts, or even the sound-symbolic value of the linguistic form. In some instances, a person may reinforce his own behavior, as when a scientist agrees "with himself" to use in his own thinking a linguistic form in a particular way, that is, with a particular symbolic value. In this sense it is not strictly true that language behavior depends "entirely" upon the intervention of another person for its reinforcement, as Miller seems to claim (Miller, 1951a, p. 173).

The difficulties in applying this interpretation universally are only apparent, but they arise primarily because the denotative and, particularly, the connotative meanings of words vary from individual to individual, and also because even denotative meanings are subject to more or less gradual change in a whole speech community. It must be understood that the denotative and connotative meanings of a given linguistic form are essentially properties of a given individual's behavior at a given point of time and that they are subject to change depending upon new reinforcing conditions which may appear in that individual's environment. For example, what might be a denotative meaning in the individual on one day may become a connotative meaning on another day, or even become extinguished altogether. The fact that the denotative meaning of a form is roughly constant over a whole speech community is simply due to the fact that the reinforcing situations leading to the establishment of a conditioned discrimination have been highly similar throughout the speech community. By virtue of this fact, the linguistic scientist is able to operate on the assumption that "each linguistic form has a constant and specific meaning" (Bloomfield, 1933, p. 145). It is when the denotative meanings of forms become variant, as in the case of words like "democracy," that difficulties in communication arise. Korzybski and the general semanticists have made capital of such trends; when they speak of "extensional meaning" they are really referring to the detailed reinforcing conditions associated with a given form.

Even connotative meanings are likely to have some constancy in a speech community, again because of a rough similarity of reinforcing conditions. To the extent that connotative meanings are similar, poets and politicians are able to produce calculated effects. Osgood (1952a) has recently devised a promising technique for measuring connotative meanings. His method depends on the fact that individuals are able, with fair interindividual consistency, to rate words with respect to various attributes or dimensions of meaning. For example, "love" might be rated toward the "good" end of a "good-bad" dimension, while it might be rated toward the "soft" end of a "hard-soft" dimension. The research is proceeding in the direction of finding, by statistical factor-analysis techniques, the minimal number of independent, unrelated dimensions necessary to describe the connotative meaning of any linguistic form. Standards can be established with respect to all members of a speech community, after which individual variations, for example, in neurotics, may be investigated. There is already evidence that the basic dimensions of connotative meanings may show a close correspondence with the basic dimensions of sensory experience; if this proves to be the case, the relations between verbal behavior and other categories of behavior will become even more apparent.

The Strength of Linguistic Responses

As we have seen, the way in which linguistic response-types acquire their "meanings" can be described in terms of the theory of learning. Learning theory also states that the frequency of reinforcement and the cumulative extent to which reinforcement has satisfied the needs of the organism is directly related to the probability that the response will occur in a suitable context. This leads to the concept of the "strength" of a response, a concept useful in accounting for the selection of responses in any actual utterance. In a previous publication (Carroll, 1944), I suggested a number of methods of measuring the strength of a linguistic response-type, such as frequency counts, free-association techniques, and recognition tests. From this point of view, the statistical and mathematical methods of such investigators as Chotlos (1944), H. Fairbanks (1944), Zipf (1935, 1949), and Bousfield and Sedgewick (1944) have a decided bearing on the determination of linguistic response-type strengths. But statistical methods suffer from a disadvantage. Being statistical, they merely report average tendencies and fail to disclose the strength of a response for a given individual at a given time. Perhaps this latter is a fundamentally unobservable variable; one can only attempt to *predict* the actual occurrence of a response.

Language Development in the Child

Observations on the development of language in the child have collected in impressive amounts, as McCarthy's (1946) review will testify. The bulk of these observations have been made by psychologists. Leopold (1948, 1952) and Gregoire (1950) have reviewed the work of both psychologists and linguists and suggest that the study of child language should be further developed in linguistics as well as in psychology. Linguists who have acquainted themselves with some of the psychological work in this area report that it could have profited considerably if the investigators had been more familiar with linguistic theory. They comment, for example, that Irwin (1941, 1947), in his work on infant speech, does not adequately distinguish between the phonetic and the phonemic levels of analysis. Nevertheless, the kind of direct observation emphasized in Irwin's work is much needed if we are to validate conclusively the hypotheses put forward by the linguist Jakobson (1941) regarding the sequence in which phonemes appear in child speech.

One of the most interesting problems in child language is that of how the higher-order units represented by the phenomena of morphology and syntax are learned. Guillaume (1927) and Carroll (1939) have suggested that this learning comes about when the child learns "phrase-wholes" (sequences of words in grammatical patterns) as single patterned entities and then learns to "differentiate" the parts. In a sense, then, the child learns the grammar of his native language in somewhat the same way that the linguist analyzes that grammar by finding the substitution groups or form classes.

In theory, the language development of the child can be explained by taking full account of learning theory and of the linguistic structure being learned. In terms of our description of language behavior, child language development is the development of a tremendous number of different responses which serve to code the child's perceptions of his environment and to mediate his needs. An integrated account of this process from the standpoint of psycholinguistics and based on adequate observational and experimental evidence remains to be expounded.

The Learning of Second Languages

A bilingual person can be said to have two coding systems for his intentive behavior, and two sets of decoding responses leading into interpretive behavior. It is somewhat doubtful whether the learning of a foreign language should proceed in all respects in a manner paralleling the acquisition of language in a child, but the desired end result, it would seem, is a state of affairs similar to what we have described in bilingualism. When language teachers urge their students to try to "think in" a foreign language, they mean to say that the students should code intentive behavior as directly as possible into the foreign-language responses, without there being an intervening role for native-language responses.

Such a view of foreign-language learning cannot be encountered widely in the enormous literature dealing with objectives and methods of foreign-language teaching. Psychologists, for their part, have taken little interest in problems of foreign-language teaching, and basic learning theory has not yet been developed to cover adequately the case where alternative sets of semantic responses are learned.

The so-called "mimicry-memorization" method of language teaching developed by linguists during the last war is full of challenging problems for psycholinguistic study.

More will be said about foreign-language learning and teaching in Chapter 6, in connection with a discussion of the implications of linguistics for education. For reviews of the psychology of foreign-language learning and related matters, the reader may be referred to treatments by Powers (1929), Huse (1931), Arsenian (1945), and Dunkel (1948).

The Origin and Development of Language

In Chapter 2, we mentioned the many speculative theories about the origin of language which were developed in the eighteenth and nineteenth centuries. Even in the modern era, hardly a decade has passed without the appearance of a new theory or a new version of an old theory (e.g., Jóhanneson, 1948). All theories of the origin of language must inevitably contain some psychological elements, for there is the question of how language-like responses came to develop in early man. This is a matter of unwritten history which must obviously remain closed to empirical inquiry, but psychologists (e.g., DeLaguna, 1927; Révész, 1946) have tried to suggest, on the basis of psychological theory, ways in which language could have originated. The implications, for this problem, of recent developments in the theory of learning do not seem to have been pointed out. According to this theory, once the basic physiological apparatus had developed sufficiently, the spontaneous "operant" responses made possible thereby would inevitably become socially reinforced, and, eventually, differentiated from one another. Responses could then have become "meaningful" almost overnight; there would have been no necessity for the type of stage-by-stage development of language postulated by Révész, for example. Furthermore, according to this theory, which response got reinforced in a particular way would have been largely a matter of chance;[14] thus, there is no reason to assign any special importance to the various influences (for example, imitative gestures of the speech organs) which have been proposed to explain how sound patterns came to be associated with their referents.

Phonetic, morphological, and semantic changes in language can quite possibly be explained, or even predicted, in terms of psychological theory. As we have suggested in Chapter 2, this would be a fruitful problem for coöperative efforts of linguists and psychologists. Jespersen (1941) is among the linguists who have suggested psychological explanations of linguistic change, but his suggestions were somewhat fanciful. He proposed, for example, that the change from *Engla-land* to *England* could be explained by "fear of stuttering." Hockett (1950) gives some weight to the hypothesis that linguistic change occurs because of minor variations in children's speech patterns which in time become standard patterns when children become adults. At any rate, the psychologist would consider, as possible explanations for linguistic change, such concepts as those of stimulus generalization and discrimination, which may be found discussed in any modern psychological text, and the habit-family hierarchy (Hull, 1934).

Individual Differences in Language Behavior

We observe that people speak in different styles and that they differ in their ability to use language. In theory, these individual variations may be interpreted by saying that linguistic responses have been learned differently, or differently reinforced, in different individuals. There remains the problem of identifying and measuring the dimensions of these differences in the most useful manner. By use of the statistical technique of factor analysis, Thurstone (1938), Carroll (1941), Taylor (1947), and others have identified several such dimensions. One is the factor of general "verbal ability," which Carroll describes as "the ability to learn various conventional linguistic responses and to retain them over long periods of time." He continues, "The factor represents differences in the stock of linguistic responses possessed by the individual—the wealth of the individual's past experience and training in the English language." Other dimensions have to do with the ability of the individual to supply responses rapidly from among a series of possible alternative responses ("fluency of expression"), the ability to give a series of ideas rapidly ("ideational fluency"), and the ability to name objects rapidly ("naming ability"). In addition, there are factors having to do with smoothness and effectiveness of spontaneous speech, and with the speed of articulatory movements. The detailed results of these studies are summarized in a recent monograph by French (1951).

Some, or perhaps all, of the dimensions of verbal behavior identified by factor analysis are pertinent to the study of personality. At any rate, the study of the relation of language and personality has usually proceeded by the direct study of verbal output and the attempt to discover personality correlates of its characteristics. Boder (1940), for example, has studied the adjective-verb quotient (the ratio of number of adjectives to number of verbs in a sample of verbal output) and its possible correlation with emotional stability and other traits. Sanford (1942b) made an exhaustive analysis, using numerous linguistic categories, of the speech of two individuals obtained in an experimental situation and suggested that the descriptions of speech in many respects matched the personalities of his subjects. Sanford (1942a) has also reviewed the literature in this area. The linguist Stanley S. Newman has made several studies (Newman and Mather, 1938; Newman, 1941, 1944) of speech characteristics as related to personality traits of both normal and abnormal subjects. Thus, the obtaining of a precise sample of verbal behavior might be viewed as a projective technique, with potential utility similar to that of Rorschach or Thematic Apperception tests. The part played by linguistic analysis would be to indicate exactly which elements of the verbal response are determined by the formal characteristics of the individual's language or dialect. Psycholinguistic investigations would indicate the units of behavior which would be most useful to examine. It is perhaps not out of the way to suggest that personality may be found to be, to a considerable extent, a matter of the organization of verbal habits; such a view appears to be supported by Dollard and Miller (1950), for example.

Speech Pathology

There is wide scope for psycholinguistic studies in connection with such behavior deviations as the psychoses, the aphasias, and stuttering. Psychologists, psychiatrists, speech pathologists, and others have devoted considerable attention to language disturbances in these behavior deviations, but it remains to be seen whether the application of linguistic and psycholinguistic methods to such studies will result in a more integrated theory of language disturbances than has been seen up to the present. The linguist Jakobson (1941) has sketched the implications of certain aphasic disorders for the theory of language: in these disorders he sees the progressive loss of phonemic distinctions in a sequence which is the reverse of the sequence in which these distinctions are acquired by the child. Goldstein, a psychologist and psychiatrist noted for his organismic theory of behavior, writes in his book *Language and Language Disturbances* (1948, p. 31): "It is my conviction that philosophy of language and linguistics on the one side, and research in aphasia on the other, could profit much from each other, much more than has previously been the case."

There are many theories of stuttering, and a variety of therapeutic techniques. Wendell Johnson (1939, 1946) claims that speech defects can be effectively treated by training the patient in the principles of Korzybski's theory of general semantics (Korzybski, 1933). An interesting application of learning theory to the problem of stuttering has been made recently by Sheehan (1951). Sheehan started out with the idea that the stutterer stutters because he is "rewarded" by the achievement of uttering a word even though he has stuttered on it. He found that a technique of "non-reinforcement," in which the stutterer had to repeat a stuttered word until it is correct, seems to be an effective therapy. Fundamentally, stuttering seems to represent an error in phonemic coding. Interest in the neurological mechanisms of stuttering, and even of normal speech, has been stimulated by the recent discovery by a number of people that a normal person will often stutter or suffer speech blocks when he hears the artificially delayed feedback of his own speech (B. S. Lee, 1950).

Language and Thought

In speaking of the relation between language and thought, we are in a very difficult area, clouded with numerous semantic difficulties arising from the diverse usages of the term *thought* in popular parlance and even in psychological writings. Thought, as we would like to describe it here, is essentially a matter of how the individual handles information in central mediation processes, whether it comes to him perceptually and nonlinguistically, or already coded linguistically. Now, this information may get handled very simply and directly, as when an individual responds to a buzzer in a reaction-time experiment, or it may get handled in a much more complicated fashion. A judgment as to whether it would be better to make a trip today or defer it till tomorrow may involve the handling of a large number of bits of information, and it is this largely implicit process of responding simultaneously or serially to many items of information which is most often conceived of as "thought," but it differs from simpler response processes only in the matter of degree of complexity. The role of language in thought, then, reduces to the problem of whether or not the "information" (environmental as well as implicit stimuli) becomes linguistically coded, and, if so, what it is that influences the selection of linguistic units and the translation or recoding of these units into other units. Notice that information does not have to be coded linguistically—it may be coded in terms of some other mode of learned response, for example, in musical or kinesthetic responses. It is thus a mistake to identify language and thought, as Révész (1950) does when he concludes that "language and thought form an inseparable, multirelational duality." It would be much more satisfactory to conclude that language is one of the chief modes of thought, and that speech is one of its possible outcomes. Nevertheless, we would not mean to imply that language does not play an enormously important role in thought; on the contrary, the automaticity and multifariousness of linguistic responses, once these responses have been learned, make it impossible to conceive that language does not constantly intrude upon what we have described as thought.

It would be profitable to review the various experiments on thinking, concept formation, and problem solving in the light of this conception of the role of linguistic responses in thought, but this is hardly the place for such a review.[15] We must content ourselves with commenting on several illustrative experiments.

First let us consider that of Heidbreder (1924) on concept formation. In this experiment, which employed college women as subjects, the subject had to discover, by trial and error, a principle which would enable her to mark the "correct" alternative in pairs of geometrical figures. At the end of each trial, she was required to report "everything that went on in her mind" during the trial. (The use of introspective verbal reports in an experiment will make the results particularly amenable to the present approach.) The "principles" had to do with such things as selecting "the *inner* figure," "the *curved* figure," "the figure with *more* sides," "both figures." Now, it is significant that if we can trust the introspective reports as evidence of the implicit behavior prior to the responses, in almost every trial the subject selected a figure in accordance with some hypothesis amenable to verbal coding, like "right," "left," "curved." Even in seemingly difficult problems where the subject had almost given up hope, she would eventually hit upon some verbally expressed hypothesis which would prove to be correct. How did this happen? The experiment as such does not disclose an answer to this question, but we may venture a guess that the selection of linguistically coded hypotheses is a function of two factors: (*a*) the stock of verbal responses which the subject can call up to solve the problem, and (*b*) the relative strengths of these responses in relation to the stimulus values of the material presented to the subject. We could investigate the role of the former factor by asking the subject, prior to the trials, to cite as many "principles" as he can think of which might be used with materials of the type used in the experiment, and we could investigate the role of the latter factor by experimentally varying the strengths of the responses.

Experimental variation of response strengths is precisely what Cofer (1951) and his associates attempted to do in another experiment in reasoning. By exercising certain verbal responses prior to the presentation of a problem-solving task, they found that the nature of the solution reached by the subject was significantly influenced. In still other experiments they found considerable evidence that strong verbal associations already extant influenced problem-solving behavior.

In Chapter 2 we discussed what was termed the "linguistic *Weltanschauung* problem*," concerned with the extent to which our perceptions of the external world and our thought patterns (that is, ways of coding information) may be molded by the structure of the language we speak. Meaning has often been described as having to do with the relation between symbols and their referents, but the linguistic *Weltanschauung* hypothesis proposes, in effect, that linguistic structure intervenes between the symbol and its referent. It may be the privilege of experimental psychology to make a major contribution to this problem. The writer envisages, for example, the possibility of studying the role of language patterns in perception and thought by making cross-cultural studies, under controlled experimental conditions, of the way in which native speakers of various languages respond to various situations or describe certain arrangements of stimuli. No such experiments have yet been attempted, perhaps because psychologists have seldom been aware of the striking differences among linguistic structures with respect to their organization of reality.

IMPLICATIONS OF PSYCHOLINGUISTICS
FOR PSYCHOLOGICAL THEORY

Psychological theory may be defined as an integrated way of describing the diversified phenomena of organismic behavior, using a relatively small number of fundamental concepts. There have been a number of "systems" of psychology, including structuralism, functionalism, *Gestalttheorie,* associationism, etc.,[16] but contemporary American psychology has settled upon a form of eclectic behaviorism which is not so iconoclastic as Watsonian psychology and which incorporates some of the better features of other systems. Among the major theoretical expositions are those of Tolman (1932), Skinner (1938), and Hull (1943); their chief concern is with phenomena of learning, which may be said to constitute the central problem of psychology. There has been, nevertheless, a hiatus between these treatments and theoretical discussions of such problems as social attitudes and the organization of personality. Mowrer (1950), Dollard and Miller (1950), and Sears (1951) have recently made important advances in bridging this gap. It has been realized that language behavior is of central importance in making the transition from a theory of simple response processes and learning to a theory of the more complex forms of human behavior, but the implications of a detailed psycholinguistic theory have not been keyed in with other theoretical developments.

The description of language behavior which is offered here is intended to suggest some implications for general psychological theory. It is, indeed, a theoretical treatment of a major area of behavior, but, even aside from this, it suggests a way of dealing with units and the general structuring of behavior of all kinds.

From linguistic theory we get the notion of a hierarchy of units— from elemental units like the distinctive feature of a phoneme to large units like a sentence-type. It may be suggested that stretches of any kind of behavior may be organized in somewhat the same fashion; in this case, however, the distinctive feature of each unit, whatever its size, is a specific goal-directed character. It may also be suggested that each unit has its "random" as well as its distinctive characteristics. The particular way in which a rat presses a lever, or the way in which a human being withdraws his finger from a shock electrode, are the random features of the response; the distinctive features are that the lever is pressed and the electrode is withdrawn from.[17]

Now, an interesting possibility is that whenever we ask an individual to describe his own behavior, at least some of the linguistic units of his verbal report may correspond to the units of the behavior he is describing. To illustrate, one is inclined to think of the three words of Caesar's *"Veni, vidi, vici"* declaration as corresponding to three major units in his behavior; the detailed lower-order units were of course described in his *De Bello Gallico*. Has the verb system of a language, in effect, encapsulated the typical units of behavior which people have occasion to describe? If this is so, we can see why there is widespread popular belief in the notion of "every man his own psychologist." But what may be deceptive about all this is that the devious ways of language do not guarantee that the actions expressed by many verbs could be shown to have the properties of psychological units. Skinner (1938, pp. 33ff.) defines a unit of behavior as a class of stimuli and responses (in the case of respondent behavior) or as a class of responses alone (in the case of operant behavior) for which lawful correlations and changes can be experimentally demonstrated, particularly with respect to the reinforcement of the relevant behavior. He urges caution in accepting the units of stimulus and response suggested by words in the popular language. In any case, the fact that verbal behavior has been amenable to linguistic analysis in terms of a hierarchy of units suggests that other kinds of behavior (particularly goal-directed, "purposive" behavior) can be subjected to a similar analysis.

It may be commented at this point that the hierarchical structure of behavior makes it somewhat resistant to the kind of analysis suggested by Miller and Frick (1949) in their paper on what they call "statistical behavioristics." Statistical behavioristics is the theory of stochastic processes applied to the study of sequences of responses. This theory has been usefully applied to certain aspects of language behavior, as we have pointed out, but it would seem that it has certain limitations whenever it is applied to sequences of responses which are patterned in a hierarchy of units. Statistical behavioristics, at least in its presently developed form, studies the probability that a given response will follow upon another given response or sequence of responses. Such a probability is known as a transitional probability. But now suppose the responses are patterned in higher-order units which in turn condition the transitional probabilities of their lower-order units. Then it can be shown that the lower-order transitional probabilities are a weighted statistical average of the probabilities which are dependent on the higher-order units. The lower-order transitional probabilities do not by any means uniquely determine the higher-order probabilities nor the nature and extent of the higher-order units. Thus, statistical behavioristics is a promising approach only after the hierarchy of units has been determined by other methods, and even then its usefulness may be limited to its value as a statistical measure of behavioral stereotypy or predictability.

We may give two illustrations of the application of psycholinguistics to the psychological theory of complex behavioral processes.

Sears (1936) has suggested that the Freudian concept of repression can be restated in terms of learning theory; "the process of repression," he concludes, "refers to the blockage of an excitatory tendency toward verbal activity; this blockage is evidenced by (a) verification of the existence of the excitatory tendency, and (b) by the known lack of a congruous verbal action." But the process of repression "occurs uniquely to two kinds of excitatory tendencies: (a) those which may be or have been accompanied by verbal activity which represents them symbolically, and (b) those which lead to verbal activity that is itself mutually incompatible with some other verbal activity." He equates "verbal activity" with Freud's "consciousness," and notes that "the meaningful content of verbal activity may pass through several developmental forms before being translated into language." Now, if Sears's conception is correct, psycholinguistics may make a contribution to behavior theory in this area by specifying how the relevant verbal behavior may be described and in what sense different kinds of verbal activity are incompatible with each other.

A brilliant application of learning theory to problems of personality and psychotherapy has been made by Dollard and Miller (1950). Desiring to integrate "the vitality of psychoanalysis, the rigor of the natural science laboratory, and the facts of culture" to aid in "the creation of a psychological base for a general science of human behavior" (p. 3), they credit verbal behavior, both implicit and overt, with playing a large role in arousing drives, mediating rewards, and facilitating the on-going activity of the human organism in learning, problem solving, and planning. After reviewing "the normal use of the mind in solving emotional problems," they apply the basic principles of learning and verbal behavior to the study and treatment of neurosis. One of the most important concepts is that of verbal labeling. Verbal labels are described as responses which permit the transfer of discriminations from one stimulus to a large class of stimuli. "Part of the effectiveness of the verbal labels," they write, "probably comes from the nonverbal cue-producing responses which are attached to them in the course of extensive social learning. As the result of this learning, words and sentences become able to direct attention toward relevant differences, to influence perception, and to elicit images and other verbal cue-producing responses. . . The verbal responses of labeling are especially important because language contains those discriminations and equivalences that have been found useful by generations of trial and error in a given society" (p. 103). But verbal labels have important functions in psychotherapy: "The neurotic is a person who is in need of a stock of sentences that will match the events going on within and without him" (p. 281).

A further elaboration of what Dollard and Miller have to say is of course precluded here, but we may close this section with a quotation from their book (p. 124) which is especially relevant here:

> Only a modest and uncertain start has been made toward understanding the marvelous intricacies of language and the higher mental processes. In this extremely important area there is a great need for more detailed observations of patients in therapy and of the socialization of children in the home, for a more rigorous theoretical formulation and a more penetrating experimental analysis. (By permission from *Personality and Psychotherapy,* by John Dollard and Neal E. Miller, copyright 1950, McGraw-Hill Book Company, Inc.)

IMPLICATIONS OF PSYCHOLOGY FOR LINGUISTICS

If we define linguistics narrowly, that is, as a body of knowledge and method concerned with the analysis of linguistic structures, the implications of psychology for linguistics are nonexistent, for linguistic analysis is a procedure which does not depend on any uniquely psychological theory or methodology. If, however, linguistics is defined more broadly, as a discipline concerned with the nature of language and the numerous explanatory problems connected with it, it should be obvious from what has been said here that linguistics must often appeal to psychological theory and experimental methods.

IMPLICATIONS OF LINGUISTICS FOR THE CONDUCT OF PSYCHOLOGICAL RESEARCH

Many psychological experiments and research investigations involve verbal stimuli and verbal responses, even when the problem being studied has no direct bearing on linguistic psychology. Psychologists need to be more fully aware of the cultural elements which partly determine responses to verbal stimuli, and occasionally they will need to be aware of the exact linguistic description of the materials with which they are working.

It would be relatively easy to go through the literature of psychological experimentation to find many cases where the conclusions and interpretations may have been at least partly in error or misleading because the investigator failed to take into account the factor of linguistic structure. If one is truly going to standardize or hold constant the verbal instructions in an experiment, they would have to be acoustically recorded and mechanically reproduced on every occasion on which they are needed. Presenting typed verbal instructions to a subject is not really enough, for it leaves unstandardized the intonation and stress patterns which the subject may impose implicitly, and such variations might be of crucial importance. Psychologists have too often confused the spoken and the written word, or at least they have assumed too freely that spoken and written words are equivalent stimuli. For example, in his review of association experiments, Woodworth (1938, Chap. 15) has little or nothing to say on the differential effects of spoken and written stimulus words on free-association responses. Hollingworth (1935) performed experiments designed to find whether a word could be regarded as a configuration in the sense defined in Gestalt theory, but these experiments concerned only printed words and therefore the results cannot be generalized to apply to spoken words.

There is developing in contemporary psychology, largely through the influence of the anthropologists, an emphasis on what is known as the "cross-cultural" approach. The psychologist wants to see whether his results, as often as not obtained by the use of college sophomores as subjects, are universally valid and reproducible for other cultures than his own. Experiments which involve verbal behavior must certainly be cross-checked in this way for different cultures, or at least for speakers of different languages.

SUMMARY

Psychology and linguistics have never been closely associated in the study of language phenomena, but, if linguistic science is broadly defined, there are surely many problems which are common to the two disciplines. While problems of linguistic structures have been largely overlooked, the psychological study of verbal behavior has in the past concentrated on attempts to interpret simple language responses in terms of the theory of learning. Linguists have mistrusted psychological interpretations because they feel, perhaps justifiably, that such interpretations are not necessary in their discipline.

In recent years, many experimental studies have been devoted to the role of language in communication. These studies have been oriented toward the theory of communication and the measurement of information as developed by Shannon and Wiener, rather than toward linguistic science.

It is believed that the further study of verbal behavior can proceed soundly only if the role of language structure in communicative behavior is properly taken into account. Psycholinguistics, as this study may be called, should be conceived as being chiefly concerned with the way in which the speaker of a language encodes his behavior into linguistic responses, depending on the structure of his language, and, as a hearer, decodes linguistically coded messages into further behavior. The highly advanced state of contemporary linguistic science as well as of psychological learning theory should make possible the integration of results from the two sciences in the study of the individual's acquisition and use of all types of linguistic responses, from the simple to the most complex. It seems evident that learning theory can account for most of the phenomena which have been discussed under the heading of "meaning." There are many areas where further research in psycholinguistics is needed, such as child language learning, the learning of second languages, personality structure, and thought and problem solving.

Psycholinguistics is seen to have important implications for general psychological theory, particularly because the notion of verbal behavior as structured in a hierarchy of units suggests a similar organization of behavior in general. It is also suggested that experimental psychology can improve the precision of numerous types of experiments if the design and interpretation of these experiments properly takes linguistic structure into account.

LINGUISTICS AND PSYCHOLOGY

Chapter 4 LINGUISTICS AND THE SOCIAL SCIENCES

INTRODUCTION

Language is without doubt cultural in nature and determination. This is true whether one believes, with some, that language must be distinguished from culture, or, with others, that language is one major aspect of culture and hence is to be included in culture. Furthermore, it is true regardless of whether one considers linguistics primarily as a social science or as one of the humanistic studies. Controversies on such problems are mainly terminological; they do not obscure the important role which linguistics may play when applied to various social sciences.

For one thing, a language system may be regarded as a cultural "marker." Hence, as a guide in indicating the boundaries of a culture area or as an aid in tracing the spread of culture by migration and by cultural borrowing, linguistic facts are often far more reliable than other cultural markers, such as the tools used by a culture, or its style of architecture. Tools and styles of architecture are much more readily borrowed than certain aspects of language.

Moreover, the members of a culture are usually aware, consciously or unconsciously, of language as a cultural marker. In the United States, we are in the habit of identifying people with a "Southern accent" as belonging to a particular subculture; likewise, individuals in the educated classes are likely to identify persons with substandard speech as belonging to "inferior" social classes. When dialectal differences become the basis for invidious comparisons, their relevance in social interaction becomes painfully obvious.

Finally, it is overwhelmingly significant that every facet of a language system contributes to the way in which a community uses language in social control. Not only everyday conversation and address but also all the varieties of mass communication, such as propaganda and advertising, depend upon the precarious standards of a common language system.

Linguistics thus appears to have a bearing on all the social sciences which are concerned with studying the behavior of groups or the behavior of individuals in relation to those groups. There is even a possibility that linguistics may play a part in the solution of certain social problems. If so, a new kind of applied science—"language engineering," as it has recently been termed—may come into being.

In this chapter we will consider the relations between linguistic science, on the one hand, and anthropology, sociology, and social psychology on the other. We will also attempt to sketch the possible implications of linguistic studies for certain problems of social engineering, such as the resolution of problems caused by linguistic diversity throughout the world and the adjustment of social conditions in communities where the folk language is not accorded its proper status.

LINGUISTICS IN RELATION TO ANTHROPOLOGY

In anthropological literature, there are many expressions of confidence in the idea that there are intimate connections between linguistics and ethnology.[1] Olmsted (1950) has sorted out some of these connections in his survey of what he recognizes as "ethnolinguistics." He points out that ethnolinguistics has been understood in several senses, as referring to (*a*) the use, in ethnology, of findings in linguistics, (*b*) the use, in linguistics, of findings from ethnology, (*c*) the interchange between linguistics and ethnology of certain features of their respective methodologies, (*d*) studies of problems clearly requiring data from both ethnology and linguistics, and (*e*) an integrative approach in the social sciences made possible by the combined forces of ethnology and linguistics. It is wise to agree, as Olmsted seems to imply, that ethnolinguistics embraces all these things.

The ethnologist, whose job is to describe the traits of a given culture, is under a routine obligation to list the language system or systems prevalent in the culture. Usually the ethnologist is not a technical linguist, but, depending upon the thoroughness with which he wishes to conduct his work, he may find it necessary to acquire at least some skill in speaking and understanding the language of the community whose culture he is studying. If the language has already been described by a linguist, the ethnologist is obviously benefited; if only in this trivial and operational sense, linguistic results can be applied in ethnology. Although ethnologists occasionally disparage the value of linguistic training, Sapir's remarks on the subject are convincing:

> Some day the attempt to master a primitive culture without the help of the language of its society will seem as amateurish as the labors of a historian who cannot handle the original documents of the civilization which he is describing (Mandelbaum, 1949, p. 162).

The relevance of linguistics to ethnology goes far beyond the mere operational necessities mentioned in the last paragraph. In both the structural and the lexical and semantic aspects of a language system, there exist correlations with traits of the culture either as it exists at any given moment or as it has existed at some previous time. Linguistic expressions of kinship and social status systems readily afford examples of such correlations,[2] and the use of kinship nomenclature as a possible clue to the establishment of linguistic families has been illustrated in a brief note by Kroeber (1941). As to the general relations between linguistics and ethnology, Kroeber concludes:

> On the whole, it is evident that of the two disciplines ethnology is the one which is dependent on linguistics. But the relations are complex and now and then it is the linguist who can profit by what the anthropologist can tender him (1941).

Greenberg (1948) has pointed out that the complete description of the semantic components of a language system is possible only by reference to cultural facts.[3] Thus, "careful compilation of a lexicon is then a field in which the linguist and ethnologist can fruitfully collaborate." Greenberg also makes the telling observation that the semantic analysis of a language should be of interest to the ethnologist because "it presents him with a practically exhaustive classification of the objects in the cultural universe of the speakers." Of course one may raise a question whether the semantic structure of a language (that is, the particular way in which potential meanings are associated with particular linguistic forms) does in fact yield information as to the "cultural universe of the speakers." Perhaps there are nonlinguistic aspects of this cultural universe, and perhaps it is not truly universal, but instead varies somewhat from speaker to speaker. In any case, Greenberg's hypothesis deserves attention; it seems to emphasize again the notion of "labeling" which Dollard and Miller (1950) have made much of in their discussion of psychological mechanisms in personality and psychotherapy.

Greenberg summarizes his rather theoretical paper as follows:

> The foregoing analysis . . . suggests that linguistics and extralinguistic segments of culture are intimately connected in a number of ways. The ethnologist may . . . view each specimen of the informants' speech as an instance of verbal behavior revealing both cultural and personal aspects. . . Altogether there is a rewarding field which awaits the linguistically oriented ethnologist and a mature science of culture is unlikely to emerge without the linguistic approach to culture having played a significant role (1948, p. 147).

An anthropologist who has found much profit in linguistic studies is Clyde Kluckhohn. In his book on the Navaho Indians, written in collaboration with Dorothea Leighton, he not only recommends that administrators, teachers, and missionaries who have to do with the Navahos should "learn something about the salient features of the linguistic structure," but also affirms that "anyone who wants to understand the Navahos at all must know something about their language and the way in which it molds thought, interest, and attitudes" (Kluckhohn and Leighton, 1946, p. 184). Later, in speaking of failures of communication between the Navahos and the whites, he writes, "Even a few days of intelligent study will show that the lack of equivalence in Navaho and English is merely the outward expression of inward differences between two people in premises, in basic categories, in training in fundamental sensitivities, and in general view of the world" (p. 215). It will be obvious at once, even from these quotations and much more from an examination of Kluckhohn's chapter on "The Tongue of the People," that the relations between linguistics and ethnology do not manifest themselves necessarily only in trivial details like the manner in which members of the culture greet each other in the morning, but also with respect to the way in which a language system may reflect the world-view of a culture. Thus, what Kluckhohn is talking about is equivalent to no less than the *"Weltanschauung"* problem which has been delineated earlier in this report.

Ethnolinguistic investigations of the kind suggested by the more or less programmatic statements cited here have thus far not been undertaken in any thoroughgoing way. This is perhaps because such investigations would probably require extremely detailed and comprehensive linguistic analyses. For example, the ethnolinguistic study of American speech would require penetrating analyses of dialectal variations, intonation patterns, and special features such as slang.

The well-known investigation of the language of gardening among the Trobriand Islanders by the anthropologist Bronisław Malinowski (1935) was severely vitiated by a lack of *expertise* in linguistics and by the adoption of a number of questionable premises. Malinowski gained a reputation for the view that it is impossible to study the language of a community without knowing its culture—indeed, that if one desires to specify the meaning of an utterance one must refer to the total situational and cultural context of that utterance. From this it would appear that while ethnological data would be crucial in linguistics, the reverse would not be true. Malinowski was, in fact, strongly opposed to traditional linguistics with its alleged emphasis on the study of texts; he rejected the Saussurean distinction between language and speech, and asserted that all study of speech necessarily leads immediately to sociological investigation (Malinowski, 1937). Nevertheless, in the work which he himself called his best effort, it is amply clear that he was at all points concerned with relations between ethnological observations and the kinds of data which would be studied by a descriptive linguist; if Malinowski had been a trained descriptive linguist, the linguistic facts would no doubt have had more compelling implications.[4]

LINGUISTICS AND CULTURAL HISTORY

In the study of cultural history, particularly the history of cultures whose beginnings are not recorded in their own written documents, linguistic results are almost indispensable before final conclusions can be drawn. Several examples of such studies may be given.

If one is interested in the prehistory of Africa, one might turn to the work of the German scholar Carl Meinhof. In his book *Die Sprachen der Hamiten* (1912) he drew certain conclusions as to the prehistoric relationships between "Hamitic" tribes and the Bantus and Hottentots of South Africa. These conclusions were based on his idea that the language of the Hottentots showed certain resemblances to Hamitic languages such as Ethiopian. Present-day analysis, however, seems to show that Meinhof's theories are not tenable. Greenberg, at Columbia University, is now at work on a classification of African languages based on more modern techniques of linguistic analysis, and hopes to draw up alternative hypotheses as to the prehistory of cultures in Africa.

A similar task is being undertaken by Isidore Dyen at Yale University in connection with Malayo-Polynesian languages of the Pacific Ocean area. It is almost impossible to trace the various movements of various Pacific Ocean peoples before the advent of the white man on the basis of anthropological and ethnographic evidence alone. Dyen hopes that comparative linguistics will provide some key to this mass of confused material. Nevertheless, the case of the Malayo-Polynesian languages is one of those which Kroeber (1941) cites as illustrating the proposition that sometimes "anthropological factors have direct bearing on a broad problem of linguistic theory."

As a final case in point, the history of the westward migrations of the white man in North America seems to be a problem which cannot be solved entirely by reference to written historical documents. Nor can it be solved completely by references to such ethnographic factors as architectural styles, food habits, and the like. A number of linguists are engaged in developing the dialect geography of American English.[5] Quite apart from the intrinsic interest of such studies, they may very well have implications for the study of the migration of the white man in the pioneer days.

LINGUISTICS AND SOCIOLOGY

The subject matter of cultural anthropology overlaps with that of sociology to a considerable extent. Studies in cultural anthropology usually concern cultures other than our own, often the strange and unusual cultures of the so-called "primitive" parts of the world. Sociology, on the other hand, studies the interaction of social groups, usually in our own culture. Both of these disciplines are studying *culture*. Perhaps the only real distinction between the two disciplines is that sociology attempts to draw generalized inferences about the formation and interaction of social groups, inferences of presumed universality for all cultures, while cultural anthropology is interested primarily in the general traits and themes of particular cultures. (Even so, some anthropologists would raise objections to any such delimiting of their field of interest.)

It naturally follows that to the same extent that linguistics may have implications for cultural anthropology, it may also have implications for sociology. Such a conclusion seems to be accepted by many sociologists, at least in principle; the extent to which results of linguistic science can be applied to sociological problems in detail, however, remains almost completely unexplored.[6]

Several references may be cited for an interpretation of sociological phenomena in terms of language behavior. The philosophically inclined sociologist G. H. Mead, in *Mind, Self and Society* (1934), emphasized the role of language as a means of social control, for example, in developing a consciousness of the "generalized other" through a process of verbal role playing. Two recent textbooks in social psychology (Lindesmith and Strauss, 1949; Hartley and Hartley, 1952), are heavily weighted with an interpretation of social-psychological data by reference to verbal behavior. In my opinion, however, none of these works outlines the full scope of ways in which linguistic results might aid the study of social behavior. For example, the effect of dialect differences in marking various social groups is ignored, possibly because few concrete investigations of the problem have been attempted.

A linguist of my acquaintance suggested that an important addendum might have been made to Warner and Lunt's study of "Yankee City" (1941) by a consideration of the varieties of dialect to be found in the various social classes identified in this sociological survey. Allison Davis (1951) and his associates at the University of Chicago have thrown social class differences in verbal ability into sharp relief, but since these differences were measured almost exclusively in terms of vocabulary (that is, knowledge of lexical items), it now remains to describe the finer points of divergence. Although there has been considerable interest in developing dictionaries and glossaries of slang and underworld speech,[7] surprisingly little attention has been paid to linguistic variations within the normal range of the social class structure. This is perhaps due to the fact that the variations lie in subtler aspects, such as phonetic structure and intonation patterns, rather than in the more obvious vocabulary items.

Another line of study which remains almost completely unexplored, except by novelists and popular writers, is the matter of personal attitudes toward the speech characteristics of others. Such attitudes are undoubtedly relevant in connection with race prejudice. For example, a Negro who speaks with a New England accent (or with an Oxford accent) is likely to be viewed differently from one who speaks in a dialect of the South.

Outstanding among sociological studies for its attention to verbal behavior is the work of Bossard and his associates (1943, 1945, 1950) on family modes of expression. Bossard recorded and transcribed the dinner-table conversations of 51 families, seeking to establish dimensions of analysis. The finer details of the results have not been made available in published form, but Bossard reports that families tend to develop highly distinctive patterns of speech, not only in the content and function of table talk, but even in respect to special word meanings, idiomatic expressions, and pronunciation. There are even familial idiosyncrasies in gesture. His data give support to the notion of language as a social index of occupation, religion, and social class, and he emphasizes that "language comes in a peculiar way to serve as a symbol of home, family, class, state, status, and country."

LINGUISTICS AND THE STUDY OF MASS COMMUNICATIONS

There is a rapidly growing field concerned with the study of social attitudes and opinions and the effects of mass communications media such as propaganda and advertising.[8] The general theory of mass communications has been discussed by various writers. Harold Lasswell has put the matter in these terms: "The study of diffusion and restriction processes [in society] calls for a general theory of language as a factor in power. . . . When men want power, they act according to their expectation of how to maximize power. Hence *symbols (words and images) affect power as they affect expectations of power*" (Lasswell *et al.*, 1949, pp. 18–19).

There are at least three points where linguistic studies (broadly defined to include descriptive linguistics, psycholinguistics, etc.) may have specific application in the area of mass communications. All three involve the specification of what effect a given message is likely to have upon a hearer or receiver of that message.

In the first place, the messages must often be analyzed in terms of their purely formal characteristics; the mass communications specialist should, ideally, be aware of the linguistic system within which he is operating, particularly with respect to dialectal differences in the sounds and meanings of linguistic forms. The effect of a radio transmission over the Voice of America in the Czech language, for example, depends partly upon the extent to which it conforms in every subtle detail to the speech norms of its intended audience.

Secondly, there is the operational problem of analyzing the semantic content of messages; this step has come to be known as *content analysis*. Lasswell's book on the language of politics (Lasswell *et al.,* 1949) is addressed primarily to the efficient accomplishment of reliable and valid content analyses. Content analysis depends on the use of proper units of analysis; that is, the content has to be reduced to a manageable number of mutually exclusive categories. But what should these units be; and what rules should govern? Admittedly the units should be recognizable, and the rules should be explicitly formulated. Content analysts have experimented with "rigid" schemes in which specific linguistic forms are the units, and with "flexible" schemes in which the analyst tries to get an impression of semantic content regardless of the sign vehicles used. "Rigid" schemes give greater reliability but less validity than flexible schemes. It may be suggested that linguistic and psycholinguistic studies could aid in the formulation of more reliable and valid content-analysis categories. Linguistic analysis suggests the possibility of establishing categories based on form classes or substitution groups (for example, the range of ways in which a particular country could be referred to might be described in this way). Psycholinguistic analysis might suggest the units of selection in messages and better ways of gauging their semantic content.

A third potential application of linguistic studies in mass communications is in the conduct and analysis of public-opinion polls. One of the strategic problems in opinion polls is the formulation of the questions used in eliciting knowledge, opinion, and attitude on the part of the respondents. Pollsters have become keenly aware of the subtle changes in effect produced by seemingly inconsequential changes in the form of questions. One of them has written a book devoted to just this problem (Payne, 1951). For example, it makes a considerable difference whether one asks whether something *should* be done, *could* be done, or *might* be done. Asking the question "Where did you read that?" may elicit such diverse responses as "In the *New York Times*" or "At home in front of the fire." The question "Do you prefer A or B?" sometimes produces different statistics if changed to "Do you prefer B or A?" The way in which a question is intoned by a door-to-door interviewer is often an uncontrolled factor: "Why do you say THAT?" (with high stress on *that*) is quite different from "Why do you say that?" (with relatively even stress). The linguist, with his techniques of describing the precise formal content of messages, and the psycholinguist, with techniques of describing semantic contents and stimulus values of messages, can obviously make a contribution in public-opinion research. It is also possible that the mass statistics collected in this type of research, particularly where a split-ballot technique is used to investigate the role of different question formulations, will provide the psycholinguist with a rewarding set of material for study.

LANGUAGE ENGINEERING

In various parts of the world, either in particular cultural groups or in various aggregations of persons with special problems and interests, difficult and unfortunate situations exist for which the remedy may possibly be an adjustment of certain language factors. Difficulties arise because people do not speak a common language, because they are illiterate, or because they regard certain languages as having an inferior or debased status. The idea that linguistics, in company with other sciences, might be able to resolve some of these difficulties has been given the name "language engineering." (The first public use of such a term in America, to the writer's knowledge, was in a paper read by G. A. Miller at the conference on Speech and Communication held at the Massachusetts Institute of Technology in June 1950.[9])

Actually, efforts in "language engineering" have been in progress for some time. The American Bible Society and other missionary organizations have long been interested in the problem of literacy, and have not failed to recognize the role that linguistic science can play in their work. It is of unusual interest to know that one large group of linguistic scientists, led by such men as Pike, Nida, and George Cowan, originally came to linguistics through their interest in the dissemination of the Gospel to underdeveloped areas of the world. These men, well recognized by their colleagues as thorough linguistic scientists, have organized training schools for the purpose of teaching missionaries the elements of linguistics.[10] As a result, there is an increasing number of individuals who are going out to all continents to study so-called primitive languages and to develop systems of writing which can be used in literacy programs.

Problems of language engineering are also met in the work of the United Nations Educational, Scientific, and Cultural Organization, particularly in its program of "fundamental education." The term "fundamental education" was adopted by UNESCO (1949) to refer to the kinds of education which are deemed urgently needed in the underdeveloped areas of the world—education in literacy, in the basic skills of productivity required to raise living standards, in health and sanitation, in recreation, and in basic civic duties. The relevance of linguistic science in implementing such a program has already been recognized by UNESCO.

There are four types of problems on which a linguistic scientist should be consulted in any program of fundamental education.

1. In many cases, it will be necessary for a linguistic expert to make a fairly thorough analysis of the native language which may be involved. This will be true even when there is some knowledge of the language available through materials prepared by nonspecialists. A refined linguistic analysis will save much needless time and effort in connection with the other three problems discussed below.

2. It will frequently be necessary to develop a system of orthography for the language. Such an orthography must be constructed in the light of the phonemic system of the language as revealed by a linguistic analysis. Reading difficulties due to an inconsistent orthography, like that which exists in English, may just as well be circumvented at the outset. The linguist may on occasion be called upon to decide what kind of alphabet should be the basis of the system of writing. In this connection, a point which may perhaps too easily be neglected is that the orthography must be suitable for the making of dictionaries.

3. The advice of linguists must be sought if there arises a problem of the choice of a regional auxiliary language toward which major efforts in the literacy program will be directed.

4. The linguist may be able to offer valuable advice on methods of teaching literacy and on the preparation of instructional materials. The special virtue of the linguistic expert in this connection is that he is likely to have the most precise knowledge of what has to be taught—the language system and the orthography devised for committing it to writing. It is evident, however, that other specialists besides linguists have something to contribute to the success of literacy programs. Educational psychologists,

for example, should be consulted on such problems as the sequencing of the instructional material and the establishment of desirable conditions of learning.

It is impossible and unnecessary to spell out here the enormous scope of the problems of language engineering when applied to the problem of literacy throughout the world or to international communication.[11] The mere mention of the linguistic situation in India, for example, where local dialects run into the hundreds, will immediately bring to mind the conviction that language engineering has wide application. Some scheme for the efficient collection of information about languages (such as Lounsbury's, described in Chapter 2) is obviously pertinent to language-engineering programs. A large number of languages throughout the world remain to be described, and the manpower in linguistic science is not presently adequate to meet this task unless special ingenuity is displayed in the problem of collecting and analyzing field data. The support of such a program as Lounsbury's is especially attractive in view of the current aims of UNESCO. At the same time, these aims make urgent the necessity of developing a more adequate formulation of the problems of teaching the fundamental language arts. In Chapter 6, we shall look at the applications of linguistics in the teaching of foreign languages, as well as in the teaching of literacy in one's mother tongue.

The problem of an international auxiliary language is so complex that it deserves special attention and evaluation in this report. Before proceeding to that topic, however, it will be interesting to focus our attention on the rather special problem of language engineering which exists in certain communities.

The linguistic situation in Haiti will be our example. As it happens, this situation was investigated at first hand by the linguist R. A. Hall, Jr., under the sponsorship of UNESCO; the following remarks are based on the UNESCO monograph, "The Haiti Pilot Project—Phase One, 1947–1949," which describes UNESCO's experimental program designed to reduce illiteracy in a test area in Haiti, and which incorporates some of Hall's findings and conclusions (UNESCO, 1951).

French is the official language of Haiti, but it is used only in the upper classes. The language of the people is called Haitian Creole. It is a development from French, but it cannot be regarded simply as a dialect of French;

instead, it is an entirely independent language, about as closely related to French as modern Italian is to Latin. Its phonetics and vocabulary are largely of French origin, but it possesses many features which show the influence of West African languages. Because of the lowly origins of Haitian Creole, it is widely regarded by Haitians as inferior to French, which is of course the language of official documents, newspapers, books, legal proceedings, and higher education. Even in the lower schools, there is an unrealistic attempt to teach French as if it were the native language.

In Haiti, therefore, language distinctions lead to an open cleavage between social classes. Members of the lower classes, in particular, are put at a disadvantage in business, trade, and law because they cannot speak, read, or write French. Nevertheless, proposals to make Haitian Creole the official language, or even to publish newspapers and books in Creole, have met with much opposition. The basic difficulty is one of social attitudes concerning the status of Creole. Attempts to establish a reasonable system of spelling for Haitian Creole have met with scorn because the results do not look like French. A system of orthography originally introduced by the Rev. Ormond McConnel was endorsed by an expert in literacy campaigns, Dr. Frank C. Laubach, and subsequently, after 1943, given an official stamp of approval by the government. Vigorous efforts to accelerate the literacy program ensued but were slowed down by continuing opposition to the system, which was regarded in some quarters as "a wicked innovation threatening Haitian spiritual and political independence."

After the UNESCO pilot project was initiated in 1947, the question of orthography was again examined, because a final settlement of the issue was desirable before pouring efforts into the preparation of textbooks and other material. At this time the American linguist Dr. R. A. Hall, Jr. was called in. Upon making a thorough analysis of Haitian Creole, Hall concluded that the McConnel system was scientifically sound and wholly practical. Limited progress has now been made in preparing materials for the teaching of Haitian Creole. Further steps are being planned in order to provide a greater variety of literature in Creole, as well as to develop instructional materials for allowing pupils to pass easily from Creole to French. It is recognized that the ultimate aim of the literacy training must include the reading of French because of the established position of that language as one which links Haiti with an international culture.

In the situation we have described, the problem of the "language engineer" is twofold. First, there is a purely linguistic aspect in which scientific analyses of the languages involved had to be performed in order to make sound decisions as to what was to be done. Second, there is a psychological aspect, in that the unrealistic and emotionally toned attitudes of the populace must be changed if any real progress is to be made. The situation neatly illustrates the need for coöperative work by different kinds of social scientists.

THE PROBLEM OF AN INTERNATIONAL
AUXILIARY LANGUAGE

The problem of an international auxiliary language is charged with strong feelings and factional disputes. One runs the risk of making enemies, no matter what one says about it. It is, in any case, an extremely complex problem and any fair-minded observer must grant some validity to each of the several points of view.

There is dispute even on the question of whether there is any need for an international auxiliary language, and if so, what value it would have. The extreme point of view is held by those who claim that the lack of an international auxiliary language is the chief obstacle to the reduction of world tensions and the improvement of mutual understanding among the peoples of the world. This view can easily be refuted by the method of contrary cases. For example, the adversaries in the American Civil War spoke the same language, while the English and the French have long been at peace despite language differences. The best argument for an international auxiliary language is to suggest its promise of greater convenience and economy in the conduct of international trade and in the exchange of information between nations. In his book *Cosmopolitan Conversation* (1933) Herbert Shenton describes the linguistic problems of international conventions and urges the adoption of an international language at least for the purpose of such conventions. Rundle (1946) has carefully studied the social and political difficulties created by language barriers. Nevertheless, even if an international language could be agreed upon by those most closely associated with the various proposals, there would remain grave problems in getting it accepted by the international public at large.

The problem of an international auxiliary language is not unlike the problem of a United Nations organization. Whether it can exist and continue to be accepted is a matter not so much of its own internal structure as of the social pressures and forces which play upon it. Of course, an international language should be as simple as possible, but even an artificial language as relatively complex as Esperanto has had considerable success. When and if the world becomes ready for an international auxiliary language, the problem of its selection and construction will be relatively simple, although I believe that linguistic scientists should play a major role in the enterprise. It is interesting that UNESCO seems to put its stamp of approval on the idea of an auxiliary language: "The selection of an auxiliary language with the widest possible field of usefulness—a world language as against a purely local one—will therefore commend itself" (UNESCO, 1949, p. 36).[12]

From one standpoint, there is no reason why there could not be a single language which would be a world-wide *lingua franca,* in some future Utopian state of our civilization. Unfortunately, this seems to be one of the premises adopted by any imperialistic nation. This was true of ancient imperialism (Egyptian, Greek, Roman) as well as of modern imperialism (British, French, German, and now Russian). The first objection which any international auxiliary language proposal has to meet is that it may be a manifestation of somebody's imperialism.

Basic English, one of the major candidates for the status of an international language, walks right into this objection, on all four feet, we might say. Proponents of Basic English say that since English, especially as represented by its scientific vocabulary, is rapidly becoming the most widely used language in the world, it might easily form the basis for an international auxiliary language. Certainly Basic English has a distinct advantage in this regard. But speakers of some languages resist the notion that English, rather than their own language, should form the basis of an international tongue.

Most international languages which have been proposed have been based on the premise that a successful international language must be contrived from elements taken from the existing languages, particularly the more common and widely known languages.[13] These proposed international languages are often called "artificial" and have only a moderate resemblance to any natural language. An objective in the construction of an artificial language is to make maximal use of elements which are found in common among various natural languages. This objective was only partially realized in Esperanto, developed by the Pole Dr. Zamenhof in 1887, which to English speakers shows too many evidences of its having been based partly on languages of the Central European area. Nevertheless, for various reasons Esperanto has had the widest currency of any of the proposed artificial languages. A recent attempt to rationalize an artificial language by making maximal use of elements common to the most widely used natural languages is Interlingua, the work of the International Auxiliary Language Association of New York.[14] A sample of the most recent version of Interlingua is given below. In order to encourage the reader to make his own translation, the English translation is presented at the end of this chapter.

In le presente phase del evolution del lingua international, que es tanto necessari in nostre era de communication mundial, IALA crede que un dictionario del vocabulario international in forma general es essential por le futur disveloppamento del experimentation. Le Dictionario de IALA offere le vocabulos commun e indubitabilmente international, e sic pone les, como nunquam avante, al disposition del adherentes de omne linguas auxiliar basate super le idea fundamental que un lingua international existe potentialmente in le linguas national.

If one should ask the question, there are interesting technical problems involved in the construction of an artificial language. Some linguistic scientists, notably Sapir (1925), have taken an interest in the problem, pointing out that some of the grammatical processes and categories to be found in exotic and unusual languages may be valuable in such an enterprise. Under the sponsorship of the International Auxiliary Language Association (IALA), Sapir, Swadesh, and Collinson contributed a number of monographs (Sapir, 1930, 1944; Sapir and Swadesh, 1932; Collinson, 1937) on several conceptual categories which were thought to be of interest in connection with an international auxiliary language. These monographs possess considerable intrinsic value, quite apart from the problem of an artificial language. If one really felt the need to contrive an entirely synthetic language, the attempt to utilize the full implications of linguistic science would be a thoroughly engaging task. It seems that at one time, say around 1935, this is what IALA set out to do. More recently, however, the direction of its work has turned toward the development of an auxiliary language which "should be composed of elements and features familiar to the largest possible number of people with different mother tongues" (IALA, 1945, p. 19). Trubetskoy (1939b) addressed himself to the problem of establishing for such a language a phonetic system which would contain the most common sounds of the languages of the world.

The interests of psychologists have also at times touched on the problem of an international language. Arsenian (1945) has reviewed some of the relevant psychological facts. At the request of IALA, E. L. Thorndike[15] studied the rate at which artificial languages like Esperanto and Ido could be learned by English-speaking pupils as compared with natural languages like French, Spanish, and German. The results strongly favored the artificial languages. Whether similar results would be obtained with a different selection of the languages to be compared and with samples of learners composed of speakers of non-European languages, we do not know. Nevertheless, it is fair to make the guess that an artificial language would almost always be easier to learn than any natural language picked at random, whatever the language background of the learner.

The claim of Basic English as a possible international auxiliary language needs to be seriously examined, particularly since the British government recently threw its support to the idea. (This official recognition may turn out to be more of a hindrance than a help, because it has had the effect of identifying Basic English somewhat too closely with the interests of the British Commonwealth, thus adding fuel to the argument that Basic English is "just a form of Anglo-Saxon imperialism.") Basic English was developed by C. K. Ogden over a period of several years after the first appearance, in 1923, of Ogden and Richards's noteworthy work *The Meaning of Meaning* (1936). One of the major points made by Ogden and Richards in this book was that one way of indicating the meaning of a symbol is to give a definition of it by means of other symbols, preferably by means of a relatively small "defining vocabulary." Ogden must be accorded much honor for taking the trouble to act upon this suggestion, where many another philosopher would have been content merely with the vision that it *could* be acted upon. Ogden's project soon took the form of a major attempt to devise a limited form of language in which almost anything useful could be said and which at the same time would have a minimal vocabulary. After examining the vocabularies of several well-known languages, Ogden early came to the conclusion that English would be a suitable basis for the kind of language he had in mind. The final form of Basic English was first given to the public in 1930; there have been no official modifications in it since that time save the publication of special lists of auxiliary and scientific words useful in technical fields. The Basic word list consists of 850 words. A major simplification was achieved by the device of eliminating most English verbs and expressing verb concepts by the use of constructions involving an "operator" [16] with an accompanying noun, adjective, adverb, preposition, or other "operator." For example, in Basic English one does not *compel* a person to do something; he *makes him do it*. The following is a sample passage in Basic English (Richards and Gibson, 1945, p. 7).

> Basic is a system of everyday English words used in the regular forms of normal English. It is a selection of those English words which—taken together and used as we are all using them all the time—will among them do the most work. It is the smallest number of English words with a general enough covering power, among them, to let a man say *almost everything*—to say it well enough for his general day-to-day purposes in all the range of his interests however wide—in business, trade, industry, science, medical work—in all the arts of living and in all the exchanges of knowledge, beliefs, opinion, views, and news which a general-purpose language has to take care of.

The standard references on Basic English are Ogden's *Basic English, A General Introduction with Rules and Grammar* (1930a), *The Basic Vocabulary, A Statistical Analysis, with Special Reference to Substitution and Translation* (1930b), *The Basic Dictionary* (1932), *The System of Basic English* (1934), and I. A. Richards' *Basic English and its Uses* (1943). Richards and Gibson have recently published a useful guide to Basic English, *Learning Basic English* (1945), designed for the speaker of English who wants to learn and teach Basic English. A number of books and articles in Basic English are available. Julia E. Johnsen has compiled a useful summary of information about Basic English, including excerpts from both favorable and unfavorable accounts (1944). Haber (1948) has enthusiastically suggested the establishment of a national institute of Basic English in America.

While a good many people endorse the idea of using a limited form of English as an international auxiliary language, there has been a continuing controversy as to whether Basic English is the best form of limited English. Fries and Traver, in *English Word Lists* (1940), approve the general struc-

129

ture of the Basic English vocabulary, but there have been outspoken critics of the system. West, Swensen, and others made a violent attack on Basic English in their monograph, *A Critical Examination of Basic English* (1934), prompting an equally violent rejoinder from Ogden in his *Counter-Offensive, An Exposure of Certain Misrepresentations of Basic English* (1935). Many criticisms of Basic English *as a system* have been unsound and misleading. To criticize the Basic English vocabulary on the ground that the 850 words contain thousands of different meanings is to ignore the fact that any similar number of common English words, however chosen, will likewise contain a large number of meanings. In fact, it has been observed that in normal English there is a high correlation between the frequency of a word and the number of separate dictionary meanings associated with it. Some critics have asserted that Basic English falls far short of being truly simple because thousands of highly idiomatic expressions can be constructed from the 850-word vocabulary. This assertion fails to recognize the restrictions which have been placed upon the use of the vocabulary by Ogden himself. These critics also fail to remember that "idiomatic" expressions inevitably tend to develop even in constructed languages like Esperanto. *Fancy dress ball* is one poorly chosen example which has somehow gained currency among critics of Basic English. The facts of the matter are that *fancy* and *dress* are not in the Basic word list, and *ball* is explicitly restricted in its use to mean a spherical object.

Somewhat more cogent criticisms can be made of certain structural features of Basic English. For example, the rules of Basic English provide that derivatives in "-er," "-ing," "-ed" can be made from 300 nouns in the Basic vocabulary. The learner of Basic English has to learn which nouns these are. Actually, they happen to be the nouns which *as verbs* permit such derivatives in standard English. It will seem odd to most learners that these forms can be used as verbs in Basic English when they occur in participial or passive constructions, but not as active verbs. Since a great many non-English-speaking learners of Basic English have well-developed verb systems in their own languages, there is undoubtedly a temptation for them to use nonpermitted verbs in Basic.[17] Ogden's defense of Basic in this respect is not wholly convincing; he asserts that elimination of the verb system makes learning easier, but many persons feel that it actually compounds the learner's difficulty.

Nevertheless, these criticisms are not of crucial import. Let us grant that Basic English is a language system possessing a high degree of potential effectiveness in communication. If so, it can presumably be learned in the same way that other language systems are learned. It is true that Basic English will present some peculiar difficulties, not only because of its use of the phonology and orthography of normal English, but also because of some of its structural characteristics, acquired in the process of eliminating the verb. Furthermore, as anyone who tries to translate a passage into Basic English will soon discover, the conversion of a complex idea into Basic English calls for considerable ingenuity and a major intellectual exercise in semantics, even with the aid of the Basic English dictionary; there is some doubt whether Basic English could stand up as an international language if its use presented too much difficulty at the higher levels of discourse. It seems probable that the major languages of the world show many similarities in their selections of semantic content which are at variance with the semantic patterning of the Basic English vocabulary; if so, any international language with a vocabulary structured as in Basic English will have a somewhat lessened survival value.

Despite all these potential difficulties, however, Basic English continues to have wide appeal as a possible international language, especially if it is understood that Basic English would be regarded as a somewhat flexible and expandable medium of communication which would draw ever closer to a near-normal form of full English. There are grounds for believing that if Basic English were to be proposed as an international language to be officially approved by some international body possessing the requisite authority, the proposed initial form which the international language might take should indeed be considerably less limited and restrictive than Basic English in the form originally published by Ogden.[18] In this way account could be taken of the experience which has been gained in teaching Basic English—experience which indicates that a somewhat modified form of limited English is usually easier to learn than "pure Basic." The mere fact that Basic English as Ogden originally proposed it has a neatly self-contained definition vocabulary does not guarantee that it is ideally suited to use as an international language.

All these considerations will undoubtedly appear highly academic to many. In reply we can only reiterate the assertion made earlier in this section that the establishment and continued acceptance of an international auxiliary language is a matter connected not so much with the structure and characteristics of the language itself as with the social pressures and conditions which affect it.

We shall have more to say about Basic English in Chapter 6, in which it will be pointed out that a distinction needs to be made between Basic English viewed as an international auxiliary language and Basic English viewed as the background for a new method of teaching second languages.

SUMMARY

Linguistic scientists are becoming increasingly aware of the implications of their work for their sister sciences, sociology and anthropology. They have begun also to be impressed with the possibilities of applying the techniques and results of linguistic science to the improvement and adjustment of social conditions. Some linguists have deplored the fact that while they themselves persist in writing treatises which are unintelligible to the layman, popular writers on language have had the courage, if not always the competence, to try to relate linguistic studies to the broader problems of society which alone can make such studies profitable and worthwhile.

This is the English translation of the passage in Interlingua on page 127:

In the present phase of evolution of the international language which is so necessary in our era of world-wide communication, IALA believes that a dictionary of the international vocabulary in a general form is essential for the further development of experimentation. The dictionary of IALA offers the words [which are] common and indisputably international, and thus places them, as never before, at the disposal of the adherents of all auxiliary languages [that are] based upon the fundamental idea that an international language exists potentially in the national languages.

Chapter 5 LINGUISTICS AND PHILOSOPHY

INTRODUCTION

This will be a short chapter. It is intended merely to demonstrate that philosophers have a vested interest in language and problems of communication, and that there are many interrelations, and many mutual interests, between linguistics, philosophy, and psychology.

THE NATURE OF PHILOSOPHICAL INTEREST IN LANGUAGE

Epistemology

Some of the most vexing problems of philosophy are concerned with the nature and validity of knowledge. This branch of philosophy is *epistemology*. Because language plays a large part in the statements we make about the world as we view it, whether from a subjective or an objective point of view, it is natural to find that questions about the nature of language—in particular, questions about the nature of the signs and symbols used in language—have played a major role in epistemological discussions. From the time of Plato's *Cratylus,* through the period of the nominalist controversies of medieval scholasticism, through the period of struggle between British empiricism and German rationalism, down to the modern period in which the logical positivism of the Vienna Circle and similar doctrines have attracted much attention, philosophers have been concerned with the nature of the concepts embodied in the symbols of language. As examples of serious works devoted to these problems we may cite those of Ayer (1936) and Urban (1939).

The Theory of Signs

C. S. Peirce, an American philosopher of the late nineteenth century, contributed an elaborate account of the nature of signs which has served to influence much of present-day thinking in America.[1] He defined a sign as "something which represents or signifies an *object* to some *interpretant.*" That which is signified by a sign is its *signifiant.* Signs were classified by Peirce in numerous ways; an important classification of signs is that into *icons, index-signs,* and *symbols.* An *icon* resembles its signifiant—for example, a picture, a blueprint, or an ideographic character like some in Chinese writing. *Index-signs* are signs which serve to point out a signifiant. *Symbols* are purely arbitrary signs which come to be associated with certain signifiants. Peirce also contributed the notion of a distinction between a *token* and a *type.* A *token* is a specific instance of a sign usage, while a *type* is an abstract class of such tokens.

Moving ahead almost three-quarters of a century from Peirce's time, we find that the contemporary American philosopher C. W. Morris draws heavily from Peirce's writings in his *Foundations of the Theory of Signs* (1938), written as a part of the *International Encyclopedia of Unified Science* sponsored by a group of logical positivists. Morris reintroduced Peirce's term *semeiotic* as the name of the science of signs. Semeiotic, according to Morris, has three branches: *syntactics,* the study of the relations of signs to one another; *semantics,* the study of the relations of signs to the objects which they signify; and *pragmatics,* the study of the relations between signs and the users of those signs.[2] In a later work (1946), Morris attempted to give a behavioristically oriented account of the theory of signs, at the same time seeming to disparage his earlier formulation.

This analysis of the three branches of *semeiotic* gives us the first glimpse into the nature of the possible relations between linguistics, philosophy, and psychology. Philosophy, of course, retains the right to speculate on all three branches of semeiotic! But linguistics is a science which addresses itself primarily to *syntactics,* while psychology (particularly psycholinguistics) is concerned with *pragmatics* and *semantics.*

The Unity of Science

The movement to study the unity of science, under the aegis of Carnap, Neurath, and other followers of the so-called Vienna Circle, is based on the premise that science consists essentially of a series of verifiable statements about the universe. It is held, therefore, that science can be unified by studying the logical structure and interrelations of these statements. The possible relevance of linguistics to such an inquiry was early perceived, and the linguist Bloomfield was invited to contribute a monograph to the above-mentioned encyclopedia. In this monograph (1939), Bloomfield attempted to delineate the place of linguistics among the other sciences, and suggested that language itself is a sort of metascience because it is the vehicle of all scientific statements. The latter view has encountered certain objections from scientists, who point out that communication in science also proceeds by the use and dissemination of models or even actual specimens of the things studied in science. A more recent view of the role of linguistics in the unity of science is that of Hockett (1948a), who feels that the further development of linguistics may foster the recognition of a new science which he calls "sociobiology" which would treat of the "translation of sociological knowledge into biological terms."

From the point of view of philosophy, the term *language* must be regarded in an extremely broad sense. We must no longer restrict our attention to the so-called natural languages, such as English, French, etc., and we must broaden our definition of language to include those systems of written symbols, such as mathematics and symbolic logic, which are not "universal" inasmuch as they treat only a limited part of human experience, but which are of special utility in guiding certain lines of investigation. Morris's *semeiotic* is designed to cover all such cases.

Metaphysics

The most majestic branch of philosophy is commonly thought to be *metaphysics,* although the logical positivists (for example, Carnap, 1928) tend to hold the view that metaphysics investigates a series of unanswerable and hence meaningless questions. Could there not be such a thing as metaphilosophy of philosophy—a series of statements about philosophy? One could examine the various metaphysical positions which have been taken by philosophers in ancient and modern times. This question is sometimes discussed in the history of philosophy, but the writer has found little evidence that a cultural and linguistic point of view has been adopted in such studies.

The nature of the "linguistic *Weltanschauung*" problem has been indicated in Chapter 2. If any broad solutions for the *Weltanschauung* problem were developed (probably by linguists and psychologists working cooperatively), the results might have an important bearing on the interpretation of metaphysical positions. This remains only a faint possibility at the present time, of course.[3]

Ernst Cassirer's (1923) account of the "philosophy of symbolic forms" can be regarded as a contribution to the linguistic *Weltanschauung* problem. Cassirer states the fundamental viewpoint underlying his work as being expressed "in the conviction that language, like all basic mental functions, can find its philosophical illumination only within a comprehensive system of philosophical idealism" (p. ix). He attempts therefore to develop a synthesis of modes of thought by the analysis of concepts expressed in a variety of languages. For example, concepts of space, time, number, and subjectivity (the ego-concept, etc.) are appraised as evidence of universally valid categories of cognition (Cassirer was fundamentally a Neo-Kantian). The data amassed by Cassirer, after suitable restatements have been made, may be of value to the student of the *Weltanschauung* problem, although one may express considerable skepticism as to the relevance of these data to Cassirer's philosophical ideas.[4]

SOME SPECIAL PROBLEMS IN THE PHILOSOPHY OF LANGUAGE

We have suggested that there may be an intimate connection between linguistics and philosophy in the study of what Morris calls *syntactics*. This latter term must be understood in a broader sense than is usual in linguistic theory. In linguistic theory, syntax is usually regarded as the study of the arrangements of the larger units of a language. Syntactics in Morris's sense, however, refers to the broad study of all the signs which are contained in a language, including their structure and arrangement. In this sense, even the theory of the phoneme (the smallest unit of language which carries meaningful distinctions) is a branch of syntactics.

There is an important difference, however, between the philosophical approach to syntactics and the linguistic approach to language structure. Linguistics, on the one hand, has developed by its own methods of analysis the rules concerning the *actual* signs and sign relations to be found in any language which is under investigation. Philosophy, on the other hand, particularly in that branch of philosophy known as symbolic logic, takes the structure of the elemental sign for granted, and then goes on to concern itself with the *possible* or *potential* syntactic rules which might be conceived to govern the structure of any language, natural or artificial.[5] The variety of the syntactic rules which a symbolic logician may study is dependent solely upon his imagination and the languages he knows, while the linguist is limited to the study of the relations found in empirical data. Actually, this limitation imposed on the linguist may be more apparent than real, for with every new language studied, new aspects of linguistic structures are likely to emerge. This situation carries with it a paradoxical implication that the symbolic logician's imagination limits him in his inquiries more than the nature of empirical linguistic material limits the linguist. Thus, the philosopher may find profit in examining the complexities of linguistic structure to be found in the various natural languages of the world. The discussion of the logical analysis of tense by the philosopher Reichenbach (1947) could perhaps have been more valuable if Reichenbach had had a further acquaintance with the tense and aspect systems of a variety of non-European languages.

Conversely, use of symbolic logic may be an aid in linguistic analysis. We have seen already that linguistic analysis results in a sort of logical calculus. Proponents of symbolic logic assert that it renders easier the manipulation of highly complex systems of data which are characterized by syntactical rules, in much the same way that mathematical analysis facilitates the treatment of large masses of data. In a somewhat different field, Greenberg (1949) has illustrated the possibilities of using the axiomatic methods of symbolic logic in the analysis of kinship relations.

Zellig Harris, in conversations with the writer, has suggested a most interesting approach to the unity of science. Anyone who wants to understand the significance of Harris's approach must understand the distinction drawn between the approach of philosophy to syntactical rules and that of linguistics. Instead of taking the philosophical approach (of analyzing the *possible* relations which might exist among scientific statements), Harris proposes that we start from a representative sample of scientific statements, as they might be found in textbook discussions or in general theoretical treatises. Such a sample would then be subjected to a type of linguistic analysis in which one would attempt to find the higher-order units and consistencies in the corpus of statements under investigation. No results of such investigations have been published as yet.

The logical positivists, as we have seen, assert that metaphysical problems are generally meaningless because they cannot be put in testable form. A number of philosophers who do not take this extreme position, however, have nevertheless perceived that language may make traps for the unwary metaphysician. The lead article in a recent collection of philosophical papers edited by Antony Flew (1951) is a paper entitled "Systematically Misleading Expressions" by the British philosopher Gilbert Ryle. Ryle points out that many statements of an apparently ontological character can be at once "grammatically respectable" but "logically disrespectable." He therefore concludes that the proper business of philosophy must involve a good deal of "systematic restatement." At the same time, other philosophers have expressed doubt that the forms of linguistic statement have anything to do with philosophical problems. Two British philosophers, Basson and O'Connor (1947) have reported an attempt to resolve this issue by appealing to linguistic experts for data on certain details of linguistic structure, in a variety of languages, which they felt might be symptomatic of the linguistic conditioning of metaphysical positions. They came to the tentative conclusion that there was no reasonable evidence for inferring that language structure is a factor in the type of metaphysical position adopted by the philosophers of a given culture. They found, for example, that the major, persistent metaphysical problems can be stated equally well in a wide variety of languages. Thus, while all the ramifications of what is known as the "linguistic problem" in philosophy have not by any means been adequately investigated, we must at this time take a position of cautious skepticism.

CONCLUSION

We have been able to give only a glimpse of the possible interrelations between linguistics and philosophy. Most of the problems in this area are intimately bound to questions of meaning, and thus to various issues in exolinguistics. It is useful to ask whether these problems can fruitfully be explored solely on the borders of philosophy and linguistics; in the opinion of the writer, the answer is in the negative. There is a triadic relation between linguistics, philosophy, and psychology such that the last of these disciplines holds the key to some of the central problems of meaning. The theory of signs recognizes that a sign has no meaning unless, as C. S. Peirce would put it, there is an organism which has an "interpretant"—

some psychological process of taking account of what is signified. Further-more, in so far as philosophers have been concerned with linguistic problems in metaphysics and in logic, they have essentially been concerned with the behavior of philosophers.[6] Thus, on many counts, psychology must be regarded as one of the disciplines essential to the solution of problems in the philosophy of language. At the very least, it is urged that philosophers of language should be thoroughly conversant with the psychological approach before entering upon the kind of philosophical inquiry which is peculiarly in their province. Finally, other social sciences, such as ethnology, will surely have much to contribute to this inquiry, particularly where cross-cultural data are involved.

Chapter 6 LANGUAGE AND EDUCATION

INTRODUCTION

In this chapter we shall consider a series of problems occasioned by the all-pervasive role of language in education. Having reached a point in this report where several different approaches to the study of language can be assumed to be familiar territory for the reader, we can broaden our focus so as to discuss the implications of each of them in connection with education. The phrase "applied linguistics" seems to have won approval, in some quarters, as a convenient way of referring to educational applications of linguistics (in the narrow sense of the term); in addition, however, a considerable body of research which already stands on the books can well be thought of as falling in the area of "applied psycholinguistics."

We shall have to speak of both ends and means, but the emphasis must be on the latter. The ends desired in educational enterprises will vary widely depending upon the nature of the enterprise. The acquisition of native fluency in spoken Arabic is one thing; the achievement of a liberal education is a quite different thing. When one is considering a relatively circumscribed objective in special education, such as competence in spoken Arabic, one feels on safer ground than when one is trying to state the objectives of liberal education in a free society—if only because one senses the greater ease in recognizing the finished product. The objectives of liberal education set forth in the Harvard Report[1] were formulated only after lengthy examination and reflection, attended by much soul searching on the whole philosophy of educational efforts. This is hardly the place for comment or animadversion on the Harvard Report or similarly sincere attempts to delineate the tasks of our schools within the framework of a liberal democracy. There is, however, scope for comment on the means recommended to achieve these ends, for upon analysis we find a structure of end-means relations the validity of at least some of which may depend

140

on linguistic or psycholinguistic considerations. For example, the authors of the Harvard Report assert that the "prime function" of foreign-language teaching in general education is "to illuminate English in these two respects in which English supremely needs illumination, namely, syntax and vocabulary" (p. 124). But research results in general give little support for making such an assertion, optimistic as our own intuitions and experiences may lead us to be.

This chapter is divided into three general sections, of which the first is devoted to education *in* and *through* the pupil's own language. The second section concerns the special problem of second-language learning, and the last treats educational measurement in language learning.

THE TEACHING OF THE LANGUAGE ARTS

It seems hardly necessary to comment on the objectives of teaching in the language arts, consisting of elementary tool subjects like reading, writing, spelling, and speech, as well as subjects devoted to the furtherance of skills in oral and written expression, comprehension of meaning, and literary appreciation. There is room for controversy as to the level of skill which is necessary and desirable for different kinds of pupils, but an advanced form of language education is one of the inherent traits of any civilized society. The present discussion can restrict itself, therefore, almost wholly to methods and techniques.

In 1925, on the occasion of the founding of the Linguistic Society of America, Bloomfield wrote:

> Our schools are conducted by persons who, from professors of education down to teachers of the classrooms, know nothing of the results of linguistic science, not even the relation of writing to speech or of standard language to dialect. In short, they do not know what language is, and yet must teach it, and in consequence waste years of every child's life and reach a poor result (Bloomfield, 1925).

This statement must have been made with conviction, for Bloomfield was a product of American education.

One more quotation, this one from a linguistically minded professor of English, will demonstrate the nature of the issue:

> The rank and file even of *English* teachers are not equipped to deal with English as a language. In spite of the fact that "more time is being spent in

the high school English classes of America today upon grammar and usage than upon any other single phase of instruction," [2] prospective English teachers are given practically no training in preparation for this part of their task. Usually our English teachers know nothing of phonetics or of phonemics, and their knowledge of grammar is limited to the kind of sentence analysis to which they were subjected in the grades of primary school and the early years of high school. The views of language that prevail in the schools and among even the "educated" public still perpetuate the authoritarian attitude of the second half of the eighteenth century and serve to create a huge market for cheap dictionaries and unscholarly handbooks of "correctness" (Fries, 1945, p. v).

It is true that an inspection of recent educational literature will show little evidence that educators at large have been signally influenced by the pronouncements of linguistic scientists. In writing on the question of applying linguistics to the teaching of fundamental language skills, linguists have frequently made statements, like the one above quoted from Bloomfield, which will seem extreme and dogmatic to many educators. Bloomfield himself (1944, p. 49 fn) cites the case of a college administrator who expressed his wonder at the very "liberal" attitude of linguists in matters of "grammar" (that is, correct usage). It is also true, however, that at least a few leaders of educational thought have arrived at some of the same conclusions about the teaching of language arts as have linguistic scientists like Bloomfield and Fries, perhaps somewhat independently of the latter. Enlightened attitudes have been manifested in a number of recent textbooks in the teaching of language arts and in curriculum planning. In some of the more forward-looking schools of the present day, one can find programs in language-arts teaching which Bloomfield would probably have approved heartily.

There is, in fact, considerable evidence that contemporary education has been influenced by new doctrines on the nature of language and meaning, even though these new doctrines may not have originated directly in linguistic science as it has been defined here. Ernest Horn (1942), in a justly praised review for the National Society for the Study of Education, points to the following trends: (1) the increasing attention given language as a part of culture; (2) the rejection of psychological dualism; (3) the recognition of the predominant role of verbal symbols in thinking; (4) the acceptance of a behavioristic interpretation of meaning; (5) the search for the meaning of meaning not in formal definitions but "in the processes of meaning and in the various structures or dimensions observable in these processes"; and (6) the recognition of the social origin of meaning. Horn states his belief that most disabilities in the language arts are "basic disabilities in language symbolization." He also comments on the disparity between the style of textbook language and the style of the spoken language as the child learns it. The influence of the work of Ogden and Richards (1936) on the meaning of meaning and of Richards (1938) on the referential and emotive uses of language is everywhere apparent in a book on the teaching of the language arts in secondary schools, prepared by the Committee on the Functions of English in General Education (1940). During the last few years, a revolution has been occurring in the field of speech education; speech educators are rejecting the old routines of rhetoric and oratory and are insisting not only that integrated training must be given in all four communication skills (reading, writing, speaking, and listening) but also that this training should be directed toward increasing the student's total personal adjustment (Paul, Sorensen, and Murray, 1946). Conversation is to be taught as much as platform speaking. The influence of general semantics as delineated by Korzybski and his followers is felt not only in speech education but also in some college English departments.

To all this must be added the evidence of the very strong tradition in educational research, both in America and abroad, directed toward improved teaching of reading, spelling, oral and written composition, and literature. The files of the *Review of Educational Research* or the yearbooks of the National Society for the Study of Education may be consulted on this point. Some of this research has been astutely planned, even though there are undoubtedly many instances (as in psychological investigation generally) where the formulation of hypotheses and the interpretation of results might have profited by closer contact with linguistic science and the psychology of language.

Unfortunately, the trends of which we have been speaking are not everywhere noticeable in American education. The number of schools which have been induced to make marked improvements in language-arts instruction is undoubtedly still relatively small. The indictments made by Bloomfield, Fries, and others are therefore in some degree still applicable to the American educational scene at large. For this reason, and also because the detailed issues involved are widely misunderstood even among leaders in educational thought, it is worth while to consider the merits of linguistic science and related studies as applied to the teaching of the language arts.

In what directions can linguistics and related studies make a contribution to the formulation of ends and means in language-arts instruction? Generally speaking, all the major perspectives of language study with which we have dealt in the preceding pages are involved, but we may fix attention on the following:

(*a*) the recognition of the primacy of speech as contrasted with written communication—as a proper orientation for instruction in oral communication and in the teaching of reading;

(*b*) an acquaintance with the phonemic structure of the language and its relation (or lack of relation) to orthography—as a preparation for the teaching of reading, writing, and spelling;

(*c*) an awareness of the dynamic character of a language system and its changes through time and space—as a background for the teaching of grammar and usage;

(*d*) a knowledge of the nature of meaning and its genesis—as background for vocabulary development and the teaching of listening, understanding, and interpretation;

(*e*) an analysis of individual differences in pupils with respect to their needs and abilities in the language arts—as a basis for the adaptation of instruction to the individual child;

(*f*) a concern with the role of language in mediating virtually every kind of learning—as an aid in capitalizing on the advantages of verbal learning and at the same time avoiding the excesses of "mere verbalism"; and

(*g*) an understanding of the psychological processes involved in encoding and decoding information through a culturally determined linguistic system—as a background for the teaching of all communication skills.[3]

The Language Arts in Elementary Education

The traditional view of elementary education in terms of the hackneyed trinity of "readin', 'ritin', 'rithmetic" dies hard. Arithmetic is not immediately germane to the present discussion. Reading and writing, at any rate, happen to be of fundamental importance in our culture, and the mastery of these skills, even at a relatively simple level, multiplies the potentialities of the child for further learning and for increased self-reliance. The academic phases of school life are wholly dependent on these skills, perhaps too much dependent on them. Hence the teaching of reading and writing comes to be thought of as the principal task of the elementary school—whatever else is to be taught; the training of other linguistic competences is apt to fall by the wayside. At least, this would be a fair comment on the orientation of much of American elementary education—an orientation which, incidentally, insidiously carries over even to the teaching of foreign languages at the secondary-school and college levels. Only in rare instances is it realized that the child needs training in speaking and listening as well—that the experience and training the child gets in the family and in his general social environment do not necessarily suffice in this respect. Not only this. The conception of reading and writing as ends in themselves sometimes leads to an overweening concentration on driving the child onward and remedying his deficiencies by frontal attack, to such an extent that the precious first three or four years of schooling can be too little used for teaching art, music, science, social studies, and responsible citizenship, to say nothing of the danger of creating emotional difficulties in the child. Or, alternatively, the difficulties encountered in teaching reading and writing simply engender frustration and hopelessness in the teacher. The child is the loser in any case, and the present appetite of our populace for pictures and graphics is perhaps traceable, at least in part, to the muddled state of literacy training.

At the other extreme we sometimes find that reading and writing are laid aside and postponed, or otherwise underemphasized, in elementary-school curricula. The principles of progressive education (to the effect that the child must learn for himself, by his own activity, and through his inner needs) are surely misinterpreted when, as occasionally happens, the early years of schooling are given over exclusively to "child-centered" projects not involving written-language skills.[4] While we know that children whose introduction to written language is postponed can readily catch up with their compeers at a later time, there is no guarantee that they have not missed some of the fruits of early reading competence.

Happily, in the last ten or fifteen years there have been signs that American elementary education is achieving a balanced view on the role of the language arts. It is increasingly true (aside from difficulties arising from serious lack of funds and personnel) that elementary-school programs are being devised to insure a many-sided development of the child. Language arts, particularly reading and writing, retain a key position but not an overbearing one. Oral-aural skills are just beginning to come into their own as educational objectives.[5] The new programs demand greater efficiency and smoothness in the teaching of the language arts. Any contribution which linguistic or psycholinguistic studies can make in this direction should be seriously considered, not only by educational authorities but also, at least in broad perspectives, by the public which supports the educational enterprise.

The Teaching of Reading

Merely to clear the ground, it must be said again that English orthography appears to present special difficulties to the learner, both in reading and in writing. Covertly, some linguists (but not all) are enthusiastic advocates of spelling reform. In fact, support has come from many quarters. The late George Bernard Shaw left part of his estate toward the encouragement of spelling reform; despite his questionable ideas as to what changes should be made, there are some merits in his arguments on behalf of revision.[6] However, we must recognize realistically that hardly any power short of the hand of a dictator could achieve spelling reform in the English-speaking condominium. In any case, a revised spelling would have some obvious disadvantages (for example, materials using the conventional spelling would become less accessible, and reform might have to become a continuous process to keep step with language change), and it might become less necessary if the teaching of reading can be planned so as to circumvent the difficulties of our present system, as seems quite possible.

Bloomfield (1933), Hall (1950), and other linguistic scientists have stated their conviction that instruction in reading can be improved only if it is founded on a correct analysis of the relation between speech sounds and orthography. They point out that the reality of language is represented by its sounds and not by the letters which may be used to represent the sounds of words. Thus, the stable norm is the phoneme instead of the alphabetic character. They complain that teaching sometimes seems to be based on the premise that given letters are "pronounced" in a number of ways, whereas it would be more proper to say that given sounds may be graphically represented in a number of ways. Thus, when the child is taught to "spell out" words it is as if he were being taught to speak, where instead he should be taught to associate letter groups with previously established phonetic habits.

It is hard to evaluate the soundness of this type of criticism of instruction in reading. It is true that there is a well-established misconception in our culture as to the primacy of written language, but this misconception has a valid basis, namely, that written forms serve to refresh our memories where we mistrust the spoken word. Even linguists recognize a tendency to form spelling pronunciations (for example, the continued sounding of the *t* in *often* contrary to regular sound changes). Some linguists have gone so far as to recommend that a teacher should never refer to a written word as being "pronounced" in such-and-such a manner, but this locution is an established part of our language, doubtless used by the very linguists who decry it. The essential merits in the recommendations of Bloomfield are these: (*a*) Whatever the rationale, the learning situation in early stages should be designed so that the perception of a printed word is conditioned to a previously established phonetic habit, instead of trying to condition an oral response to the printed word. The latter procedure may set up a *new* oral response which has no connection with the previously established oral response. For example, the child may make the mistake of responding to "know" as /knɑw/ without realizing its connection with /now/. (*b*) The child should be given an inkling of awareness about the nature of English orthography, even at the earliest stages. This is true even when a method emphasizing the learning of words as wholes is employed, for the child may easily develop letter-sound generalizations earlier than he is expected to according to this method, and he may need reassurance when his generalizations seem to misfire.

At any rate, teachers and pupils can hardly be said to be unaware of inconsistencies in English orthography. Bloomfield recommended that these inconsistencies be taught systematically and analytically, and with reference to a proper phonemic analysis of English. He suggested the outlines of an instructional method so designed (1933, pp. 500–501). We are told by Bloch (1949) that Bloomfield's system was once tried in certain Chicago parochial schools, but I have been unable to find evidence on the success of the experiment. Bloomfield published a more complete description of the method in an educational journal (1942a), drawing the fire of an educator who has specialized in reading pedagogy. This educator was W. S. Gray of the Department of Education at the University of Chicago, who devoted several pages of his book *On Their Own in Reading* (1948) to a consideration of Bloomfield's proposals. To quote Gray:

> One fairly recent proposal [Bloomfield's] for a mechanical approach roundly denounces any learning of words as wholes in the early stages, and proposes instead, use of the alphabetical principle. . .

> .   .   .   .

> The recent trend toward reinstating the purely mechanical word-perception programs of the old alphabetic or phonic methods is viewed with alarm by educators who are interested in promoting growth in reading power. Skill in phonetic analysis is essential for independence in identifying new printed words, but this skill should be based on fundamental understandings of how sounds in their letter symbols develop as generalizations based on the child's experience with words—words which he learns visually as meaningful wholes, rather than mechanically as a series of letter sounds. And finally, the use of phonetic understanding and skills should be geared into the total process of word perception (Gray, 1948, p. 32; reprinted by permission from *On Their Own in Reading,* by William S. Gray, copyright 1948 by Scott, Foresman and Company).

Later, Gray presents several chapters devoted to his own views on teaching phonetic analysis as an aid in developing reading skill. From a technical standpoint, Gray's discussion could have been improved through closer attention to phonetic and orthographic facts. In matters of detail, a linguist could have stated much more accurately the kinds of habits and skills which the reading student needs to develop in order to recognize new words. Apart from this, the major distinction between the views of Gray and of Bloomfield seems to be that the former wishes the child to acquire phonetic word-analysis skills by generalizing from his experience in learning words as wholes, while Bloomfield is willing to present at least some of the bare facts about phonemic word analysis in the earliest reading lessons. While Gray may scorn Bloomfield's approach as "old-fashioned," it is possible that a partially alphabetic approach, seasoned with refinements contributed by linguists and psychologists, may have considerable merit.

It is not true, as Gray alleges, that a linguist would denounce learning of words as wholes in the early steps. The linguist would merely wish to give the child every kind of assistance in developing word-perception skills; he would regard instruction in the nature of sound-symbol relations as a highly effective kind of assistance. What the linguist does denounce is the inaccurate statements about sound-symbol relations made by educators and teachers. When Gray says, on p. 88 of his book, "In our language a printed word is actually a recording of the series of sounds that we use in the spoken word," the linguist can justly plead for qualification.

To summarize this discussion let us try to state a balanced view on the teaching of reading. It would seem desirable to plan elementary reading instruction so as to train the child as directly as possible in the skills manifested by the trained reader. Research studies of trained readers have established firmly that printed words are perceived as visual wholes; words are never recognized by being spelled out (Woodworth, 1938, pp. 737–745). The cues for word perception, however, consist of single dominant letters, groups of letters, or general word shapes. It follows that the child should be trained in perception of words as wholes, but every advantage should be taken of alphabetical cues. This can be done by teaching a small initial "sight" vocabulary through such procedures as the presentation of cards containing single words; concurrently, a start can be made in training for recognition of letters, syllables, and letter groups by systematically presenting series of highly similar words and pointing out the similarities. Bloomfield's proposals in this respect have particular merit; by presenting a series like *man, fan, can, pan, ran,* one can insure rather early generalization for the common elements in these words, while at the same time a basis is laid for the differentiation of letter cues. There is nothing wrong in teaching the child to recognize single letters provided he is given the impression that sounds are not always represented by the same letters.

It is obvious that progress in reading depends upon progress in speech, and particularly upon vocabulary development. Oral-language development should be allowed to run ahead of reading development at all stages, and there must be much talking about new words and meanings before they are met in reading. The influence of the home can undoubtedly be highly beneficial when parents take pains to expose the child to a suitable range of verbal experiences in meaningful contexts—by reading and telling stories to the child, and in many other ways. Much can be done in the preschool in this respect, and while the preschool is not a proper place to begin formal reading instruction, printed words can be introduced into the child's environment in a number of informal ways.

It should also be obvious that progress in spelling depends upon progress in reading. The child should not be allowed to take an active part in the construction of words until he is thoroughly able to recognize the correct forms. If this precaution is taken, phonetic explanations and spelling rules can be held to a minimum.

The fact of wide individual differences in learning ability must be faced. Through the use of reading-readiness tests, reasonably sound decisions can be made as to when a child may start learning to read. It is of interest that the research leading to these tests has indicated the importance of visual-perception skills and auditory-discrimination abilities. These results are in harmony with the notion that the child learns to read by perceiving printed words as wholes and by acquiring habitual associations between sounds and letters or letter groups. There are indications that teaching methods should be varied according to the child's particular pattern of abilities; for example, children with visual defects are best taught by methods emphasizing "phonetic" skills, while children with certain types of auditory deficiency should be taught by methods emphasizing visual perception (Bond, 1935; Fendrick, 1935). There is need for further research on this point, however, as well as on the whole field of remedial reading techniques.[7]

The Doctrine of Correctness in English Grammar and Usage

Sooner or later in the elementary school, the child is confronted with the task of learning what is regarded as correct language usage. He finds that certain habitual language patterns of his everyday experience are for some reason not wholly acceptable in the classroom (especially in written compositions), and that he must replace these habits with patterns which in many cases seem strange to him. His teachers bombard him with attempted grammatical explanations, or with inflexible appeals to authority, but their efforts often go unrewarded, for even his secondary-school and college English teachers still find his verbal habits objectionable in many ways. These teachers are imbued with the doctrine that correct usage is defined by dictionaries and grammar books, and they are determined to secure conformity on the part of their pupils. More often than not, these same teachers fail to refer extensively enough to dictionaries and other collections of factual data about language use. If they did, they might be surprised and disillusioned to find, for example, that Fowler's *Modern English Usage* (1926) sanctions the use of the split infinitive in circumstances where ambiguity might otherwise result, as in *Our object is to further cement trade relations.*

We have drawn a picture of a situation which is all too common in American education. Fortunately, there are signs of reform. Enlightened English teachers, influenced in part by the writings of linguistic scientists, are putting the doctrine of correct usage in its proper perspective[8] and are revising content and method in the teaching of English. It will probably take another generation for these reforms to spread to every rampart of American education, for they have met not only apathy but even active resistance.

Bloomfield (1933, p. 300) and more recently Robert A. Hall, Jr. (1950, p. 189) are among the linguists who have urged reform in the attitudes of educators on the matter of correctness in usage. They specifically object to English teachers who persist in handing down such dogmas as those about the use of *shall* and *will,* and who fail to recognize that the "incorrect" forms of speech used by pupils may simply be manifestations of natural linguistic changes or dialectal variations. Furthermore, as Hall writes:

> The really fundamental problem is to get rid of the undemocratic attitude that underlies the whole situation, that makes us condemn variant speech-forms, and that makes such teaching necessary. This is a question of basic attitudes, which it will undoubtedly take generations and centuries to outgrow. From the short-run point of view, we still have with us the fact that standard speech is regarded as desirable and necessary by a dominant portion of our community, and that a substandard speaker is going to find certain doors closed against him, certain opportunities denied him, until he acquires standard speech-patterns (1950, p. 189).

Linguists have another complaint. Admitting that the usages of standard speech must be taught, they argue nevertheless that the notions of English grammar which are conventionally used in this teaching are often unnecessarily complicated and even unsound. Textbooks of English grammar are frequently wrong in numerous details. For example, some texts attempt to classify all verbs as either active or passive, and the teacher is faced with the necessity of trying to explain how such a classification could mean anything in the case of copulative verbs. Linguists object to the use of unnecessary terminology which has been handed down from ancient grammarians. They feel that English grammar should be taught on the basis of those linguistic principles properly needed to describe English. As yet, however, there is a paucity of text materials based strictly on the results of descriptive linguistics and designed for use in elementary and secondary schools. One feels that pupils would very much appreciate texts in which different varieties of usage are catalogued, and in which grammar is expounded in a self-consistent manner.

There is a fundamental question whether English grammar should be taught, and if so, how it should be taught, and how much of it. One would think that the primary purpose of such teaching should be to illuminate, where necessary, the statements that will have to be made about the characteristics of standard speech; however, it is not known (on the basis of controlled research, say) whether an appeal to grammar is necessary at all. It may be, for example, that imitation, practice, and repetition of standard speech patterns will be as effective as grammatical explanations. On the other hand, the teaching of grammar may serve an important secondary purpose of giving the pupil an immediate awareness of the structure of his language. Perhaps this objective is more important than the former one from the standpoint of general education. It may also have some utility in connection with the study of foreign languages, although one must avoid overoptimism as to the possibility of transfer, differences in linguistic structures being what they are.

Something should be said about the sources of information on English usage which have been developed to meet the needs of a changed orientation in English teaching. Publishers of dictionaries, of course, continue to compile information on past and present usage in morphology, meaning, spelling, and (occasionally) phrase patterns. Sometimes they are able to note a change in usage even before it has come into very general acceptance, for there is cultural lag in language as in other aspects of our civilization. Surveys of usage in grammar and syntax have been made by Leonard (1932), who obtained his data primarily by a questionnaire method, and by Marckwardt and Walcott (1938), who addressed themselves more directly to actual occurrences in literary materials. These surveys were sponsored by the National Council of Teachers of English. A work which comes highly recommended as a scientifically oriented description of actual usage in C. C. Fries's *American English Grammar* (1940). Though it is not designed as a textbook for secondary schools, it would serve as an excellent reference work for the teacher. Fries's analysis is based on the examination of letters in War Department files, classified according to various nonlinguistic criteria of the social status of the writers. Thus, it was possible to assign each usage to one or more levels of standard, colloquial, or nonstandard language.

The problem of correct usage is complex. Linguistic analysis of the various levels of standard and colloquial speech, with their changes in the course of time, shows that "correctness" is a relativistic concept. A given form is "correct" for a given variety of speech in a given historical period. But since language usage is a marker of cultural, social, and educational status (whether one likes it or not), a speaker must presumably be careful in choosing his forms of expression if he wants social approval from a given group. These are facts which linguists have stressed. An issue which has frequently been overlooked is the bearing of "correctness" on efficiency in communication. Will efficiency of communication be increased or decreased by acceptance or rejection of a given usage? It can be (and has been) argued, for example, that the confusion of the words *disinterested* and *uninterested,* if not checked, will lead to a loss of accuracy, with the eventual necessity of developing still another phrase or two to carry the lost meanings. A proposed criterion of whether a given usage is "correct" is whether it is capable of conveying all the intended information without lowering the hearer's opinion of the speaker. Thus, if I use nonstandard language patterns, I must calculate the risk of being misunderstood (or not understood at all), as well as the risk of being disapproved by my audience. Of course, some hearers and readers will be hard to please, particularly those who have highly conservative views on language correctness. In fact, most persons, depending on the extent of their education, behave as if they have a vested interest in the stability of language. It is as if they fear that efficiency of communication will otherwise be endangered. All this is unconscious, but it makes good sense to preserve a measure of stability in language. Many people are fastidious not only about the enduringly significant aspects of language usage, but also, by unconscious generalization, about relatively trivial matters such as spelling. And even in spelling, there is perhaps some reason to be fastidious; what reader has not experienced at least a momentary blockage upon coming across a mispelled word? Language may be allowed to change, but not by fits and starts, and not in such a way as to cause serious leakages in our communication channels.

It must be concluded that every problem of correct usage will have to be evaluated from several standpoints.[9]

First, one has to decide whether one is dealing with something which makes a real difference in the efficiency of communication (such as the use of a comma to distinguish *The policeman, who was there, . . .* from *The policeman who was there . . .*, corresponding of course to certain differences in the spoken utterances) or one which is a trivial matter of fashion or of arbitrary decision by unenlightened grammarians (such as whether prepositions can be used at the end of clauses, as in *The difficulty I found myself in* contrasted with *The difficulty in which I found myself*).

Next, one has to determine the facts of usage in different varieties and levels of speech. But the appeal to usage makes sense only on the assumption—a reasonable one in most cases—that natural forces in the development of language have produced patterns of speech or writing which cause no great difficulty in communication. It is implied here that among these forces is one compelling a certain measure of stability—a steady state, to use the chemists' phrase. Linguistic habits must be rather highly standardized if communication is to be efficient. Even minor deviations from the norm may cause delay or difficulty in decoding. It is only with the accumulation of minor variations that a new or modified linguistic habit gets learned and established in the speech community.

Finally, we must ask which variety of speech is of most general use as the standard for pupils in our schools. Assuming that a level of "highbrow literary American English" could be defined and described, should it be held out as the norm of English to be taught in the elementary school, or even in secondary schools and colleges? Obviously not. But there is undoubtedly some set of moderately flexible standards which could serve. To a degree, these are the standards of colloquial and of written English already described in the works of Leonard, Marckwardt, and Fries previously cited. A reasonably high common denominator in these standards can be reached, depending upon the eventual educational level of the student. I would not want to be misunderstood on this matter. I agree with Hall (quoted on p. 151) in rejecting the undemocratic and socially immature attitudes whereby variant and substandard language patterns are condemned; I would even go further and say that pupils should be taught under what circumstances such language patterns can be used appropriately and effectively. Overinsistence on rigid standards of usage may be detrimental to the development of personal styles of oral and written communication. Nevertheless, I believe that the teaching of sensible standards of English usage in schools will make possible a fuller realization of our democratic ideal, in that all our citizens will be better able to communicate with one another. The criterion of correctness is fundamentally a social one: it depends on the total effectiveness of communication in a given society.

Advanced Language Skills

While he is mastering the basic tool skills, the pupil is gradually introduced to more and more complex tasks in the use of language. Through reading and other experiences, his vocabulary increases enormously;[10] on the surface, the child's comprehension of verbal material develops apace, and he attains a certain measure of skill in oral and written composition. In bright children, the results may be remarkable.

Nevertheless, much is left to be desired in the average product of our schools and even in the more promising segments of the school population. There are, for example, undoubtedly tens of thousands of secondary-school students or graduates who can read with understanding nothing more difficult than articles in the *Readers Digest* or the *Saturday Evening Post* —who would find documents like the Declaration of Independence or the Bill of Rights quite beyond their comprehension. This discussion can concern itself only with whether linguistic studies can suggest certain steps toward even a small improvement in the verbal competence and level of comprehension shown by the population at large.[11] The implications will probably be more relevant in the language training of the better students.

The things which have been said previously in connection with the doctrine of correctness in usage will apply with even greater force at

155

the higher stages of education. Hayakawa (1950) is ready to suggest that the phobia which some people seem to have about putting their thoughts on paper in any formal way is traceable to a fear of writing incorrectly. Concern over linguistic proprieties, in such cases, completely overshadows the purpose of English composition, namely, to communicate ideas.

Hayakawa's more general proposals as to a more effective method of teaching English composition appear sound and workable. He would have pupils address their themes not to the teacher but to their fellow students, who would even be allowed to grade them. In this way, students would learn to have something useful to communicate, and class discussion would point up failure of communication caused by inaccurate wording and phraseology. Even matters of linguistic propriety would be taken care of, for the student writer would be subject to a realistic kind of criticism from his fellows, many of whom would comment on what they would regard as poor taste. An approach somewhat similar to Hayakawa's, but more specifically influenced by linguistics, has been suggested by Lloyd (1950).

The effective teaching of reading comprehension undoubtedly depends to a large extent on the introduction of material in a properly graded sequence. This fact has long been recognized by educators, who have developed word-frequency lists (Thorndike, 1932) and formulas for measuring the readability of prose (Dale and Chall, 1948; Flesch, 1949) with a view to controlling the ease of learning at various stages.[12] One of the chief obstacles here is that of vocabulary development. Grove (1950) has pointed out that the vocabulary of English (as compared to German, say) is made unnecessarily difficult for the common man because of its dependence on a large number of foreign roots—mainly from Latin and Greek. His proposals to surmount the difficulty by extensive teaching of etymology can hardly be accepted, however, for etymological teachings would probably impose a wholly extraneous burden on most learners; the bright students do not need this teaching anyway. The answer to vocabulary development lies simply in the recognition that progress can be made only by prolonged and systematic effort; psychologists should investigate the rate at which words at the growing edge of vocabulary can be learned. Language simplification and the grading of material will, of course, aid vocabulary development, but it is more important to recognize that meanings and concepts are acquired only by a process of abstraction from numerous experiences of either concrete objects and relations or verbal contexts. The materials of instruction must therefore be designed to enable the student to make abstractions more readily. In this way, the psychological theory of meaning becomes available for application to practical educational problems.

The application of a theory of language and meaning to the teaching of English is in fact the underlying motive of I. A. Richards in a notable series of works, including *Interpretation in Teaching* (1938) and *How to Read a Page* (1942a). Richards is concerned not only with the student's knowledge of the linguistic elements constituting a piece of writing, but also with his ability to appreciate its total effect. He wants to show the student how to dissect a passage by finding the literal or plain-sense meaning, the mood, intention, and tone of the writer, and the writer's attitude toward his subject, his reader, and himself. Such dissection, it is hoped, will give the student a keener sensitivity and a fuller appreciation when he begins to roll these elements together again for a synoptic view of what he is reading. An approach of this sort seems to offer great promise in the teaching of reading comprehension even as early as the junior-high-school stage; its advantages in the teaching of literature are obvious and have been widely acclaimed.

The teaching of scientific views about language ought to find a larger place in secondary-school and college curricula. It is odd that the high-school student is taught branches of science like physics, chemistry, biology, and (in recent years) even psychology and sociology, while at the same time he gets little scientific instruction about something which is of such immediate interest as language. Certainly some of the ideas about the nature and function of language which have been discussed in these pages are not beyond the grasp of the high-school student; a more extensive treatment of linguistic science and related studies would be of undoubted interest to the college student, as well as a significant contribution to his general education.[13] Courses in specific languages, as presently given in our schools, do not alone suffice in this respect, since the mere mechanics of learning a second language will tend to push aside the broader perspectives of language study unless time is reserved for them.

Language arts have such a far-reaching significance in the educational program that as the child matures he has increasing need of guidance as to how he can best develop his linguistic potentialities. These potentialities need to be diagnosed and fostered by every means at our disposal. For example, aptitudes for particular types of written expression (expository writing, literary expression, etc.) need to be recognized early and encouraged. Deficiencies in oral communication, such as diffidence in conversation or in speaking to groups, must be diagnosed before they become too much congealed in the child's total personality. Questions of whether a pupil should take instruction in foreign languages, and, if so, which languages he should study, can be decided only in the light of his abilities and interests. It is obvious that the kind of educational guidance which is implied here cannot always be given satisfactorily by teachers in single academic departments. Ideally, it could be given best by specially trained counselors equipped with all the knowledge and techniques that the psychology of language, clinical psychology, and the science of educational measurement can bring to bear on these problems. Furthermore, educational guidance in the language arts should begin in the early years of elementary education and continue through the college years. Unfortunately, lack of trained personnel and gaps in our scientific knowledge make this ideal program difficult to realize at present, but as the concept of educational guidance develops it will be necessary to give increasing attention to guidance in language arts.

It remains to discuss two additional aspects of instruction in advanced language skills: speech education and semantics.

Speech Education

Any analysis of the nature and functions of language will show that oral communication, in both its expressive and its receptive phases, is of prime importance. This is one of the facts emphasized by linguistic scientists but strangely neglected, at least until recently, in our whole scheme of education. It is true that declamation, "elocution," and rhetoric were widely taught in traditional education, but these were viewed as independent subjects and were seldom integrated with other phases of the curriculum devoted to language arts. There was also a frequent tendency for speech education to be too much preoccupied with the study of dramatic art, to the neglect of the needs of boys and girls who did not happen to be inclined toward the theater. The teaching of speech has been predominantly restricted to the colleges, and then not in all colleges. Finally, speech departments have often found themselves in the position of being "poor relations" of the English department. This neglect of education in spoken communication in English thus parallels in a curious manner the traditional neglect of oral communication in foreign-language teaching, on which we will comment later in this chapter.

Many have desired to see a change. In fact, some speech teachers are now insisting that with a fourfold approach to language (speaking, listening, reading, and written composition) centered in their departments they are able to do a better all-around job of teaching the use of the English language than English departments of the traditional sort were ever able to do. There is at least some merit in this belief, particularly if speech departments are willing to undertake the task of teaching English composition—a task which is notoriously tedious to young English instructors who are really more interested in teaching literature. If a sufficiently high standard of instruction could be maintained, there would be every reason to recommend that the teaching of those basic language skills which must be taught at the college level be placed in a combined department of written and spoken English. (This has, in fact, already happened in several institutions of higher learning.) There are elements common to the two enterprises of teaching oral and written English: the structural features of the language are the same, and there are the same problems of meaning, creativity, and interpretation. Furthermore, if we accept the notion that competence in spoken language somehow underlies competence in writing it, an integrated program makes much sense. On the other hand, certain special requirements in each phase would make complete integration difficult. For example, criteria for the evaluation of written and of oral productions differ. Making a good speaker and making a good writer demand different sets of techniques. In the former case there are delicate psychological problems affecting the speaker's ease in the communication situation. Indeed, the speech educator sometimes comes dangerously close to being a practitioner of clinical psychology, even when he is dealing with "normal" students of speech and not with cases of speech defect (stuttering, etc.); the act of speaking in a sense involves the whole personality (Murray, 1944).[14]

The preparation of the public speaker is nevertheless still the dominant theme of speech education at the college level. The substantial basis for this instruction has been derived largely from an experience which extends back as far as the times of Demosthenes, Cicero, and Quintilian. Textbooks are much occupied with analyses of great speeches—their form, content and delivery. An attempt is made to advise the student how he can go and do likewise. At the same time, speech educators have developed a considerable body of research on methods of instruction, evaluation, and diagnosis. Some of this research has already been mentioned in Chapter 3. Psycholinguistic investigations of all kinds will be of great value in the teaching of speech. Speech educators also recognize the value of certain data from linguistic science. Hultzén (1947), for example, recommends that teachers of speech must be acquainted with phonemics in order to "get rid of phonemic interferences with phonetic procedures." But a whole range of linguistic phenomena, particularly those connected with suprasegmental phonemes of stress and intonation, will also be of value in speech education when these phenomena have been more adequately catalogued through linguistic analysis.

Speech education is being extended in two directions. First, attention is being directed to types of communication situations which are less formal than the public address. There is a desire to teach skill and smoothness in ordinary conversation, as well as good habits of listening. Secondly, there is some evidence that speech education will become a more regular part of secondary-school curricula. At some point there will eventually be a joining of forces with the efforts of elementary-school teachers, who as we have said previously are themselves showing increased interest in the young child as a speaker as well as a reader and a writer. It seems reasonable to hope that if speech education were to be taken up more generally in the elementary school, the type of instruction presently found necessary at the college level would no longer have to be of such a remedial character.[15]

Semantics and Education

In the mind of the layman, disturbed about seemingly protean variations in the meanings of words, the study of language is probably most closely associated with "semantics." Popularized treatments of semantics by Chase (1938) and Hayakawa (1941) have, of course, helped in creating this illusion, but the problems of meaning as perceived by the layman can hardly be shrugged off.

The problem of meaning is an ageless one, as we have noted, but from ancient times until recently it has remained largely in the hands of philosophers, logicians, and gifted amateurs. The twentieth century has seen the rise of several movements inspired by a desire to enable the common man to rectify his thinking about the nature of meaning. Not only this. These movements have also been founded on the faith that a knowledge of semantic principles will help an individual gain a more realistic orientation toward all sorts of everyday problems—from problems of personal adjustment to problems relating to the nature of the universe. The scientific underpinnings of these movements have not always been sound, but the least that can be said is that their proponents have been sincere in their faith and amazingly effective in their teachings. We use the word *teachings* advisedly, for these movements must be regarded primarily as educational enterprises. These teachings have had the virtue of containing many truths which need to be pointed out to the common man again and again—truths which may be regarded as either obvious or not obvious, depending on one's point of view. Perhaps one may summarize the total effect of these doctrines by saying that they tend to make one adopt what might be called a scientific orientation toward the dynamic and changing character of one's environment. This scientific orientation would include a proper appreciation of the way in which words and symbols function in thought and communication. In particular, an attention to the *actual referents* of words and the attitudes of their users, rather than to the words themselves and their stereotyped meanings, would compel greater sensitivity and keener discrimination as to the meaning of any verbal statement. It may be because certain semantic movements preach a form of watered-down scientism that they have failed to impress large numbers of scientists, particularly linguists, psychologists, and philosophers. In the first place, the major assertions of semanticists are already obvious to such persons and taken for granted, and in the second place, these persons can easily find imperfections in the logical and empirical structures of the systems which have been offered thus far.

The statements of the preceding paragraph are perhaps unfair if we begin to apply them too sweepingly. Certainly they are somewhat unfair if we are speaking of several streams of thought which have emerged in England, but they may be applied with particular aptness to the movement known in America as "general semantics." First, however, let us mention developments abroad.

Movements devoted to semantics have had their philosophical antecedents. Ogden and Richards (1936, p. ix) point out that, in reference to the problem of meaning, "since the lost work of Antisthenes and Plato's *Cratylus* there have been seven chief methods of attack—the Grammatical (Aristotle, Dionysius Thrax), the Metaphysical (The Nominalists, Meinong), the Philological (Horne Tooke, Max Müller), the Psychological (Locke, Stout), the Logical (Leibnitz, Russell), the Sociological (Steinthal, Wundt) and the Terminological (Baldwin, Husserl)." Yet, in 1903, Lady Victoria Welby was able to complain that her predecessors had not developed an adequate science of meaning. In a book entitled *What is Meaning?* (1903) she outlined a science of meaning to be called "significs," and it is evident from the fervor and earnestness of her writing that she confidently believed that the teachings of significs could bring about, in students and in the lay public at large, a revolutionary upswing in the quality of thought and understanding.

Better education of the public was undeniably one of Ogden and Richards's guiding motives in writing *The Meaning of Meaning* (1936). This scholarly work is based on a thorough survey of the history of semantic philosophy and on a critical examination of the requirements of effective symbolic communication. Its analysis of meaning in terms of a semantic triangle (symbol, referent, and thought or reference), its description of the causal relations in a sign situation, and its discussions of the canons of symbolism and the theory of definition have made it a classic. The psychological terminology and premises adopted by Ogden and Richards are by now somewhat outmoded, although one may venture the opinion that their conclusions would not be fundamentally altered even if the analysis were to be re-undertaken along the lines suggested in Chapter 3 of the present work.[16] It is not our present objective to comment further on Ogden and Richards's book, except to draw attention to its purpose and its implications in the light of the work accomplished since its publication.

As to the purpose of a science of meaning, Ogden and Richards have this to say (1936, p. x):

> The practical importance of a science of Symbolism even in its present undeveloped form needs little emphasis. All the more elaborate forms of social and intellectual life are effected by changes in our attitude towards, and our use of, words. . . None but those who shut their eyes to the hasty re-adaptation to totally new circumstances which the human race has during the last century been blindly endeavoring to achieve, can pretend that there is no need to examine critically the most important of all the instruments of civilization. . . [It is necessary to] raise the level of communication through a direct study of its conditions, its dangers and its difficulties. The practical side of this undertaking is, if communication be taken in its widest sense, Education. (This and the preceding extract are reprinted by permission from *The Meaning of Meaning,* by C. K. Ogden and I. A. Richards, published by Harcourt, Brace and Company.)

The collaborative work of Ogden and Richards has borne fruit in several directions. The development of Basic English was an outcome of the finding that the designation of meaning by definitions leads to a relatively small number of referents which can be used as starting points for defining any symbol. The translation of a communication into Basic English, it is averred, compels the translator to dissect its meaning into basic elements and thus provides a kind of exercise in semantics. It is admitted that Basic English will not cure all semantic ills, for a passage in Basic English may exemplify wrong-headed thinking as much as any in full English. It remains true, however, that the spelling out of meanings by means of definition is one of the chief avenues to semantic rectitude, and this is a technique which needs to be taught widely in the schools—in such a way that the student becomes conscious of what he is doing and of its utility.

In our discussion (p. 157) of the implications of a theory of language and meaning for education in the advanced language skills, we have already alluded to another direction in which Ogden and Richards's work has had an influence. This is the use of semantics in interpretation, which in this context may be defined as the analysis of the total content and effect of any verbal communication into elements relating to its "plain sense," its "feeling," its "tone," and its "intention." In this way, both the symbolic and the emotive contents with which a message is charged are to be taken account of. In the hands of a teacher who has thoroughly mastered the ideas in Richards's *Practical Criticism* (1929), pupils find interpretation an illuminating exercise. If nothing else, it forces pupils to ask questions which might not otherwise occur to them about the meaning and intention of a message—whether it be a piece of propaganda, a poem, or simply a plain statement of a scientific fact. Along the way, questions of the meanings of particular words will present themselves, providing the pupil with an opportunity to try his hand at definition. A knowledge of semantics has its value also in writing and English composition, as Hartog's book *Words in Action* (1947) makes plain.

The work of Ogden and Richards has, then, had a large and useful influence. In publishing *The Meaning of Meaning,* they laid a good foundation for later undertakings. However one may feel about Basic English as a linguistic system, one must admire the ingenuity displayed in its construction and the arresting quality of the questions which arise in any attempt to make use of it in teaching. Richards's work on interpretation provides a sound and tangible direction for educational efforts in the fields of reading, English composition, and literature. There is, regrettably, little research of a scientific character which has sought to measure the potential impact of these methods on a student's mind; such research is urgently needed. Fortunately, there is a good-natured modesty about the claims which Ogden and Richards have permitted themselves to make concerning the values of their teachings.[17]

The case is quite different when we consider the doctrines of Alfred Korzybski and his followers. These doctrines have come to be known, in their aggregate, as *general semantics;* since this designation has been adopted so widely by Korzybski's disciples, it is probably wise to use it only in connection with the stream of activity set in motion by Korzybski.[18]

The history of general semantics provides a fascinating study in the dissemination of ideas. Korzybski, who began his professional career in Poland as an engineer, spent the latter part of his life in America. In *The Manhood of Humanity* (1921), he drew attention to the "time-binding" character of the human organism as contrasted with the animal, who can be only "space-binding." Now, time-bindingness is hardly a profound concept—it alludes merely to the obvious fact that civilization exists by virtue of communication through successive generations—but it has been seized upon by general semanticists as one of their cardinal principles. It was not until after 1933, when he was able to put in print his magnum opus, *Sci-*

ence and Sanity (1933), that Korzybski attracted any considerable number of adherents. *Science and Sanity* even in its later editions has remained an abstruse and almost deliberately disorganized book. (Korzybski took pains to advise his readers to reread it a number of times in order to arrive at an integrated view of its multiply connected ideas.) Whether it was because of the very abstruseness of the book, providing an intellectual challenge to the reader, or because of the enthusiastic testimonials which came from the pens of several established scientists (for example, Keyser, 1934; Campbell, 1937), or because of the novel manner in which Korzybski clothed his ideas, the book attracted wide attention. Perhaps none of these explanations is sufficient, for one may also offer the opinion that if Korzybski's book had been devoted merely to the theory of meaning, it would have had only a small audience. It was, rather, its emphasis on the possible contributions of semantics to mental health and its continual allusions to the "un-sanity" of our society which made it the object of much admiration. It has become the bible of the general-semantics movement, despite the fact that Korzybski's doctrines have been presented by subsequent writers in much more digestible and better organized form, for example, by Chisholm (1947), Hayakawa (1941, 1949), Irving Lee (1941), and Wendell Johnson (1946).

The central ideas of general semantics are concerned with the importance, for mental health, of adopting a scientific orientation toward reality. Such an orientation would have to involve a proper appreciation of the function of symbolic systems in perception and in communication. Korzybski would begin by pointing out the various levels of organization existing in the material world—from the nuclear and molecular levels up to levels of social organization. (This idea, of course, can be traced back at least as far as the positivism of Auguste Comte.) He would then point out that any symbolic system nearly always has to represent the infinitely varied facts and processes of the material world by means of abstractions. Just as a map must perforce omit the finer details of the territory it represents, verbal abstractions cannot of themselves give any idea of the complexity and diversity of the things they refer to. Even within verbal systems one finds levels of abstraction—abstractions of abstractions. Mental ailments come about largely because the individual is likely to perceive reality too much in terms of symbols and abstractions rather than in terms of the actualities represented so inaccurately by those symbols. Indeed, Korzybski thought the

165

major ills of the world are due in large measure to a two-valued logic where reality is seen only in black and white, as it were, whereas a correct evaluation would emphasize a multivalued logic of shades and tints on a practically endless number of dimensions. Korzybski was convinced that the situation could be remedied by education in semantics.

To this end, an Institute of General Semantics was founded, offering courses, seminars, and conferences to all who would take an interest. The Institute was never officially affiliated with a university, but for a period it operated in the vicinity of the University of Chicago. Its headquarters are now at Lakeville, Connecticut. A journal with the unusual title *Etc., A Review of General Semantics* was founded in 1943; under the editorship of S. I. Hayakawa this has served as a forum for the discussion of numerous issues in semantics and related fields. In recent years the pages of *Etc.* have shown evidences of a desire on the part of its sponsors to rectify the careless, vague, and inexact statements made in the early days of the movement. In addition to provocative original articles on a variety of subjects, it has been publishing reprints of papers, selected from external sources, which are deemed by its editor to provide a fresh slant on problems of general semantics.

General semantics, despite the catholicity of its professed aims, seems to have had an appeal mainly to a particular segment of the intellectual world. It has been most warmly received by certain speech educators, speech pathologists, and remedial-reading experts. A number of psychiatrists have shown an interest in its doctrines on semantics and mental health. On the other hand, general semantics has been coldly ignored by most psychologists, linguists, anthropologists, and philosophers. For one thing, these latter groups by nature dislike the oddly assorted terminology and the aura of cultism and missionary zeal which have been characteristic of the movement. More fundamentally, they recognize that general semantics is not an investigative discipline in the true sense of the term. In the nearly twenty years of its existence it has produced very little which can qualify as scientific research.[19]

The statements of general semanticists themselves testify that the movement is an educational enterprise rather than an investigative discipline. In his *Introductory Lectures on General Semantics,* Chisholm (1947) states at the outset that he is "trying to teach modern, scientific, physico-mathematical method." In his report as retiring president of the International Society for General Semantics, Chisholm (1949) states that the object of the society "implies the task of *training* the nervous systems of as many people as possible to act in terms of the order empirically known to be *healthy.*" Thus, it must be "more than merely a scholarly society." Irving J. Lee (1950) admits that while "in the past the society has tried to spread its ideas mainly by personal enthusiasm," tough-minded unbelievers will remain unconvinced until research findings on the effectiveness of general-semantics teachings are forthcoming. It is to be hoped that Lee's remarks will help to usher in a period in general semantics of greater caution and appeal to scientific evidence. Otherwise, general semantics as an avowed scientifically oriented doctrine will continue to be a monstrous self-contradiction.[20]

If general semantics is then to be evaluated chiefly as an educational undertaking, what are the chances that it can succeed in its objectives? Provided that general semanticists can carry through a housecleaning in their premises, the prognosis is favorable. Upon analysis, the doctrines of general semantics turn out to be nothing more or less than a sprightly though somewhat muddied interpretation of facts and principles taught in various sciences. But where the scientist will ordinarily offer only cold facts and principles, the general semanticist with his customary buoyancy, arresting phrases, and clever audio-visual devices can perhaps come to closer grips with the minds of his pupils. If general semanticists will cease appearing to claim that almost any psychological or social problem can be solved by semantic reconditioning, the way will be open for a more intelligent diagnosis of these problems in the light of the various sciences which may be relevant.

There is undoubtedly a place in education for semantics (in the general sense of the term). Indeed, as Ernest Horn (1942) has pointed out, the major part of all education is concerned with the development of meanings and concepts. Teaching methods must be planned so that the difficult constructs we require pupils to learn can be connected with concrete experience; field trips, audio-visual aids, and other constructive activities can aid in serving this function. The principle of learning meanings by concrete experience has been recognized by every major educational theorist, including, for example, Comenius, Pestalozzi, and John Dewey, although it can too easily be forgotten in the day-to-day stress of teaching. Nevertheless, the use of language will remain supremely important in all instruction; concrete experience without verbal interpretation will help little. As Horn remarks, it is not the use of language but its abuse that should be eliminated. An abuse of language in education is represented by the mere memorization of verbal symbols and formulae; while such memorization has its place, its value is obviously limited.

Perhaps educators like Horn have not gone far enough. They write as if a knowledge of semantic principles were useful only for teachers. But these principles are presumably useful for pupils as well. One of the virtues of the semantic movements discussed here may be that they have attempted to put semantics teachings directly in the curriculum. If we may believe a report by Semmelmeyer (1940), this can be done even in the first grade. At the very least, the nature of a symbol and an abstraction can be pointed out to young children; bright children are sometimes observed to develop these ideas for themselves. Some of the instructional techniques and devices —such as the "structural differential"—developed by Korzybski and his followers appear to be of considerable promise in this respect.

SECOND-LANGUAGE TEACHING

The problem of teaching a second language (that is, a language which is not the learner's native tongue) is extraordinarily complex and hence has a truly enormous literature.[21] The most recent broad survey of the problem is Dunkel's *Second-Language Learning* (1948). Unfortunately, Dunkel's survey shows that we are little better off in our knowledge of the problem than we were, say, thirty years ago, that is, before the flush of wide-scale investigations which started about that time. Perhaps we are better off in a negative sense—we know better the extent of our ignorance. We are also in a better position correctly to evaluate certain elements of the problem, but we are not at all sure that we have any better methods of teaching foreign languages than the traditional ones.

Any discussion of second-language teaching must begin by a consideration of the purpose of such teaching. We must also distinguish between avowed objectives of teaching and actual objectives of teaching as displayed in the learning situation itself. The avowed objectives of second-language teaching vary widely, if we consider the total range of situations in which foreign languages are learned in formalized instruction—from the teaching of languages by the Berlitz system to the teaching of languages and literatures in any representative Eastern liberal-arts college. One group of objectives has to do with the command of a language. We must then inquire what kind of command is sought. Is the emphasis on a speaking knowledge of a language, and if so, is it a knowledge simply sufficient to "get along" in a foreign country as a tourist, or is it a type of knowledge which would enable the speaker to "pass as a native"? Another group of objectives has to do with the humanistic values which are supposed to accrue from the study of foreign languages; again, the objectives seem to range all the way from a simple knowledge of the geography of a foreign area to a deep appreciation of great works of literature. A third group of objectives, less often mentioned in discussions of the subject, is concerned with varying degrees of knowledge and appreciation of the role of language as a cultural institution. This may extend from "an appreciation of how ideas look when put in a foreign language" to a rather sophisticated knowledge of linguistic analysis.

This is not the place to try to evaluate these varying objectives of second-language learning. It must be pointed out, however, that there is little agreement as to the proper objectives of language teaching, that second-language instruction does not always conform to its avowed objectives, and that the evaluation of any method of instruction must be made in the light of the objectives it presumes to attain. The following discussion assumes that the learning of a second language is a desirable educational objective, at least for many students—either as a tool or as the means of opening up new vistas in general education.

It is difficult to sort out the various methods of instruction which have been proposed. Any distinction between recently proposed methods of instruction and the more traditional methods can be made to seem great on paper but the distinction is not necessarily present to any significant degree in actual practice. Methods of instruction are too often defined in terms of relatively superficial elements, such as whether the "direct" or the "reading" method is emphasized, whether audio-visual aids are used, whether an "informant" is used, whether the "mimicry-memorization" method is used, etc. We may call these things superficial because they indicate little about the way in which the individual learns, or about the nature of the things he learns. This is not to discount the importance of observing these superficial aspects of instructional methods and of trying to take account of them in research in language learning. The demonstration that improved results seem to be obtained under certain conditions of instruction may occasionally lead to a recognition of more fundamental factors in the learning process. A truly adequate description of a method of instruction would, as it were, look over the student's shoulder in the classroom and then follow him home to watch him do his homework.

Certain factors in the student must be considered in the evaluation of any given program of instruction. We must consider the student's age, his intelligence, his "aptitude for language," his motivation, his prior experience with languages (including his own), and so on. Even these factors have to be considered in relation to the purposes and methods of instruction. As one looks over the relatively extensive literature on the relation of intelligence to achievement in learning foreign languages, one can draw only the rather trivial conclusion that a certain level of intelligence is required to learn foreign languages successfully *under the conditions of instruction which commonly obtain in our schools and colleges.* The literature says nothing about the intelligence required, for example, for a sailor to learn a bit of everyday French while his ship is in port at Marseilles, to give a rather unusual illustration (even though the case in point may not be at all infrequent).

A Short History of Developments in Second-Language Teaching

Probably most readers of this book are familiar with the traditional approach to second-language teaching, with its emphasis on the study of paradigms, word lists, and extensive translations from written literature. Often, the meager treatment of the sounds of the living languages is designed only to enable the student to give a reasonably accurate pronunciation of the written text being studied. It is assumed that a student who wants a speaking knowledge of the language can "pick it up" whenever he might need to. Such a system may of course work reasonably well in Europe, where the student has ample opportunity to acquire speaking knowledge of a language through contacts with travelers from neighboring countries. Yet it may be questioned whether the traditional approach is satisfactory even for providing a reading knowledge of a language.

Commercial methods such as the Berlitz and the Linguaphone systems have capitalized on the failure of American education to equip students with a practical knowledge of the languages they study. These commercial systems have apparently been quite successful, and have been based upon a direct, oral approach which uses simple auditory and visual aids. Native speakers of the language are often employed as instructors. One can scarcely resist pointing out that these native instructors only infrequently know anything about linguistic science. Persevering students of foreign languages in commercial schools somehow seem to have been able to attain their goals, even in the absence of phoneme theory and the apparatus of modern linguistic analysis. Of course, our evidence for the success of these commercial language-teaching systems is primarily hearsay, and, even if we had better evidence, we would have to take into account the intensive character of the instruction, the student's motivation (he pays as he goes), and the small size of the classes.

It is curious to note that what is often called the traditional approach may not be so traditional after all. It is a development which probably dates from relatively recent times. In the Colonial days of America, language instruction seems to have included considerably more attention to oral aspects of language, even when the language was Latin, Greek, or Hebrew. The "traditional" approach, then, seems to have been developed to meet the needs of rapidly expanding popular education in the latter part of the nineteenth century. Before 1875, say, members of the elite classes learned foreign languages through individualized instruction by native instructors. After that time there were simply not enough native speakers of foreign languages available to meet the demands of ever-increasing numbers of students in high schools and colleges who wanted education in the liberal arts.

It may have been the first World War, when Americans in large numbers were put in contact with Europeans for the first time, which really focused attention on the sad state of foreign-language teaching in America. In any case, it became recognized in the 1920's that the deadening pattern of language instruction, both in the classical and in the modern languages, needed a thorough overhauling. The Classical Investigation (American Classical League, 1924–25) and the series of reports of the Modern Language Study (Fife, 1931) made recommendations which were the storm centers of controversy for many of the ensuing years. It must be emphasized that both these reports were primarily concerned with language teaching in secondary schools. The combined effect of these investigations was to lay renewed stress on the reading-knowledge objective. In the Classical Investigation, supported by the General Education Board of the Rockefeller Foundation, the "direct" method, emphasizing the use of Latin or Greek in oral drill and classroom conversation, was not recommended because, among other reasons, there were too few teachers qualified to use such a method. Algernon Coleman's final report (1929) on the Modern Language Study, a study supported by the Carnegie Foundation, recommended an emphasis on a reading-knowledge objective on the ground that this objective was all one could expect high-school students to attain in the two years of study to which most of them limited themselves. Use of the oral approach was recommended only to the extent necessary to progress toward the "ultimate" objective of "ability to use orally and in intelligible fashion a small stock of the foreign words, phrases and sentences." Coleman's conclusions were supposed to have been buttressed by large amounts of experimental evidence.

There is considerable reason to believe, at this time, that the Modern Language Study was a fiasco. Louis Mercier (1930) adduced evidence to show not only that the Coleman report was the work of one individual (Coleman) and not fully endorsed by the whole committee responsible for the study, but also that Coleman's conclusions were not adequately supported by his data. Mercier's criticisms were echoed in many other polemic writings of the early thirties. Nevertheless, the Coleman report probably exerted considerable influence on language teaching, not only in secondary schools but also in colleges and universities. One might say, however, that it served chiefly to justify and rationalize existing practices rather than to promote new trends.

Thus far, linguistic scientists had had relatively little influence in the language-teaching movement except in so far as some of them also happened to be language teachers in colleges. There is reason to believe that they rejected traditional grammar-translation methods, at least if they followed the advice of Bloomfield, who wrote as follows (1933, pp. 503, 505):

The large part of the work in high schools and colleges that has been devoted to foreign-language study, includes an appalling waste of effort; not one pupil in a hundred learns to speak and understand, or even to read a foreign language. The mere disciplinary or "transfer" value of learning the arbitrary glossemes of a foreign language can be safely estimated at almost nil. The realization of all this has led to much dispute, particularly as to the methods of foreign-language teaching. The various "methods" which have been elaborated differ greatly in the mere exposition, but far less in actual class room practice. The result depends very little upon the theoretical basis of presentation, and very much upon the conditions of teaching and on the competence of the teacher; it is only necessary to avoid certain errors to which our tradition inclines. . .

The pupil who takes up his first foreign language at high school age or later, is likely to substitute an analysis for mere repetition, and thus to meet halfway the incompetent teacher, who talks about the foreign language instead of using it. Between the two, they have kept alive the eighteenth-century scheme of pseudo-grammatical doctrine and puzzle-solving translation.

Language Teaching During World War II

It may have been Bloomfield's statement that "the matter that is to be presented, the thousands of morphemes and tagmemes of the foreign language, can be mastered only by constant repetition" (1933, p. 505) which influenced the form and direction of a number of language-teaching programs in which linguistic scientists became directly or indirectly involved during World War II.

The credit for providing the initial impetus for many of these programs belongs largely to Mortimer Graves, executive secretary of the American Council of Learned Societies, who some time before Pearl Harbor foresaw a developing need for the study and teaching of unusual languages of possible military and diplomatic usefulness. Early in 1941, the ACLS established an Intensive Language Program, with funds provided by the Rockefeller Foundation, which served as an administrative base of operations until after the war. (In fact, the ACLS still maintains a Committee on the Language Program which offers a guiding hand to a number of linguistic enterprises.) The Intensive Language Program began by supporting descriptive analyses of several unusual languages for which teaching materials were woefully insufficient. Shortly after Pearl Harbor, these results were turned to good account when the work of Mary Haas with the Thai language was applied to an intensive course in that language at the University of Michigan. This course represented the first case in which a linguistic scientist, without necessarily having personal fluency in the language in question, directed the classroom teaching process and used native informants as models for drill purposes (Haas, 1943). The chief objective of this teaching, of course, was command of the spoken language.

The success of the initial trials gave impetus to the expansion of the program. The linguist J M. Cowan was put in charge in April 1942, and in the following summer courses in some twenty-six languages were established at a number of universities, all utilizing the linguist-informant setup. Also, about this time, ACLS personnel were consulting on the operation of various language programs in the U. S. Government and armed services. Of these programs, the most important were the following:

1. *The "Army Language Section."* This enterprise developed primarily in an effort to provide language-learning materials for men of the armed services to use in their spare time. The Education Branch of the Special Services Division (concerned chiefly with recreational activities) had primary responsibility for this program. A corps of linguists under the direction of Henry Lee Smith, Jr., produced a series of instructional materials, including manuals, dictionaries, phrase books, and phonograph records. The series of Technical Manuals called *Language Guides* and *Phrase Books* were of an elementary character; accompanied by two 78-rpm phonograph records, they were available in nearly forty languages. The series of Education Manuals, referred to as Basic Courses, were self-contained and reasonably well-graded texts providing for about the equivalent of a full year of instruction in the normal college course. They were supplemented by twenty-four 78-rpm phonograph records and were available in several dozen languages. During the war they were issued by the United States Armed Forces Institute, and after the war they were put on the civilian market by Henry Holt and Company under the designation "Spoken Language Series." It must be emphasized that these materials were designed largely for self-study purposes, or at least for situations in which a native informant might be present but certainly not a linguistic scientist. It was with this type of program in mind that Bloomfield prepared his *Outline Guide for the Practical Study of Foreign Languages* (1942b).

2. *The Army Specialized Training Program: Language and Area Section.* This was a large program involving some 15,000 Army enlisted men assigned to college training in languages for periods of (usually) nine months. Although this program has been widely supposed to have been closely supervised by linguistic scientists, the latter actually played only a small part in it. Cowan, it is true, was consulted on its planning, and the directive which set the tone of its instructional methods bore evidences of

the notions of linguists. Emphasis was to be given to the spoken, colloquial form of the language, grammar was to be explained only when necessary, and, above all, practice and repetition were to be used almost to the point of exhaustion. The languages studied included common ones like French and German as well as a number of unusual ones. The methods actually used in ASTP classrooms varied widely, depending considerably upon the predilections of the persons in charge, who were more apt to be language teachers of conventional background and training than linguistic scientists. It may be said that in many cases the procedure was simply a matter of following traditional methods with an increased emphasis on the spoken language. Trained linguists were in charge in only a few of the courses. Furthermore, conventional text materials were the rule; the manuals of the Spoken Language Series were not widely used—but in fairness it must be noted that not all of them were available at the time.[22]

3. *The Foreign Language and Area Programs of the Provost Marshal General's Office, Department of the Army.* This program involved linguistic training of occupation and military government officers. The teaching methods used in it were a good approximation to the methods previously worked out by linguists in the early stages of the Intensive Language Program. The results have been favorably commented on by Hyneman (1945).

It can be realized from the foregoing discussion that the language programs conducted during the late war were exceedingly varied in objective and method. The courses which naturally attracted most attention from the language-teaching profession were those of the ASTP, but, as noted, the connection of these with linguistic science was often tenuous. The significant thing about the ACLS Intensive Language Program in its original form was that linguistic scientists were put directly in control of the language-learning process.

The Intensive Language Program and its offshoots were greeted with much enthusiasm by the educators in whose institutions courses had been conducted. Many of them saw in these programs important implications for postwar educational practice in foreign-language teaching. Many of the principles of the Intensive Language Program were therefore adopted in postwar education, particularly in colleges; its influence extended even into some high schools. Generally, the foreign-language instruction in these colleges and high schools took the form of a somewhat intensified program of study, the foreign-language course often being a double course, or even a triple course. The oral approach, including the "mim-mem" procedures, was stressed; most colleges and schools, however, did not find it practical to use a native informant in addition to the instructor. Where possible, drill sections were organized under the leadership of fluent speakers of the language being studied.

Some of the popular articles (for example, in the magazine *Fortune,* 1944) on the Intensive Language Program or its variants may have given the public the impression that the program could produce "miracles." Rumors circulated to the effect that a person could learn a foreign language in a few weeks, or even in a few days. That, of course, was far from the truth. In most cases, students in the intensive courses acquired a mastery of a foreign language (and then only within certain limits) after nine months of instruction which occupied a large part of their waking hours. To an outsider, they may have seemed glib even after only a month or so of instruction, but most language systems are too complex to be mastered even reasonably well in nine months. There is a large difference between uttering pat phrases and actively using a language in spontaneous communication.

Partly as a consequence of ill-informed journalistic articles which made exaggerated claims for them, the wartime language-teaching programs have been subjected to a barrage of criticism, both constructive and destructive. For example, Mario Pei (1946), a Romance philologist and author of several books on language, charged that the intensive courses did not yield the results claimed for them, and ridiculed the idea of using linguistic analysis —allegedly designed chiefly for field work with unknown languages—in teaching widely studied languages. (The former criticism must be held invalid if it was intended to refer to the majority of ASTP courses; the latter is valid only if it is accepted that linguistic analysis is solely an investigative technique.) Other critics have been concerned with the very real difficulties of applying intensive language methods in the usual secondary-school or college situation—difficulties arising from lack of time and shortcomings of personnel. Still other critics have rejected the spoken-language aims of the intensive programs as being inappropriate for the usual school program. Finally, there has been the not unexpected criticism that the intensive language programs contributed nothing really new in language teaching—that for many years previously, progressive language teachers had been using oral-aural methods and drills.

On this last point, it is true that the intensive language courses represented a particular combination of methods and procedures, nearly all of which had appeared at some time previously. These methods can be described almost completely in the terms outlined in the *Report of the Committee of Twelve,* published at the end of the last century under the sponsorship of the Modern Language Association (1900). The emphasis on modern linguistic analysis and upon large amounts of drill on graded materials represented new departures, but only in degree. But then, in these highly advanced times it could hardly be expected that a new method would represent anything more than a new combination of procedures. In many cases the application of scientific linguistic analysis represented an enormous advance. Linguists cannot yet be completely certain that their teaching programs are superior to traditional methods, but they have a reasonable expectation that they *will* prove superior.

The Investigation of the Teaching of a Second Language

Contrasted with the methods of teaching in greatest vogue up to 1940, the methods of the Intensive Language Program appeared so novel that it seemed to be time for a reëxamination of the whole problem of language teaching. Accordingly, an Investigation of the Teaching of a Second Language was established in 1944 with the support of the Rockefeller Foundation. The principal investigators, F. B. Agard (a linguist and language teacher) and H. B. Dunkel (an educational research specialist), published their final reports four years later (Agard and Dunkel, 1948; Dunkel, 1948).

The plan of the investigation was to make what experimental comparisons might be made between (*a*) classes using a conventional approach not stressing aural-oral objectives and (*b*) experimental classes stressing aural-oral skills. No attempt was made to set up a rigorous experimental design with adequate matching of students in the experimental and control groups. Instead, effects of the control variables were to be randomized by making studies in a number of colleges and in a number of different situations. Special achievement tests were developed in French, German, Russian, and Spanish to measure the results of the instruction. The tests yielded scores on both reading comprehension and aural comprehension.

The persons responsible for the design of the investigation were keenly aware of the requirements for an ideal experimental comparison, but apparently felt unable even to approach the fulfilment of these requirements. Thus, in analyzing their results they were forced to give weight to those comparisons which *happened* to approach conditions of experimental rigor. But even for these comparisons, they failed to make, or at least to publish, all the measurements which would enable them to know more positively to what extent ideal experimental conditions had been attained. There was also a failure to put enough effort into the construction and use of tests of "oral production," that is, tests of the student's ability to pronounce and speak the foreign language.

It is not surprising, therefore, that the results of the investigation were either negative or inconclusive. "The experimental courses evaluated by the Investigation," write Agard and Dunkel (1948, pp. 293 ff), "generally failed to produce near-native oral-aural or reading proficiency in the American student of a second language in one or two years. In other words, within the total instructional time available for these experiments, the newer procedures and techniques have not proved themselves impressively in training students of average aptitude and motivation. Perhaps the goal was unrealistically high, but it was that sought by many experimenters; and only a near-native ability will justify some of the advantages claimed for the skills." Nevertheless, "with few exceptions language students claim to be more highly motivated by oral-aural than by grammar and reading goals. Many elect the experimental courses eagerly with the purpose of getting a speaking knowledge" (p. 292). But, "by and large, experimental students failed to understand the phonographically recorded utterances of an unfamiliar native speaker, delivering unfamiliar though easy material, significantly better than did conventional students" (p. 289). At the end, the investigators could do nothing more than point to "the need for more precisely planned experiments." "There is still a serious need," they write, "for experiments designed to test one by one in carefully controlled situations these fundamental problems which confront the language teacher in his search for perfection" (p. 300).

The experimental design of the Agard-Dunkel investigation leaves something to be desired. There were many instances in which the new methods appeared to yield significantly superior results; a more carefully planned experimental design might have indicated the conditions under which these methods were superior. In the present state of knowledge concerning experimental design and statistical method, it would have been possible to conduct the investigation so as to enable fairly precise inferences as to the effect of the experimental variables to be drawn, even in the face of rather widely varying methods of instruction. The reader interested in the statistical methods which might have been used may be referred to a study of shorthand systems by Deemer and Rulon (1942), which is a model study in educational method. As in the Agard-Dunkel investigation, this study compared two instructional procedures in a variety of conditions, but detailed control measurements were made at the outset of the experiment. Use was made of the so-called Johnson-Neyman technique (P. Johnson and J. Neyman, 1936), a statistical procedure which enables the investigator to determine for what ranges of values of the control variables the differences between the methods can be taken as significant. Use of this technique may sometimes suggest that the methods being compared are differentially effective for different types of students—that is, that one method is more effective for certain kinds of students and the other is more effective for other kinds of students.

There have been other experimental studies on foreign-language instruction, though not as extensive as the Agard-Dunkel investigation. Among these, the studies by Hohlfeld (1950) and Hamilton and Haden (1950) are notable—the former for its careful, though limited, experimental design, and the latter for its scope and the care with which the problems to be investigated were formulated. A general comment on all these studies, however, is that they fail on either or both of two counts: (*a*) the questions put to the test have not been adequately thought through, with the result that the methods being compared are not different in any important way, and (*b*) the experiments do not meet the standards of modern educational research, with adequate controls, valid pretest and posttest measurements of ability and achievement, and rigorous and searching statistical analysis of the data.

Recent Developments in Language Teaching

Educational research takes much time, energy, and care. In the strict sense, it cannot create new instructional methods; it can only evaluate them.

It must wait upon the development of new ideas. It is fitting, therefore, that linguists and language teachers have been constantly trying to devise new procedures in accordance with their best judgment and experience, and to suit those procedures to the various situations in which demands are made upon them. The subsequent paragraphs describe only a few of the new projects under way.

The Cornell Language Program

In the Division of Modern Languages at Cornell University, an attempt has been made to realize the implications of the wartime Intensive Language Program for language instruction in the peacetime setting of a liberal-arts college. The program was established on a trial basis with the support of the Rockefeller Foundation during the academic years 1945–1951. As Cowan (1947) and Agard (1949) have recounted, courses were developed in several languages, including French, Spanish, German, Italian, and even Chinese. The main features were: (*a*) intensiveness, involving a year's study with two hours per week of lectures on structure and grammar by a linguistic scientist and six hours per week of drill conducted by native informants; (*b*) primary emphasis on command of the spoken language, with practice in reading brought in only in later phases; (*c*) use of the Holt Spoken Language Series as text materials;[23] (*d*) the setting of proficiency examinations at the end of the year's work, students having to pass these examinations to meet academic language requirements; (*e*) use of "linguistic analysis," in order to make students aware of the phonemic and morphological structure of the language, and (*f*) enormous emphasis on imitation and practice of language patterns. This last aspect embodied the principle of mimicry-memorization, familiarly known as the "mim-mem" principle. Audio-visual aids were not extensively used, most instruction being conducted in a bare classroom.

One of the major premises of the Cornell Plan, as of similar programs, was that a command of the spoken language is the best avenue toward a truly fluent reading knowledge. This premise is strikingly manifest in the *Russian Area Reader* by Fairbanks, Shadick, and Yedigar (1951), designed for second- or third-semester work. Each lesson begins with a series of sentences which are to be thoroughly learned, orally, before the subsequent text is read.

Since this was not an experiment in the strict sense of the term, no control groups were used, although careful records of progress and achievement were kept. Thus, the evaluation of the project's success rested chiefly on subjective judgment, except where matters of comparative costs and personnel needs were concerned. Nevertheless, an independent faculty committee assigned to examine the merits of the program concluded that it had been in most respects successful and that it should be continued as a regular part of the instructional program at Cornell.[24] At any rate, the persons responsible for the courses were impressed with their apparent success, and students have been openly enthusiastic in regarding the method as "the only sensible way to learn a language." Most students seem willing to endure the drill sessions in order to achieve long-range gains. Large numbers of them were able to pass their language requirements without having to repeat courses. Members of literature departments apparently adopted a somewhat ambivalent attitude, admitting on the one hand that those students who came to their courses after completing the language requirement were better prepared than formerly, but complaining on the other hand that the effect of the program had been to bring fewer students to their literature courses. (The departmental structure at Cornell, it should be explained, places language teaching and linguistic science in a Division of Modern Languages, while literature and related studies are taught in departments entirely separate from this division.) It should be recognized, however, that there has been a nationwide decline in the numbers of students taking advanced literature courses.

Language Teaching at the Foreign Service Institute, Department of State

Under the direction of the linguists H. L. Smith, Jr., and G. L. Trager, the School of Languages and Linguistics in the Foreign Service Institute, U. S. Department of State, Washington, is engaged in teaching various languages to Foreign Service Officers and occasional persons from other governmental agencies. Some courses are of relatively brief duration, but in the longer, intensive courses, the application of linguistic analysis is extremely thorough. Students are taught the principles of linguistic analysis, elementary techniques of linguistic field work, and an advanced treatment of the linguistic analysis of English. Smith and Trager believe that a knowledge of linguistic science can frequently be essential in the work of a Foreign Service Officer. For example, they have reprinted for training purposes several of Whorf's papers (1939, 1940a, 1940b, 1941) under the title of *Four Articles on Metalinguistics*. Leary (1952) has described the important role of "metalinguistic" teachings in the current program of the Foreign Service Institute.

As might be expected, aural-oral skills are emphasized, since the primary objective is to give the student a speaking knowledge of the language being taught. Instruction in the written language plays a secondary role. The program could almost be characterized as carrying the Intensive Language Program to its logical extreme. What differentiates this instruction from the wartime methods is its even greater emphasis on linguistic analysis. It may be added that in order to support a language-teaching program of this sort, the School of Languages and Linguistics has become one of the major centers of linguistic research in the United States.

Georgetown University's Institute of Languages and Linguistics

A program of instruction in modern foreign languages whose purpose is very similar to that of the Foreign Service Institute has been organized in the School of Foreign Service at Georgetown University (Washington, D. C.). Dr. Leon Dostert, who was in charge of simultaneous translation at the Nuremberg trials, is the director of this program, embodied in what is called the Institute of Languages and Linguistics. The instruction emphasizes oral-aural skills, and utilizes audio-visual materials to an unusual degree. Several dozen tape-recording machines in semisoundproof booths are provided in the instruction rooms, and students are encouraged to practice imitating the recorded speech of the instructors and to record their own speech for comparison. Few other universities, if any, can boast such complete facilities, which with proper use can be of considerable aid to language instruction. The Institute has also set up facilities, similar to those used at the Nuremberg trials, where advanced students practice the art of simultaneous translation. Further, the Institute has expanded its activities to embrace the supervision of the language courses in the undergraduate division of Georgetown University; these courses are conducted in a manner similar to those designed for students enrolled directly in the Institute. The Institute has also manifested considerable interest in the use of its pedagogical methods at the high-school level.

Principles of descriptive linguistics have been actively introduced into the preparation of instructional materials and even into the classroom itself. Several courses in descriptive linguistics are offered, and a number of seminars have been held for faculty members who have not had the benefit of training in descriptive linguistics and its application to language pedagogy. In this matter, there has been collaboration with Trager and Smith at the Foreign Service Institute.

Members of the Institute, in conjunction with sound engineers, have conducted much research and experimentation in the use of electronic equipment (tape recorders, oscillographs, etc.) in language teaching.

The Institute is exercising a large measure of leadership in the language-teaching field. It has held, for example, several round-table conferences to which numerous members of the profession throughout the country were invited. Résumés of the second and third of these conferences have recently been published under the editorship of John DeFrancis (1951) and Salvatore Castiglione (1952).

The English Language Institute at the University of Michigan

Under the direction of Charles C. Fries and Robert Lado, the English Language Institute of the University of Michigan has been concerned chiefly with the teaching of English as a second language. Fries (1945) sets forth the outlines of a procedure based upon the premise that, at least in the preparation of materials, a linguistic analysis of English and of the learner's native language must be made at the outset in order to show in exactly what respects the two languages are different, and hence to indicate the kinds of things the student must unlearn and the kinds of novel habits he must acquire. This is clearly a sound approach. Fries finds that it is necessary to prepare different materials for speakers of different foreign languages. Thus, he has developed separate series of materials for Spanish speakers and for Japanese speakers who come to learn English. An outstanding feature of Fries's method is its emphasis upon the oral approach and upon the extensive use of imitation and analogy in setting up appropriate habits in the learner. It should also be pointed out that Fries, with the aid of Kenneth Pike, has pioneered in the study of English intonation patterns and in the use of the resulting knowledge in pedagogy.

THE STUDY OF LANGUAGE

English Language Research at Harvard University

In the course of his long experience with the teaching of Basic English to various groups (mainly speakers of languages other than English), I. A. Richards developed a number of highly interesting notions about second-language teaching in general. For the past few years, an organization now known as English Language Research, Inc., of which Professor Richards is director, has been devoting increased attention to the implementation of these notions in the teaching of foreign languages, as well as English. In this work, Professor Richards has been assisted by Miss Christine Gibson.

Two principles are fundamental to the work now being done by Richards and Gibson.

First, proper grading and ordering of the material to be learned is held to be of prime importance. At any stage of the learning process, new items must be introduced when and only when the student is ready for them. If this principle is followed, it is presumed that no new item will present any real difficulty—for difficulty is only relative to the learner's state of readiness.

Second, linguistic meanings can be learned most adequately when they are presented in proper verbal and nonverbal contexts. Richards and Gibson use the term "sen-sit" in referring to the presentation of words in such a context, that is, a word is to be presented in a *sen*tence and in a *sit*uation.

It is probably true that many other language teachers have been intuitively guided by these principles, but Richards and Gibson have put them in the very foreground of attention, as we may see if we examine their methods.

Before any teaching is done, careful work must go into the preparation of instructional materials. The choice of a limited vocabulary is a crucial first stage, for words and forms must be selected so that (*a*) the sounds and letters of early lessons will present the least difficulty to the student, (*b*) the referents can be built into pictures of objects and actions, and (*c*) the materials can be arranged in a meaningful sequence. In the case of English as a second language, it is held that use of the vocabulary of Basic English, with certain modifications, makes grading a relatively easy task.[25] The second step in preparing teaching materials is to develop the content of instruction in full detail, and the final step is to transfer this content to film strips, motion pictures, sound recordings, or suitable combinations thereof.

In the classroom, work is preferably conducted with relatively small groups under the direct supervision of a specially trained instructor. The first step in the learning process is the imitation of extremely simple sentences in the language, whose meaning can be demonstrated by the use of pantomime, "props," or drawings projected on a screen. Later steps simply carry the student to more complicated materials, using much the same types of procedures. At every stage, the teaching is conducted entirely in the vocabulary and constructions taught up to that time, and meaning is allowed to arise from the context of carefully prepared concrete situations. The learner is encouraged to construct simple sentences as early as possible. There is, of course, much necessity for practice and imitation.

It will be evident from the above that the spoken form of the language is emphasized in the instruction. The teaching of reading, however, can be done by much the same methods, sometimes concurrently with the instruction in speaking and understanding. Richards, Gibson, and their collaborators have worked most intensively with instructional problems in elementary phases of a language—say the first year's work, the objective of which is regarded as the control of a vocabulary of some 800–1000 words. From this point the student may easily go on to advanced work.

"Linguistic analysis" of the sort emphasized at Cornell or at the Foreign Service Institute has not up to now played an explicit role in the work of Richards and Gibson. For example, in the classes observed by the writer little attention has been paid to teaching the sounds of the language beyond what can be done by imitation of complete words and phrases. As the methods are further developed, however, it is anticipated that more emphasis will be given to this matter.

To implement more fully the visual aspect of these methods, several instructional manuals have been published: for English (Richards, 1945), French (Richards, Ilsley, and Gibson, 1950), and Spanish (Richards, Metcalf, and Gibson, 1950). In these manuals, which are offered even for self-teaching purposes, the learner is guided by simple pictures and schematic drawings, carrying appropriate captions and explanations. A series of phonograph records, motion pictures, and other aids are being prepared for more general circulation.

On solely an impressionistic basis, the writer would point to the following virtues in the work of Richards and Gibson:

1. The emphasis on the introduction and use of words in immediately

recognizable contexts as provided by concrete objects, pantomimic actions of the instructor, film strips, etc.

2. The extreme care which appears to have been taken in the grading of the material for difficulty and in presenting it in proper order.

3. The extensive use of audio-visual materials which are intimately tied in with the content of the instruction.

An Evaluation of the Present Situation in Second-Language Teaching

There is an enormous literature on the problem of second-language teaching. There is a multitude of theories about proper methods of instruction, and a host of special techniques which have been proposed. As we have seen, at least three or four major investigations have been conducted in the hope of throwing light on improved policies and practices. Nevertheless, few conclusions can be drawn with confidence. No method has emerged as clearly the best method, and there seems to be no end to the arguments as to the proper objectives of foreign-language instruction in our schools. Under reasonably favorable conditions, each of the methods clearly produces significant amounts of learning. Oral-aural approaches produce considerable speaking knowledge and aural comprehension of the language; the "reading method" produces considerable reading knowledge in the student. But the direct method also produces some reading knowledge, and the reading method often seems to produce some speaking knowledge. It is difficult, therefore, to find clear differences in the results achieved by the two presumably contrasting methods. Finally, no method succeeds with all students. No method, as far as we know, is able to iron out the large individual differences in rate of learning which are always encountered.

What are the causes of our ignorance? First, there is a lack of agreement among foreign-language teachers as to the proper objectives of their instruction, due partly to an understandable failure to ask themselves questions which might be embarrassing, and partly to an unsureness about broader educational goals which is, for that matter, characteristic of much of contemporary American educational thought. One's educational philosophy is bound to color one's feelings about the claims made and the results reported by the proponents of various programs of language instruction.

In the matter of technique, research studies appear to have missed the point that contrasting methods of instruction cannot be differentiated solely in terms of their over-all results. What is needed is a more precise knowledge of the conditions under which the various methods succeed. It is reasonable to suppose that one method will succeed under certain conditions, while another method will succeed under other conditions. It is also conceivable that the efficiency of a teaching method varies with the type of student. In the last analysis, we are fundamentally ignorant of the psychology of language learning. If we look at the studies in this field, we find many on such questions as whether one should teach languages in fifteen-, thirty-, forty-five-, or sixty-minute periods, but very few investigations of such matters as the process by which an individual comes to acquire a new set of phonetic habits, for example.

There is probably no need, at the present time, for another large-scale investigation of second-language teaching like the Modern Language Study or the more recent Investigation of Second-Language Teaching. The possibilities of this type of study have been, for the moment, exhausted. A choice between various teaching methods cannot be made on the basis of any presently available evidence, and it is doubtful that any future large-scale study would have much to contribute until the new methods of instruction have become better crystallized and until adequate experimental designs can be planned. What is needed now is a series of small-scale, carefully controlled educational experiments, in which some of the best minds in linguistics, foreign-language teaching, psychology, education, experimental design, and measurement would be brought to bear on the problem. These experiments should be designed so as to display the effect of a wide range of variables upon the resulting achievement. Only a few of these variables need be concerned directly with the method of instruction. Every effort should be put forth to develop and test hypotheses about the psychological processes involved in the learning of various aspects of language systems. Above all, there is little point in performing these experiments at all unless the experimental conditions can be adequately controlled.

As an example of the kind of specific hypothesis that ought to be tested, the writer will offer one of his own. He would like to find out whether methods emphasizing the aural-oral approach might not be made to succeed better if, instead of presenting the student with a fixed, pre-determined lesson to be learned, the teacher created a "problem-solving" situation in which the student must find, by inquiring of either the teacher or the dictionary, appropriate verbal responses for solving the problem—which might be, for example, finding a hidden object, or getting an offending window closed, or choosing a satisfying meal from a foreign-language menu. At later stages, the problems set would be of a more purely verbal character. The essential point is that the student would early be forced to learn, by a kind of trial-and-error process, to *communicate* rather than merely to utter the speech patterns in the lesson plans. Instruction conducted in this way might more realistically parallel the student's actual or potential needs. This hypothesis is based on fairly well-established principles of what the psychologist Skinner (1938) calls "operant conditioning." At the same time it contains certain features based on what is believed to occur in the language learning of the child.

Here are several other questions for which definitive answers are needed through experimental research:

In the "mim-mem" approach, is it better to introduce meanings concurrently with linguistic patterns, or only after the patterns themselves have been learned? That is, should sounds and meanings be presented simultaneously or successively?

To what extent are visual aids necessary? For what purposes are they most useful, and how should they be introduced in the instruction? Should associations be established directly between foreign words and picturable objects and actions, or will it suffice to mediate meanings by the use of words in the learner's native language? After basic concepts are learned, can meanings be mediated just as well by verbal definitions as by pictures and concrete materials?

What psychological factors come into play with the use of standard orthographies, phonemic transcriptions, "parlay-voo" transcriptions, and the like? Are these a help or a hindrance in learning? When and how should they be introduced? Are the results the same for all languages?

If it is not always true that learning to speak and understand transfers to learning to read, how can this transfer be facilitated? Is it solely a matter of vocabulary differences, or what?

What difference does it make whether the learner's native language is used in the instruction? Under what conditions does use of the native language delay or facilitate learning?

How much help is grammar and linguistic analysis when injected into the teaching process itself? (It may be taken for granted that linguistic analysis should be involved in the preparation of instructional materials.) When can linguistic structure be taught solely by getting students to make inductions from varying patterns, and when do linguistic explanations facilitate learning?

At what rate can new materials be introduced, and what factors affect this rate?

What psychological factors hinder students from passing beyond the mere repetition of set patterns to the more active stage of making variations in these patterns spontaneously?

Pending the availability of clear-cut experimental evidence which would enable one to choose confidently among the various teaching methods in use, one can be guided only by the apparent satisfaction of teachers that they are accomplishing what they have set out to accomplish, and by the apparent satisfaction of students that they are learning something potentially valuable to them in a reasonably efficient way. From this point of view, methods which emphasize the use of the spoken language seem to have a considerable advantage.

If I had to recommend a "best" method for teaching command of a foreign language as a tool, purely on the basis of personal hunches I would recommend for a first-year's course something like this: The preparation of the verbal content would be guided by linguistic analysis, but the sequencing of the instruction would be done along the lines of I. A. Richards's plan. The initial presentation of the material in each lesson would also be conducted somewhat in Richards's manner, auditory aids supplying the voice of a native speaker to be imitated and visual aids supplying meaningful contexts. Then, however, features from the Cornell and Georgetown plans would be utilized. Native informants would take over to conduct drill in linguistic patterns, and information from linguistic science would be employed to describe the characteristics of the new linguistic habits which have to be formed. Further drill by students working alone would be provided for by a language laboratory equipped with tape-recording machines. After phonetic patterns have been learned, recourse would again be had to film strips for additional semantic reinforcement. Results of psycholinguistic investigations would guide the exact sequencing of imitation and reinforcement processes. In the later phases of instruction —but I need not go on! Such a "best" method as this is impossible of fulfilment in ordinary circumstances. This bit of fantasy is valuable in illustrating the fact that all the recent programs have certain merits, but that from a realistic point of view their features are, often, mutually incompatible. Nevertheless, depending upon the circumstances surrounding any given situation, it may be possible to approach an ideal method in a good many respects. If a knowledge of linguistic science, a fluent command of the language, and sound pedagogy can be combined in one teacher, the results should be outstanding. The procedures described by Delattre (1947) would appear to come rather close to the attainment of such an ideal.

The Contribution of Linguistics to Second-Language Teaching

The impression seems to have been gained in some quarters that the linguist has a special and unique contribution to make to the problem of teaching a second language. Even if we discount all the popular notions about the supposed "miracles" which the linguists had wrought in the Intensive Language Program, it remains that the language-teaching profession looks upon programs like the Cornell plan as based on the approach of technical linguistics.

It is only a half-truth to say that the new programs are fundamentally based on the teachings of linguistic science. Though linguistic analysis has played an important role in these new language-teaching programs, *linguistic analysis is not a method of instruction;* linguistic analysis merely has something to say about *what is to be taught.* If an individual wants to learn a language, he may well appeal to the linguist as the best authority on the characteristics of that language. The linguist has made a thorough study of the sounds of the language, the grammar, the syntax, and so on, and can indicate to the learner a number of rules which will help him acquire the language more rapidly than if he had to work out these rules for himself. The linguist can also point out the relation between the sounds of a language and its orthography, and many other details about the structure of the language system which is to be learned. In case the language is one about which little is known, the linguist provides a technique for ascertaining the details of the language system.

The value of the native informant, where used, consists initially in the fact that he represents a model of what the linguist is talking about; the speech of a native informant may be more accurate than any that the teacher himself can demonstrate. Thus, a native informant, or anyone who speaks the language accurately and fluently, has the status of an "audio-visual aid," but a good phonograph record or tape recording will do just as well for certain purposes. On the other hand, the speaker of the native language represents someone to talk to, and can therefore catalyze the student's readiness to communicate in the language being learned.

Moreover, the linguist can point out some of the characteristics of the learner's native language, with particular attention to those aspects of it which can be transferred to the second language, and likewise to those aspects which will have to be unlearned or replaced by novel habits.

The linguist can also contribute his knowledge of the history of a language, when that happens to be involved in the teaching. The linguist has much more up-to-date information on this score than a person could acquire by reading, let us say, some of the popular presentations of "phil-ology" published in the nineteenth century.

To repeat, linguistic analysis does not provide a method of instruction. This statement, of course, does not in any degree disparage the role which linguistic analysis may have in the planning of instruction, for certainly everyone would agree that the right things ought to be taught, and the linguist can tell us in an analytical way what these right things are, usually even better than a native informant can. For example, the linguist can make the learner aware of the proper stress and intonation patterns of the foreign language; the ordinary teacher is not likely to have made an adequate analysis of such items, and the native informant is often hardly aware of them at all.

It is not surprising that the linguist emphasizes command of the spoken language, because he realizes that the essential character of a modern language is represented in the fact that it is a *system of sounds,* not of letters or ideographic characters written on a page. It is also not surprising that the linguists have recommended a "mimicry-memorization" method designed to fix new linguistic habits firmly in the behavior of the learner, because the linguist is enough of a psychologist to realize that language is a system of extremely well-learned habitual responses. But it is gratuitous on the part of the linguist to affirm that endless drill and repetition constitutes the *only* way in which new linguistic habits may be strengthened. The educational psychologist has asserted that the only virtue in practice and repetition is that it allows adequate opportunity for other factors to have an effect. The psychologist can cite many cases in which learning occurs after only one trial. The writer is forced to the conclusion, therefore, that the methods of the linguistic scientist *as a teacher* are not necessarily the most effective methods. We are fundamentally in ignorance as to the best ways of strengthening new linguistic habits, and must therefore appeal to the psychologist to give us new evidence on this score.

The methods of language instruction utilized in the Intensive Language Program, as well as in other programs described here, provide a healthy reaction to the dictionary-thumbing and paradigm-parroting tactics of many language teachers in the first forty years of this century. Despite certain features whose value may be questioned, these methods should be allowed to have a strong influence on the future evolution of language teaching in our schools. The writer specifically wishes to express disapproval of the reactionary and hypercritical trend of opinion which just now seems to be setting in.

LINGUISTIC PROBLEMS IN EDUCATIONAL MEASUREMENT

There are many possibilities for more fully realizing the implications of linguistic science and related studies in psychological and educational measurement. Improved measuring devices are vitally needed in order to make thoroughgoing diagnoses of students' linguistic potentialities and in order to assess their achievements.

Applications of Linguistics in the Measurement of Psychological Traits

Almost all psychological tests are based either directly or indirectly on language responses. It has already been found, by factor analysis and other methods, that some psychological traits are specifically related to the ability of the individual to handle his language. The acquisition of a large vocabulary in one's native language seems to be an index of intelligence. Vocabulary, however, is only one aspect of a language system; it is most nearly like what the linguists call the *lexicon* of a language. Would it not be interesting to investigate, therefore, the extent to which one might develop measurements of the ways in which individuals handle other aspects of their language systems? The number of investigations which bear on this possibility is so extremely small that the field can be regarded as unexplored.

Despite the lack of any real evidence on the question, the following proposition may be offered: that when any psychologist or test constructor sets out to make a test which bears upon the verbal responses of the individual, it would be well for him to know at least something about what linguistic analysis has to say concerning the structure of those responses.

The Measurement of Aptitude for Foreign-Language Learning

Foreign-language teachers, psychologists, and even linguistic scientists have speculated on the possibility that there may be differences among individuals with respect to their aptitude for learning foreign languages. The linguist, of course, points out that any individual of reasonably normal intelligence can learn any language *in time,* but he has noticed certain differences in the rate at which different people learn. He has noticed that some people have particular difficulty in imitating strange sounds, for example. These considerations have led to interest in the possibility of constructing "foreign-language aptitude" tests.

There is urgent need of improved foreign-language aptitude tests, not only in public and private schools and colleges but also in government and military situations, where decisions have to be made on the selection of individuals for relatively long courses of language study, and where failures are costly.

In the course of the Modern Language Study, completed in 1928, several investigations of foreign-language aptitude were carried out (Henmon, 1929). The results of these studies were largely inconclusive on the question of whether there are special aptitudes in language learning. The investigators did not, of course, have available the theory and knowledge concerning the construction of aptitude tests which was to be gained only in the thirties and forties with the advent of Thurstone's techniques of multiple-factor analysis.[26] Moreover, they were handicapped by the fact that their tests had to be tried out largely in situations where the methods of instruction and of testing emphasized the reading-knowledge objective and detailed lessons in grammar and syntax. Traditional methods of teaching make the learning of foreign languages primarily an intellectual enterprise; indeed, the intellectual benefits have often been deemed to constitute the most important objective of such learning. It is not surprising, therefore, that the tests found of most general use in the prediction of achievement in foreign languages have been intelligence tests of one kind or another.[27]

Courses of language instruction which emphasize oral-aural skills may conceivably put demands on certain abilities which are not measured by the usual intelligence tests. Unfortunately, relatively little effort has thus far been expended in an attempt to discover and measure such abilities. Some of the oral-production tests studied by the writer (Carroll, 1941) seem to offer possibilities as predictors of foreign-language success. More recently, the writer has had occasion to speculate in greater detail as to the traits which should be investigated in this connection. The following partial list is presented here for what it may be worth:

1. Tests of the ability to mimic sounds and stretches of sounds. These tests would measure (*a*) the length of the "mimicry span"—as in tests of memory span—and (*b*) the accuracy with which unusual sounds can be imitated. Attention would also be directed to the subject's accuracy or control in imitating patterns of stress and intonation.

2. Measures of speech style in native-language oral-production tests. For example, cohesiveness and directness of style can be evaluated in situations where the subject responds verbally to pictures, stories, etc. Some of the measures could be patterned after those used by Sanford (1942a).

3. Various dimensions isolated by factor analysis. The rote-memory factor and the various fluency factors would seem to be of particular promise.

4. Tests of phonetic discrimination. Some of these could be patterned after the well-known Seashore tests of musical ability.

5. Work-sample tests in learning oral production and aural comprehension of simple materials in a foreign language.

6. Measurements of the ability to persist in phonemically accurate utterances even when attention is directed to another aspect of the utterance.

7. Tests of the ability to imitate foreign accents.

8. Tests of flexibility in adapting to a foreign-language orthography.

9. Tests of the ability to develop meanings inductively.

The Measurement of Achievement in Foreign Languages

All the large-scale investigations of second-language teaching have had to face the problem of a criterion of success against which the results of the instruction could be evaluated. Unfortunately, most available measures of foreign-language achievement have emphasized the command of the written language. The tests constructed by the College Entrance Examination Board, and likewise by the recently inaugurated Educational Testing Service, are typically pencil-and-paper tests of vocabulary, reading comprehension, and grammar. The Agard-Dunkel investigation of second-language teaching (1948) had to construct and standardize new tests in aural comprehension, but the construction of these tests presented many technical difficulties which could hardly have been quickly solved in view of the lack of previous research on the problem. It also proved difficult to develop reliable and valid tests of oral production; students' ability to speak a foreign language accordingly had to be evaluated by impressionistic means.

One significant development is represented by the work of Robert Lado (1950, 1951) at the University of Michigan, who completed a doctoral thesis on the construction of achievement tests in English for Latin-American students. In constructing his tests, he paid great attention to the kinds of linguistic learning with which the students had been found to have most difficulty. In commenting on previously developed tests of aural comprehension of English as a foreign language, Lado asserted that all of them failed to incorporate the findings and techniques of linguistic science, and that they showed other serious deficiencies. Lado summarized his doctoral thesis as follows:

A number of conclusions are reached. They are (1) that a great lag exists in measurement in English as a foreign language, (2) that the lag is connected with unscientific views of language, (3) that the science of language should be used in defining what to test, (4) that the native language of the student must be considered in foreign language tests, (5) that more tests are needed adapting the techniques to students of other language backgrounds and measuring more completely some of the variables, and (6) that the factor of entrance level is significant for research based on rate of improvement. The study gives procedures for the application of linguistics to the development of foreign language tests.

We may expand Lado's conclusions by noting that a great lag exists in all foreign-language measurement.

Chapter 7 COMMUNICATION ENGINEERING AND THE STUDY OF SPEECH

INTRODUCTION

It is traditional to think of engineering as the application of science toward the better utilization of machines and other material objects, but the concept of engineering has been progressively broadened in recent years. There is now a tendency to speak of engineering as the application of scientific knowledge to any sphere of human experience where greater productivity and efficiency can be attained thereby, whether machines are involved or not. (For example, applied psychology has sometimes been called human engineering;[1] in Europe applied psychology is widely identified as psychotechnology.) Some will deplore this semantic change; others, recognizing it as an inevitable and irreversible trend, will welcome it as a means of breaking down interdisciplinary barriers in applied science.

This broadening of the concept of engineering is well exemplified in the study of language. The development had its origin in the work of communications engineers concerned with the design of equipment for the transmission of speech (Fletcher, 1929). It was found necessary to make extensive analyses of speech sounds and indeed of all characteristics of speech which are essential to intelligibility. It was also found necessary to find means of measuring the amount of information in a message so that the efficiency of a communication channel could be assayed by comparing the information at the source with that at the destination. In the last few years, this work has led to the development of a general mathematical theory of communication. It would appear that some of these developments have implications for linguistic analysis and more generally for all sciences concerned with the study of communication. We have already spoken, in Chapter 3, of the influence of communication theory on contemporary trends in psychology, and in Chapter 4, of the promising field of "language engineering" as an applied social science.

As a parallel development, the advance of technology in electronics has suggested numerous possibilities for the construction of special devices for the analysis and synthesis of speech and for the mechanical encoding and decoding of messages. Some of these devices have already become a great boon to linguistic investigations in acoustic phonetics.

THE THEORY OF COMMUNICATION

Although the possibility of a general theory of communication was suggested by certain communication engineers in the 1920's, the first systematic exposition of such a theory was presented by Shannon in 1948 in the *Bell System Technical Journal*. This exposition has now been reprinted as the first part of a book, *The Mathematical Theory of Communication* (Shannon and Weaver, 1949). In the latter part of the same publication, Warren Weaver of the Rockefeller Foundation essays an interpretation of Shannon's communication theory in a broader setting.[2]

The possible generality of communication theory is indicated by Weaver in defining what he means by *communication:*

The word communication will be used here in a very broad sense to include all the procedures by which one mind may affect another. This, of course, involves not only written and oral speech, but also music, the pictorial arts, the theater, the ballet, and in fact all human behavior. In some connections it may be desirable to use a still broader definition of communication, namely, one which would include the procedures by means of which one mechanism (say automatic equipment to track an airplane and to compute its probable future positions) affects another mechanism (say a guided missile chasing this airplane).

Weaver continues by setting up three levels of communication theory:

LEVEL A. How accurately can the symbols of communication be transmitted? (The technical problem.)

LEVEL B. How precisely do the transmitted symbols convey the desired meaning? (The semantic problem.)

LEVEL C. How effectively does the received meaning affect conduct in the desired way? (The effectiveness problem.)

Thus far, only LEVEL A has received systematic formulation in Shannon's work.

The fundamental problem in this aspect of communication theory is the measurement of the *efficiency* of a given communication channel. This entails at the outset the measurement of the amount of information in a given message, because, as we have mentioned, efficiency must be evaluated by seeing how much information gets through from the source to the destination. The word *information* is used here in a special sense. The amount of information in a given symbol of a message is a function of the number of potential symbols which might occur in its place. If only one symbol could occur in a given position of a message, that symbol would be said to transmit no information, since the receiver of the message could expects its transmission with absolute certainty—if we assume, as we must in communication theory, that the receiver knows the statistical structure of the code being used, that is, the statistical probabilities of the various symbols which may occur in various positions of messages. Thus in the telegraphic transmission of normal English printed texts, the symbol U following the symbol Q contains, for all practical purposes, no information whatsoever, since the receiver of a message knows that a Q must be followed by U. If, however, a large number of symbols may potentially occur in a given position in a message, the symbol which *does* occur helps out, or "informs," the receiver of the message roughly in proportion to the number of possible symbols. For example, in the transmission of a message encoded in a secret cipher, it is conceivable that *any* letter of the alphabet might occur as the *first* symbol of the message and that the probabilities of all the letters might be equal. In this case, the transmission of whatever *is* the first symbol may be said to convey a large amount of information. Communication theorists like to say that the amount of information is a function of the sender's freedom of choice in selecting the symbols of a message; his freedom of choice is, as it were, limited only by the statistical characteristics of the code being employed. The word *code* is used in a broad sense to include not only the secret codes that we ordinarily think of in this connection but also the linguistic systems of ordinary speech and writing.

Shannon has suggested that a convenient unit for measuring information is the *bit* (a contraction of "binary digit" proposed by the Princeton statistician John W. Tukey). To explain why binary digits are relevant here, we must enter into a short digression. Suppose we have sixteen symbols and our problem is to specify just one of these symbols. To make this illustration concrete, suppose we have the letters of the alphabet from A to P and we have to specify the letter K. How many items of yes-or-no information would we have to transmit in order to do this? The most efficient procedure is as follows: Let us divide the set of sixteen symbols into two halves, the first eight and the second eight. Our first specification can be in the form of the answer "Yes" to the question, "Is the symbol in the second eight?" Now let us divide the second eight symbols again into two halves, those from I to L and those from M to P; we can now say "No" to the question, "Is it a letter from M to P?" One finds that the procedure of specification needs to be carried out two more times, so that the whole sequence of questions and answers looks like this:

Is the symbol a letter from I to P (not A to H)? Yes.

Is the symbol a letter from M to P (not I to L)? No.

Is the symbol a letter from K to L (not I to J)? Yes.

Is the symbol the letter L (not K)? No.

Then the symbol must be K, and its specification has required four yes-or-no pieces of information. Of course, if we had to specify a given symbol from a larger number of alternatives, we would have had to give more pieces of information. The reader may be reminded of the popular parlor game called "Twenty Questions." If this game were played according to strict logical principles, the answers to twenty yes-or-no questions should suffice to enable one to identify which one of 2^{20} or 1,048,576 different things one's opponent is thinking of.

Now it happens that the number of yes-or-no answers necessary to specify a given alternative from among a given number of alternatives can be computed as the logarithm to the base 2 of that number. In the case cited above, $\log_2 16 = 4$. This logarithm also gives the minimum number of digits, less one, needed to represent a given number in the binary number system, widely used in connection with electronic computing machinery. (The preceding statements need the added qualification that nonintegral logarithms must be "rounded off" to the next highest whole number.) The binary number system uses only the digits 1 and 0 (which may be thought of as corresponding to "Yes" and "No," respectively). The reader may educe the properties of this system from the following sample list, which also gives logarithms to the base 2.

Decimal Number	Binary Number	$\log_2 N$
0	0	—
1	1	0.0000
2	10	1.0000
3	11	1.5850
4	100	2.0000
5	101	2.3219
6	110	2.5850
7	111	2.8074
8	1000	3.0000
16	10000	4.0000
32	100000	5.0000

From this, one may see why information (in the special sense required in communication theory) may be measured in *bits*.

The amount of information may be analyzed in various ways depending upon the symbol units which one regards as the alternative choices. For example, in the analysis of written messages, one could choose the alphabetic letter as the symbol unit. In teletypewriter transmission, there are thirty-two characters (including a space) which can be transmitted; if these characters are regarded as equiprobable, the transmission of one character represents five units of information, five being the logarithm of 32 to the base 2. On the other hand, we could choose *words* as our symbol unit. If there were 65,536 equiprobable words in the language of transmission, transmission of one of these words would constitute sixteen units of information.

If not all choices are equally likely, the average information-carrying capacity per symbol unit, in *bits,* may be found by evaluating the expression $-\sum_{j=1}^{n} p_j \log_2 p_j$, where p_j is the probability of occurrence of symbol unit j, and the summation is over all n symbol units. It should be said that this and other calculations can be made only if one has tabulated frequencies from a large corpus of material.

The average information-carrying capacity of symbol units is decreased if the occurrences of these symbol units can be predicted to some significant extent from a knowledge of the preceding symbol units. If we take any given sequence, i, of symbol units, we can determine the average information capacity of a following symbol unit as equal to $-\sum_j p_{i(j)} \log_2 p_{i(j)}$, where $p_{i(j)}$ is the transitional probability that sequence i will be followed by j. Then, by summing these quantities over all i's, weighted by their respective probabilities of occurrence, we can find the average informational capacity of symbol units when a preceding sequence is known. These considerations lead to the notion of *redundancy* in a message. Redundancy occurs when the average information carried by symbol units is less than the maximum possible under conditions of equiprobable and independent symbols. It may be measured by the ratio $(I_{max} - I_{obs})/I_{max}$, where I_{obs} is the observed amount of information and I_{max} is the maximum amount. The case of the symbol U preceded by Q in normal printed English is an illustration of redundancy, for a message can be transmitted without any loss of information by omitting all U's which follow Q's.

The analysis of messages by these procedures brings into bold relief the fact that the structure of the code has an important bearing on the efficiency with which messages can be transmitted. If the code itself implies considerable redundancy (as does the "code" represented by English orthography, for example), efficiency of communication is reduced, *ceteris paribus*. On the other hand, a certain amount of redundancy is desirable in order that messages can be accurately received over a "noisy" channel. It is therefore necessary to study the effect of the *signal-to-noise ratio* on the efficiency of communication, noise being defined as that part of a received transmission which is extraneous to the original message.

The mathematical theory of communication has found considerable usefulness in a number of engineering applications. Its relevance in psychological investigations of communication has already been discussed in Chapter 3. Thus far, there has been little contact between communication theory and linguistics if one considers the national scene as a whole.

Warren Weaver has already suggested some of the ways in which linguistic studies might take advantage of communication theory. He writes (Shannon and Weaver, 1949, p. 117):

> The concept of the information to be associated with a source leads directly, as we have seen, to a study of the statistical structure of language; and this study reveals about the English language, as an example, information which seems surely significant to students of every phase of language and communication. The idea of utilizing the powerful body of theory concerning Markoff

201

processes seems particularly promising for semantic studies, since this theory is specifically adapted to handle one of the most significant but difficult aspects of meaning, namely the influence of context.

The first thing that should be done in trying to analyze language from the standpoint of communication theory is to use as symbol units in the analysis the fundamental units which have already been isolated by linguistic science, namely distinctive features, phonemes, morphemes, sentence types, etc. An analysis of the written aspect of a language may be useful for some purposes, but it would seem much more pertinent to evaluate the characteristics of a language *as spoken*.

One approach to the analysis of linguistic structure which is suggested by communication theory would be the determination of conditional probabilities inherent in the sequence of phonemes and other units of analysis in normal speech. Such an investigation would lead immediately to a difficult problem: to what extent are the conditional probabilities found in a long series of utterances due to (*a*) the inherent formal characteristics of the language, or to (*b*) the semantic aspects of the utterances, that is, what the speaker happens to be talking about? Another problem, for which communication theory as it now stands apparently has no answer, would concern the extent to which the *sequences themselves* (that is, apart from the symbols) carry meanings. Both these questions are crucial in linguistic analysis, and, as we have seen, they have not yet been satisfactorily solved. It is conceivable, therefore, that the application of communication theory to linguistic analysis would make for progress in the field of linguistics, at the same time requiring an expansion of communication theory.[3]

Another problem which can be only dimly envisaged at the present time would have to do with the role of the compulsory grammatical features of a language. We have seen in Chapter 2 that in English it is virtually mandatory to indicate the number—singular or plural—of things being talked about, while Chinese does not make such a requirement. How should such linguistic features be viewed from the standpoint of communication theory? Would they constitute redundancy, or should they be regarded as noise in the communication system?

It is becoming evident that communication theory provides a neat parallel for Jakobson's theory of binary opposition. According to Jakobson, as we have seen, many linguistic features can be analyzed in terms of sets of mutually contrasted pairs of items. For example, an item is either a vowel or a consonant; a consonant is either voiced or unvoiced; and so on. (The precise nature of these oppositions is currently under discussion.) Similarly, a form is either singular or plural; a singular noun is either animate or inanimate (for example, in Algonkian); and so on. Now, in communication theory the basis for measuring information is the binary digit, or "bit." In a situation where there are two equiprobable messages, such as "yes" and "no," transmission of either one of these messages constitutes one unit of information. The parallelism between Jakobson's formulation and the measurement of information is obvious: the elementary symbols of language are themselves of a binary nature, and thus the number of bits of information communicated by a linguistic form is (at least partly) a function of the number of binary oppositions it contains. Jakobson, Fant, and Halle (1952) are at this writing proposing to investigate this problem in detail.

In Chapter 2, in the discussion of linguistic typology, we saw how several linguists are attempting to compare language structures by means of certain quantitative measures. The measurement of amount of information by Shannon's formulae now suggests that linguistic structures may be compared with respect to their information-carrying capacity. Some languages may require, on the average, more symbols to convey a certain amount of information than other languages do. G. A. Miller (1951b, p. 792) has already made a crude estimate that a statement in Basic English must be about 36 per cent longer than a statement in full English in order to convey the same information.

One major reservation concerning the implications of communication theory for linguistic analysis must be stated, however. Communication theory, at least in that phase which has been most fully developed at the present time, concentrates its attention on the *receiving* end of a communication channel. It pays attention to the analysis of a message only in order to measure the efficiency of the communication channel in terms of how much of the message gets through to the receiving end. It says nothing about how the message got selected at the sending end, nor does it care. Linguistic analysis, on the other hand, is very much concerned with the selection of messages at the sending end of a communication channel. It is concerned not only with the nature of the symbols which were selected, but also with the sets of formal rules inherent in the structuring of those symbols. The individual who analyzes a message at the receiving end (for example, a decoder) may very well use conditional probabilities to help him decipher the message or find its meaning, but the sender of the message does not, in any immediate sense, use conditional probabilities in selecting his messages. That is, he does not choose his message by looking up conditional probabilities in a table, as it were. Instead, his message is formulated in terms of a definite linguistic structure, whose rules could be stated usually as all-or-none probabilities. It is stimulated by a definite situational context: if an English speaker adds the phoneme /z/ to the form /dɔg/, it is because he wishes to talk about a plurality of dogs (which may be in his environment, for example), and not because there is a certain conditional probability leading to the phoneme /z/ in this case. Furthermore, the fact that phoneme /z/ occurs instead of /s/ is more parsimoniously accounted for in linguistic analysis by a structural rule than by a conditional probability, for a conditional probability makes sense only in terms of *all possible* symbol units which might occur immediately after /dɔg/. Linguistic analysis considers messages as actual occurrences, while communication theory is forced to regard messages as random processes.[4] The interests of linguists and of communication theorists are in this sense fundamentally divergent.

It is understandable, however, that communication theory should have appeal to psychologists. The statistical structure of a language, when determined on large sequences of utterances, may be presumed to parallel in some respects the verbal response tendencies of a speaker. Some of these response tendencies are admittedly a function of the structure of the language, but, over and above this, some response tendencies have been built up in accordance with the inherent conditional probabilities of the environment. For example, the speaker may tend to say that something is as *blue* as the *sky,* as *cold* as *ice,* or as *sparkling* as *diamonds,* simply because these associations come from frequent experiences. It is in this way that communication theory can be applied to the measurement of verbal contexts, as suggested in Chapter 3.

Perhaps the whole process of communication can be regarded as a series of communication channels. Thus, if I am walking across the street with a companion and suddenly exclaim "watch out," and if my companion stops suddenly, there are at least three communication channels involved. First, there is a communication channel between the external world (a rapidly moving bus approaching) and my vocal mechanism—a communication channel which chiefly involves the encoding of some sort of message into the linguistic pattern "watch out." Secondly, there is the communication channel between my vocal mechanism and the hearer's auditory mechanism. A third channel connects my companion's auditory receptors with his motor responses. Indeed, it might be said that all interaction between situations and individuals can be regarded as communication and can be studied with the techniques of communication theory. This is the perspective which has been adopted by Norbert Wiener in his *Cybernetics* (1948) and in *The Human Use of Human Beings* (1950). Various issues bearing on such a perspective have been discussed at several conferences sponsored by the Josiah Macy, Jr., Foundation (Von Foerster, 1951, 1952).

ELECTRONIC DEVICES FOR THE ANALYSIS, SYNTHESIS, AND CONVERSION OF LINGUISTIC DATA

A number of new devices for the analysis and synthesis of speech sounds have recently become available. Furthermore, the development of large-scale electronic computing devices seems to make it possible to look forward to special kinds of machines for analyzing systems of messages or converting them into other kinds of messages. We shall describe a number of these electronic devices and attempt to evaluate their possible usefulness either in linguistic analysis or in practical applications of linguistics.

The Sound Spectrograph

As an aid in experimental phonetics, the sound spectrograph (developed during World War II) is without parallel. For the first time it has become easy to make rapid analyses of the physical characteristics of speech sounds. What the machine[5] does is to make a permanent graphic record of the sound frequencies present at every instant of a 2.4-second sample of speech. Inspection of this graphic record enables one to isolate the periods over which the vowels and consonants were present in the utterance, to determine the frequencies of the formants which contribute to the vowel qualities, and to study the nature of the changes which occur in vowel quality, in diphthongs, and in the neighborhood of consonants. Joos, in a monograph based on his use of the sound spectrograph (1948), demonstrates that the instrument can be of great usefulness in linguistic work. For example, the spectrograph will give highly objective measurements of the variations in vowel quality which are found in various dialects of a language. It will also make it possible to state the probable phonetic range of variation for any given phoneme. The salient details of a sample record produced by the sound spectrograph are featured in Fig. 1 (*upper*).

A related development is the "visible-speech" machine developed in the Bell Telephone Laboratories and described by Potter, Kopp, and Green (1947). This machine produces the same type of record as does the Sonagraph, but on a continuous, transitory basis. It is thus designed to enable a deaf person, after suitable training, to see and interpret a graphical representation of speech as it is uttered.

The Speech Stretcher

The speech stretcher (for details, see Gould, 1951) is a device which makes it possible to play back a sample of speech at some rate other than that at which it was originally uttered, but still retaining the original pitch of the utterance. Thus, it does not have the disadvantage of a phonograph record played at half speed, which would give a slowed-down speech one octave below the original pitch. The speech stretcher is useful not only for experimental phonetics but also for the phonetic analysis of new and unrecorded languages. Joos writes (1948, p. 129):

The usefulness of the Speech Stretcher for phonetic demonstrations is immense. Untrained listeners using it hear far more than skilled phoneticians hear in normal-tempo speech, and they make rapid progress toward hearing normal speech details. The time available for reflection about what is heard is far more than twice as much as with normal speech. It is noteworthy that the result is always totally different from what happens when one deliberately attempts to speak slowly without altering normal phonetic patterns.

There are as yet very few speech stretchers in existence, but one can foresee considerable usefulness for the device in connection with linguistic field work and language teaching. For example, if samples of a new and unrecorded language were recorded at normal speed, it is believed that it might be possible, by the use of the speech stretcher, to have them

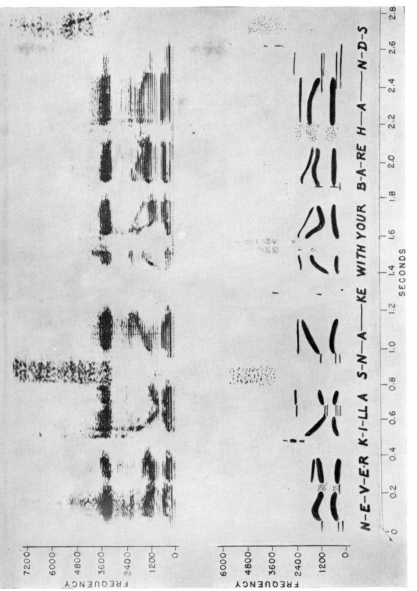

Fig. 1. (*upper*) A sound-spectrograph recording of the utterance *Never kill a snake with your bare hands.* The relative darkness at a given time and at a given frequency represents the amplitude or strength of sound waves at that frequency. (*lower*) The hand-painted pattern playback version of the same utterance. (Courtesy of Haskins Laboratories, New York.)

transcribed phonemically with considerable accuracy even by persons with a minimum of training in linguistics and phonetics. Thus, scarce linguistic manpower would be saved for the job of analyzing the text after it had been phonemically transcribed.

A Formant-Graphing Machine

A formant-graphing machine has to the writer's knowledge not yet been constructed,[6] but it has been suggested by Joos as a device which would have considerable utility both in experimental phonetics and in the teaching of foreign languages.

In order to explain what this machine would do, we must first describe what is meant by a *formant*. It is generally agreed that vowel quality is due to the particular combination of higher partials present in the sound wave which is emitted by the vocal mechanism. It is interesting to note that vowel quality is not dependent upon the fundamental pitch of the tone generated by the vocal cords; instead, it is due to the resonance features of the mouth and nose. Furthermore, these resonance features are manifested in humps in the spectrum of the sound wave. The humps which are crucial for vowel quality are called formants; of these, two are of major importance. Thus, for the *e* in *hotel,* the first formant is approximately at 600 cycles, and the second formant is approximately at 1700 cycles; these figures hold for adult male speakers. Now, if we take a piece of graph paper and represent the first formant along one axis and the second formant along the other axis, it is possible to plot the position of any vowel, using its two formants as coördinates. The diagram in Fig. 2 illustrates the kind of graph that might be employed in a formant-graphing machine; it also shows the approximate positions of certain English and non-English vowel sounds (as spoken by adult males). The coördinates have been arranged so that the configuration corresponds to the conventional vowel quadrilateral, with front-back and high-low dimensions. Thus, [i] is a high-front vowel and [o] is a low-back vowel.

At present, if we want to plot vowels on a formant chart, we have to get a sample of speech recorded on a sound spectrograph; then we must make measurements of the spectrograph record. The whole process might take ten or twenty minutes. What is wanted is a machine which would do it instantaneously, that is, while someone is uttering a vowel which

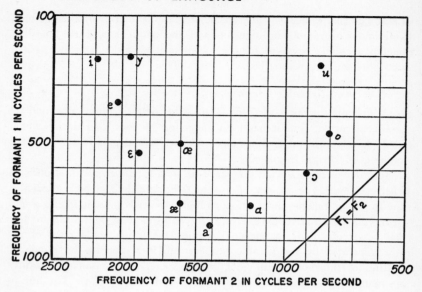

Fig. 2. A plot of formant 1 versus formant 2 for sustained vowels pronounced by a phonetician who is a male native speaker of English. The phonetic values of the vowels are approximately as follows: [i] as in *heed*, but without diphthongization; [e] as in *hey*, but without diphthongization; [ɛ] as in *head*; [æ] as in *hat*; [a] as in *ask* (Eastern U.S.); [ɑ] as in *harm*; [ɔ] as in *hawed*; [o] as in *hoe*, but without diphthongization; [u] as in *who*, but without diphthongization; [y] as in Fr. *lune*; [œ] as in Fr. *oeil*. (Adapted from data presented by Gordon Peterson, *Language* 27:541–553 (1951), and used by permission of the author and the Linguistic Society of America.)

we want to analyze. Joos proposes an electronic gadget which would plot the formants of a vowel instantaneously—for example, as a light at a certain position of a display board, or as a "blip" at some point on the surface of an oscilloscope screen. The light would also move as vowel quality changes, tracing a certain pattern, for example, for the diphthong in the word *loud*.

The utility of such a machine in the teaching of the sounds of a foreign language is obvious. If a student is having trouble with the German *ü* in the word *müde*, for example, we would simply sit him down before the formant-graphing machine and tell him to try to make noises so that the light will come as near as possible to a certain area which we have indicated on the display. Of course, he would need some guidance, but he would be able to see the results of his attempts in a concrete way.

The "Electrical Vocal Tract"

H. K. Dunn (1950) of the Bell Telephone Laboratories recently demonstrated what he calls "an electrical vocal tract," which is a device for the synthesis of vowel sounds. The operation of Dunn's device is based upon the use of electronic circuits which attempt to duplicate the resonating and filtering characteristics of the human speech organs. It is capable of producing highly naturalistic vowel sounds. In this respect it is much more successful than the "Voder" which was demonstrated at the New York World's Fair in 1940. This device is not generally available, but it might have considerable usefulness in experimental phonetics.

The "Pattern-Playback" Device as a Speech Synthesizer

Drs. Franklin S. Cooper and John M. Borst of the Haskins Laboratories (305 E. 43rd Street, New York City) have recently developed a highly ingenious and promising device for converting the graphic records of sound spectrography back into sound. By means of this device, it is possible to "play back" (that is, to hear) not only a sound-spectrographic record of actual speech, but also any artificial graphic pattern traced on a film. For example, it is possible to paint a simplified and somewhat schematized representation (see Fig. 1, *lower*) of an actual spectrographic record and then to determine whether the result yields the expected speech sounds when "played back" through the machine. It is found that the painted simulation of the original spectrograph may vary within moderately wide limits and still yield an intelligible rendition of the original utterance when played back. Obviously, the machine provides an admirable means of producing, varying, and controlling the physical sound stimuli in experiments in audition, phonetics, and the perception of speech. On account of its versatility and flexibility, the machine promises to serve most of the purposes of such devices as Dunn's electrical vocal tract and other speech synthesizers. Delattre (1951) and Liberman, Delattre, and Cooper (1952) have already come out with some interesting results based on the use of the pattern-playback device.

Linguistic Machines

Suggestions have been made in many quarters that it might be possible to construct a machine which would translate one kind of symbol into another kind of symbol. In a crude way, such a machine as the teletypewriter already does this, converting certain kinds of coded signals into movements of the various alphabetic print bars on the typewriter at the receiving end. Moreover, an ordinary IBM tabulating machine can be wired to perform certain simple coding problems. What is envisaged here, however, is a considerably more complex machine, such as an "automatic stenographer" whereby one would be able to talk into a machine which would print out the message in stenographic or alphabetic characters. Edmund C. Berkeley, a specialist in electronic computing machines, has proposed what he calls an "automatic recognizer" (1949, p. 186). The following paragraph looks like pure fantasy, but some of its suggestions may be within the realm of the possible:

The automatic recognizer will be capable of extraordinary tasks. With microphones and a large memory, this type of machine would be able to hear a foreign language spoken and translate it into spoken or written English. With phototubes and with an expanded filtering and decoding capacity as in deciphering machines, the automatic recognizer should be able to read a dead language, even one (such as Minoan or Etruscan) that has so far resisted attempts to read it. The machine would derive rules for the translation of the language and translate any sample.

Linguists point out that the linguistic rules which would have to be incorporated in any machine which would translate from one language to another or type out "your letters written and spaced as they should be" as Berkeley suggests, are so complex that the machine would have to have a very large capacity. Present-day computing machines are in some ways remarkably stupid, even when they fill several large-size rooms, as compared with the capacity of a reasonably intelligent human brain.[7] Furthermore, the writer doubts very much that any computing machine would be able to decipher an unknown language like Minoan, because such decipherment would depend upon the discovery of a "Rosetta stone" providing a translation in a known language, or at least upon some kind of external evidence (as we have in the case of the Maya hieroglyphs). We have no Rosetta stone or external evidence of any real helpfulness for Minoan.

The writer knows of only one such linguistic machine which has thus far been brought to any stage of perfection. This is the phonetic steno-sonograph described by Dreyfus-Graf (1950) of Switzerland at a recent conference at the Massachusetts Institute of Technology. After several years of research, Dreyfus-Graf has been able to perfect a machine which converts speech sounds as spoken into a microphone into a graphic record composed of recognizable characters similar to those used in stenography. Dreyfus-Graf also looks forward to being able to convert speech sounds into printed characters by a further process of electronic coding. Such a "sonograph" would have obvious uses not only in linguistic field work but also in many educational and commercial applications.

Preliminary work on the construction of linguistic machines is being carried on at a number of institutions, notably at the Massachusetts Institute of Technology and at Northeastern University. The proper construction of electronic components for such machines presents difficult problems in linguistic analysis, since the machine must be able, for example, to recognize variant allophones as members of the same phoneme. C. P. Smith (1951) has developed what he calls a "phoneme detector," based on electronic matching of the typical sound patterns ("envelopes") of standard phonemes.

There is much interest already in the possibility of constructing electronic machines for translating messages from one language to another. Oswald and Fletcher (1951) have attacked some of the linguistic problems which would have to be solved to make such a machine possible. They recognize two general types of problems, lexical and syntactical. The lexical problems have to do with the size of the vocabulary which would have to be established in the machine and with the comparative ranges of meanings of words in two languages; with these they are not immediately concerned. They have, however, conducted an illustrative analysis of comparative syntactical patterns in German and in English. In brief, their technique consists of determining what English syntactical patterns are implied by given sequences of morphemes in German. The rules so determined could presumably be set into a machine for translating German into English. In translating, the machine would proceed along a line of print until it had enough information to decode the German properly and encode it into English.

It may be suggested here that the translation problem might be handled with greater generality if it were possible to decode any language into some general set of semantic units—perhaps comparable to the units of selection postulated in Chapter 3. One would attempt to find a set of semantic units into which any language could be decoded by definite rules, although once we move outside languages of the Indo-European pattern the difficulties would become formidable. This set of semantic units, in what we might call "Basic Communicese," would then become the common denominator for mechanical translation devices. For example, a passage in Arabic would be translated into "Basic Communicese" and then into any other standard language we please. In this connection, it should be pointed out that what is commonly called a "literal" translation, in the pejorative sense of the term, is usually a bad translation simply because it takes account of only the lower-order units of selection—these being strung out in the order in which they stood in the original, without taking into account the higher-order units of selection which condition the choice and sequencing of lower-order units. A mechanical translator must take into account units as high as possible in the selection hierarchy.

SUMMARY

The theory of communication as developed by Shannon promises to have many implications for linguistic analysis. Thus far, linguistic scientists have not fully explored these implications. It is possible, however, that the theory of communication has somewhat more relevance for the psychology of language than for linguistic science itself. Developments in this field are too new to allow one to foresee exactly what kind of research should be done or where the results would lead.

Certain devices made possible by modern electronic techniques, notably the sound spectrograph, the speech stretcher, and various forms of speech synthesizers, promise to have considerable usefulness not only in linguistic analysis but also in certain educational applications. A formant-graphing machine, suggested by Joos in conversations with the writer, would be an especially useful device. Electronic machines for doing such jobs as converting speech into writing or translating from one language to another are already in the blueprint stage and will probably be perfected in the foreseeable future. There needs to be much collaboration between linguistic scientists and communication engineers in the development of such devices.

Chapter 8 ORGANIZATIONS, PERSONNEL, AND PUBLICATIONS

It is time now to examine the facilities—organizations, personnel, and periodical publications—which support the advance of language studies in America. The facilities of which we shall speak are primarily those organized in the field of linguistic science, but some attention will be given to related fields.

ORGANIZATIONS AND PERIODICALS IN LINGUISTICS

The Linguistic Society of America

The major learned society in linguistics is the Linguistic Society of America, often abbreviated LSA. The LSA was organized in 1925 and has seen a continual growth in membership. In 1950, 829 "personal members" were on the rolls; this figure excludes 23 "honorary members" in foreign countries. The LSA has established no requirements for membership other than the customary payment of annual dues. It may be estimated that not more than 30 to 35 per cent of the membership could be classified as "linguistic scientists," a linguistic scientist being defined as a person who displays a scientific interest in general linguistics and who has made scholarly contributions to this field. The membership rolls include many persons with peripheral interests in general linguistics, such as professors of Latin and Greek, Romance languages, etc. The "inner circle" of linguistic scientists probably does not number much over 200; this is reflected partly in the fact that the attendance at professional meetings of the LSA has been about 100 in recent years.

The annual meeting of the Linguistic Society is usually held in December; in addition, there is usually a summer meeting held in connection with the Linguistic Institute.

The Linguistic Institute

The Linguistic Institute is conducted annually for six or eight weeks during the summer. It is sponsored jointly by the LSA and the institution where it is held. Among these host institutions have been Yale University, the University of North Carolina, the University of Wisconsin, the University of Michigan, and the University of California. In 1952 and 1953 the Linguistic Institute is scheduled to be held at Indiana University.[1]

The Linguistic Institute offers credit in a broad range of courses in linguistic science and in the study of specific languages. Such courses as Introduction to Linguistic Science, Descriptive Linguistics, Phonetics and Phonemics, and Field Methods in Linguistics are regularly taught. Such courses as Problems of Indo-European Grammar, Comparative Grammar of Semitic Languages, Hittite, Old Persian, and Algonkian Languages are also likely to be found in the curriculum. Attendance is relatively large: in 1950, there was an enrollment of 193, of whom 95 were enrolled in two or more courses. The Linguistic Institute provides a meeting place for scholars in linguistic science, many of whom quite regularly attend the sessions to sit in on one anothers' courses or to do collaborative work with colleagues from other universities. The Institute has also followed a policy of inviting foreign scholars to give special lectures or even full courses.[2]

The Summer Institute of Linguistics

The Summer Institute of Linguistics, not to be confused with the Linguistic Institute, is supported by certain religious groups and is organized primarily for the purpose of teaching those aspects of linguistics which are of use to missionaries and Bible translators. Staff members have shown much interest in general questions of theoretical linguistics, and courses in general linguistics, phonemics, etc., are taught as a background for practical work. At present there are two branches of the Summer Institute of Linguistics. One is at Norman, Oklahoma; the other is held at Caronport, Saskatchewan.

Other Organizations in Linguistics

The Linguistic Circle of New York is composed of linguistic scholars residing within a comfortable radius of New York, where meetings are held every month or so for the presentation and discussion of papers. Similar local organizations have been formed in Washington, D. C., in Michigan, and elsewhere.

Linguistic "clubs" and seminars exist at a number of universities, at Yale and Indiana, for example. These are organized on an informal basis.

Periodicals

In contrast to the situation abroad, where there are perhaps ten or more periodicals devoted primarily to general linguistics, there are in the United States only four periodicals of any importance which could be said to be addressed to general linguistics as such.

Language is a quarterly journal founded in 1925 and published by the Linguistic Society of America. Its present editor is Bernard Bloch of Yale University. Normally, it accepts articles only from members of the LSA; its contents cover the whole range of linguistic studies, and its standards of scholarship are of the highest. In addition, *Language Monographs* ("studies too long to appear as articles in the journal *Language*") and *Language Dissertations* (Ph.D. dissertations in American universities editorially passed on as being "upon linguistic subjects") are occasional publications distributed to subscribers of *Language*.

The *International Journal of American Linguistics* is a quarterly journal, originally founded by Franz Boas in 1917; it ceased publication in 1939 but was reëstablished in 1944 by C. F. Voegelin, of Indiana, who now serves as its editor. Space is largely devoted to articles on American Indian languages, but there are also discussions of problems in general linguistics.

Appearing three times a year, *Word* was founded by the Linguistic Circle of New York. Joseph Greenberg and André Martinet of Columbia University are now its joint editors. It publishes articles both on general linguistics and on a wide range of special topics. Not all its articles are as technical as the norm of those in *Language* or *IJAL,* and there seems to be a disposition on the part of its editorial board to admit articles in borderline fields such as the psychology of language. Beginning in 1952, *Word* will publish annually a fourth issue devoted to Slavic studies.

Studies in Linguistics, founded in 1942 by G. L. Trager and others, is a quarterly publication somewhat less formal in appearance than the periodicals mentioned above, but it has a content which roughly parallels that of *Language.* A series of *Occasional Papers* have been issued as supplements to *Studies in Linguistics.*

While there is no organized bibliographical or abstracting service in linguistics to compare with, say, *Psychological Abstracts, Biological Abstracts,* or the *Education Index,* the needs are now being met in a very large measure by a bibliographical project initiated in Europe by an international committee of linguists with the aid of a subvention from UNESCO. A two-volume bibliography of linguistics for the years 1939–1947 has already been published (Comité International Permanent des Linguistes, 1949–1950), and this is being followed by a series of annual bibliographies.[3] With text in English and in French, these bibliographies provide listings of books, reviews, periodicals, and journal articles classified under general linguistics, phonetics, language families, and specific languages. The coverage seems to extend fairly deep into borderline areas such as the psychology of language. Writings from all parts of the world, including the United States, are represented, and added usefulness comes from the fact that there is an alphabetical list of authors' names.

ORGANIZATIONS AND PERIODICALS IN RELATED DISCIPLINES

Philological Organizations

In each of several fields of language study, there are one or more learned societies devoted to philological and literary inquiries. Materials of import for scientific linguistics not infrequently appear in their publications.

Foremost among these philological societies, to speak only of those in the United States, is the Modern Language Association, founded in 1883. The contents of the *Publications of the Modern Language Association* cover a broad field of studies, but reflect an emphasis on what B. L. Whorf was fond of calling "standard average European" languages and literatures—English, French, German, Italian, and Spanish, in the main.

The American Philological Association is an old and respected learned society (founded in 1869) specializing in classical philology and publishing *Transactions,* and *Proceedings, of the American Philological Association.* The interests of Sanskritists and orientalists are served by the American Oriental Society, with its publication, the *Journal of the American Oriental Society.* Semitics and related topics are covered in the *Journal of Near Eastern Studies,* published by the Oriental Institute at the University of Chicago.

216

The American Dialect Society, which specializes in the study of dialects of American English, published a journal *Dialect Notes* during the period 1889–1939. It now issues only occasional publications in monograph form.

There are numerous philological journals which have no direct affiliation with learned societies. *American Speech* is devoted to the study of American English and its dialects; its phonetic transcriptions of speech samples from various parts of the country are of special interest. The *Journal of English and German Philology* is published at the University of Illinois. Other periodicals devoted to modern-language philology are *Modern Philology*, *Modern Language Notes*, the *Romanic Review*, and the *Hispanic Review*. Periodicals specializing in classical philology are the *American Journal of Philology* and *Classical Philology*. Several universities publish their own series of studies in English, modern language, and classical philology. The *Harvard Journal of Asiatic Studies* contains much of linguistic importance.

Organizations of Language Teachers

Each of the major academic branches of language teaching is represented by one or more national and regional organizations. While the periodical and other publications of these organizations reflect much concern with strictly pedagogical problems, they also contain material of linguistic or philological interest.

The National Council of Teachers of English publishes journals at each of three educational levels: *Elementary English*, for the elementary-school teacher; the *English Journal*, for the secondary-school teacher; and *College English*, for the college teacher. All of them, but particularly *Elementary English*, have shown considerable awareness of the need for research in pedagogical problems. In addition, the NCTE has sponsored a series of *English Monographs* in book form; these have included, for example, Marckwardt and Walcott's *Facts about Current English Usage* (1938), Fries's *American English Grammar* (1940), and Pooley's *Teaching English Usage* (1946), which have already been cited in these pages.

Foreign-language teachers are banded together in the National Federation of Modern Language Teachers, which publishes the *Modern Language Journal*. The NFMLT has affiliated with it a number of regional and specialized associations, the latter including teachers of French (publishing the *French Review*), teachers of Spanish and Portuguese (publishing the journal *Hispania*), teachers of German (with the *German Quarterly*), teachers of Italian (with the journal *Italica*), and teachers of Slavic and East European languages.

Teachers of Latin and Greek are represented by a national organization, the American Classical League, and by several regional associations. The Classical Association of the Middle West and South publishes the *Classical Journal,* and the Classical Association of the Atlantic States sponsors the *Classical Weekly.*

Language Learning, a relatively new periodical, is published by linguists and language teachers at the University of Michigan.

Organizations in the Field of Speech Education

The major organization in this field is the Speech Association of America, which has published the *Quarterly Journal of Speech* since 1915 and *Speech Monographs* since 1934. The *Journal of Speech and Hearing Disorders,* founded in 1936, is published by the American Speech and Hearing Association. A new society, with a rather ambitious name and program, has recently been organized by a number of speech educators; this is the National Society for the Study of Communication, which started publication of the *Journal of Communication* in 1951.

Psychological, Social Science, and Philosophical Organizations

Founded in 1892, the American Psychological Association in 1951 had approximately 8600 members, and thus includes, according to its latest directory, "most of the qualified psychologists in the country." It now embraces numerous special-interest groups, organized as divisions: the Division of General Psychology, the Division of Experimental Psychology, etc. There is a Division of Aesthetics, but there is no division devoted to the psychology of language. The few psychologists interested in linguistic psychology are to be found scattered among a number of divisions. The journals published by the APA are too numerous to list here; of special interest, however, is *Psychological Abstracts* which since 1928 has attempted to publish, month by month, abstracts (up to 150 words or more) of all books, articles, and other materials of psychological interest appearing throughout the world.[4] There is a yearly index by subject matter and by authors' names.

Like the American Psychological Association, the American Sociological Association seems to contain no organized special-interest group devoted to problems of language and communication. In the official organ of the ASA, the *American Sociological Review,* materials directly relating to such problems are only rarely to be found.

The close connections between linguistics and anthropology are evident in the periodical *American Anthropologist,* published by the American Anthropological Association. This journal could almost be called one of the standard media for the publication of articles of linguistic interest. Many members of the Linguistic Society of America are also members of the AAA, and a Joint Committee on American Native Languages, composed of members of the two societies, constitutes an advisory board for the publication of the *International Journal of American Linguistics* mentioned earlier.

The philosophy of language is occasionally treated, directly or indirectly, in the several journals in the field of philosophy, for example, in the *Journal of Philosophy, Philosophy and Phenomenological Research* (published by the International Phenomenological Society), the *Philosophical Review,* and the *Journal of Symbolic Logic* (published by the Association for Symbolic Logic). *Philosophic Abstracts,* published by the Association for Philosophical Research, is a useful reference source, though it contains notices only of books. The American Philosophical Association, founded in 1900, is the major learned society in this field.

Most persons who have been in the vanguard in communication theory are members of the Acoustical Society of America, whose official organ, the *Journal of the Acoustical Society of America,* has published a number of articles bearing on communication theory and speech analysis.

REPRESENTATION OF LANGUAGE STUDIES IN THE RESEARCH COUNCILS AND FOUNDATIONS

There are at least four recognized research councils in the United States: the National Research Council (NRC), covering natural, biological, and psychological sciences; the Social Science Research Council (SSRC); the American Council of Learned Societies Devoted to Humanistic Studies (ACLS); and the American Council on Education (ACE). The government-sponsored National Science Foundation (NSF), is only now in the process of organization. Language studies are directly represented in the ACLS, the SSRC, and the ACE. The ACLS sponsors several committees in the field of language studies. The most important of these, the Committee on the Language Program, has played an active role in advancing various types of linguistic studies, and has often served as a liaison agency between linguistic scientists, research foundations, government departments, and others concerned with linguistics and the results of linguistic researches. The Intensive Language Program, described in Chapter 6, was sponsored by the ACLS. In the SSRC, a Committee on Linguistics and Psychology was organized in November 1952. The American Council on Education has a Committee on Modern Languages, which has issued a number of publications bearing on the teaching of modern languages.

Working largely through the above-named research councils, a number of philanthropic organizations in America have long given support and, sometimes, even active leadership in linguistic studies. For example, for several years beginning in 1927, the Carnegie Corporation of New York helped support a program of research in American Indian languages, enabling a committee composed of Franz Boas, Leonard Bloomfield, and Edward Sapir to supervise field studies of about 82 different languages. In recent years the Rockefeller Foundation has lent assistance to a broad range of linguistic studies, not only in general linguistics but also in borderline fields such as the philosophy of language. This is hardly the place to catalog all the considerable contributions which have been made to language studies by the foundations, but special mention should be made of the Wenner-Gren Foundation, whose Viking Fund has supported numerous publications in linguistics and anthropology and instigated several important conferences on linguistic problems bearing on anthropology.

CENTERS OF ACTIVITY IN LINGUISTICS

There are relatively few departments of general linguistics in American universities. Most linguistic scientists are associated with departments of Germanic philology, of Sanskrit, of Romance languages, etc., or with departments of anthropology. Even when an individual bears a title as a professor of linguistics, it does not necessarily mean that he belongs to a department of linguistics. At Yale University, for example, the "department of linguistics" is really an aggregation of individuals whose salaries come from various funds, there being no budgetary allocation to a department of linguistics as such.

A list of university departments and other centers of linguistic activity may be of use to many readers. Any such listing, of course, will inevitably run the risk of seeming overly discriminating, if not positively invidious, but it seems wise to err on the side of omission. I will therefore list only those institutions where a full-fledged linguistic program is in being and where more than one or two linguistic scientists are to be found. The reader is cautioned, however, that important activities, though of lesser extent or of more highly specialized character, are being undertaken at a number of institutions not listed. He is also cautioned that the linguistic programs to be found at each of the listed institutions vary considerably with respect to the varieties of linguistic theory which are favored and the special fields of study which are emphasized. With these reservations, the following list is offered: Columbia University, Cornell University, Department of State (School of Language Training), Harvard University, Indiana University, Princeton University, University of California, University of Chicago, University of Michigan, University of Pennsylvania, University of Wisconsin, Yale University.

PERSONNEL IN THE FIELD OF LINGUISTICS

We have already remarked above that the number of persons who could be classed as "linguistic scientists" in America is extremely small—probably not over 300, even if we include graduate students. Nearly all of them are members of the Linguistic Society of America, but that organization also includes a considerable number of persons whose interests in linguistics are peripheral.

What do we mean by a "linguistic scientist?" The distinguishing marks of a linguistic scientist are the following:

1. He has had broad training (usually leading to the Ph. D.), or the equivalent in self-instruction, in general linguistics—both descriptive and comparative—at a major center of linguistics or at least at the Linguistic Institute or one of the summer institutes.

2. He is competent to do one, or preferably several of the following things: (*a*) to make a field study of a previously unknown language and to prepare a description of it generally acceptable to other linguistic scientists;

(*b*) to make contributions to the advancement of linguistic methodology; (*c*) to make comparative studies of languages in order to discover their affinities and origins by approved methods of comparative linguistics; (*d*) to make historical studies of a single language; (*e*) to perform a number of miscellaneous tasks such as development of suitable orthographies for unwritten languages or preparation of accurate dictionaries, grammars, and instruction materials in a language.

The training of a linguistic scientist is rigorous. The course of study at Yale University, for example, makes the following requirements, among others:

1. The student must take courses in general linguistics, field methods in linguistics, phonetics and phonemics, etc.

2. The student must show a thorough knowledge of Indo-European comparative linguistics. He must know something of several Indo-European languages; a reading knowledge of French and German is required for entrance upon graduate studies, and a similar knowledge of Greek and Latin is required for beginning the second year of work.

3. The student must acquire a knowledge (that is, a fairly thorough knowledge of the structure, grammar, and lexicon, but not necessarily a "speaking knowledge") of at least one non-Indo-European language.

Generally, students specialize in some field of linguistics, such as Germanic linguistics, Slavic linguistics, American Indian linguistics, etc. Doctoral dissertations are usually studies of particular problems in the analysis of a particular language or a group of languages. At least at Yale University, students are not encouraged to write dissertations on general problems of linguistic methodology or theory, since they are not regarded as having sufficient maturity and experience in linguistics to do so.

The above program requires so much time on the part of the student that in the normal three years' course for the Ph. D. there is not much opportunity for him to take courses in allied fields of study. What extra time he may have open to him he may devote to studies in the history, literature, and culture of the peoples in whose languages he is specializing. He may take courses in cultural anthropology, but it is very unlikely that he would study psychology, education, sociology, or philosophy, for example. From one standpoint, the finished Ph. D. in linguistics may be regarded as a very narrow specialist.

The staffs at linguistic training centers feel that a person who wants to take graduate training in linguistics should come prepared with considerable training in languages of the sort usually offered in undergraduate courses, for example, Latin, Greek, French, German, Anglo-Saxon, or Middle-High German.

A minor comment may be inserted at this point. It is a fact that a student might take an undergraduate major in a foreign-language department (either in a modern or an ancient language) and never become aware that a field of linguistic science exists. If he were a major in Latin, for example, he might get the idea that "comparative philology" was an exclusively Teutonic activity of the nineteenth century. It is also significant that in a bulletin issued by the National Federation of Modern Language Teachers and entitled "Vocational Opportunities for Foreign Language Students" (Huebener, 1949) there is not a single mention of linguistic science or of any vocational opportunities in it.

It is impossible to make any generalized characterization of linguistic scientists except by characterizing the work they do. Linguistics is a most exacting field. The linguist often has tremendous masses of data to work with—and generally these masses of data can be reduced to order only by the careful examination and comparison of individual items. Whether the linguist is working in descriptive or in historical linguistics, these characteristics of the data put a premium on his memory and ingenuity. The most successful linguistic scholars—like Sapir, for example—have had a remarkable capacity to retain in memory an enormous number of linguistic facts from many languages and to bring them forth when needed to illustrate a point or to fit a missing piece into a linguistic puzzle. The pursuit of general linguistics, therefore, seems to require a rather high order of some special kind of intelligence as well as a great capacity for the painstaking and thorough work which is demanded in all fields of scholarly endeavor.

Chapter 9 THE FUTURE OF LANGUAGE STUDIES

If only by making an extrapolation of present trends, we can say that language studies have a future. But whether this future will contain anything dynamic and impressive depends on two things. First, progress depends on further and increasing support. In these days of large appropriations for research in the natural sciences, the needs in the social sciences tend to be neglected. But increased support for language studies will be justified only if the second condition for progress is satisfied. This second condition is that students of language in the various disciplines surveyed here must broaden their perspectives, pay less heed to departmental barriers, and address themselves more directly and openly to the function of language and communication in all thought and action. Nothing less is required than that a general science of communication should emerge, for only in this way can some of the broad problems of human communication, as they affect society, be solved.

Doubtless the reader will desire a greater sense of conviction that language studies can yield solutions to the larger human problems. The problems we have in mind are of two sorts: technological and educational. The technological problems have to do with making it possible for human communication to be surer and more effective. In order to solve this technological problem, we need to have precise information on linguistic codes and the manner in which they function, or can function, in the matrix of human culture. The educational problems have to do with making the members of our society more effective communicators. Here it is necessary to acquire further understanding, and a greater degree of prediction and control, with respect to those phases of human behavior which have to do with communication.

These remarks imply a bold and far-reaching program—one for which we are perhaps not yet ready. Individual scholars and scientists in various disciplines have already invested their energies—quite properly—in the pursuit of narrow and specialized questions, to such an extent that a redirecting of effort toward broader issues would in many cases be inadvisable. The tradition of free scientific investigation, too, is such that most scholars prefer to follow their own interests and curiosities, which can often be satisfied only by concentrated work in remote corners of knowledge.

What seems to be demanded, then, is a new variety of generalist. Recently, four statisticians (Bode, Mosteller, Tukey, and Winsor, 1949) have set forth the qualities needed in what they call a *scientific generalist.* The scientific generalist these men describe would span the field of the natural and biological sciences, including psychology. The unifying elements would be scientific method and statistics. Now, the kind of generalist we need in the present context is a *communications generalist.* His range of competences would have to have a center of gravity in the social rather than the natural sciences, and would have to extend far into the humanistic studies. Like the scientific generalist, the communications generalist would need a knowledge of scientific method and statistics, for he would undoubtedly be called upon to perform experiments and to analyze quantitative data. The disciplines which would have a key function in his work, however, would be linguistics, psychology, and cultural anthropology.

The major initial task of the communications generalist would be to strive toward a better theoretical integration of knowledge concerning communicative codes, behaviors, and conditions. He would acquire a thorough knowledge of the characteristics of linguistic structures, examine the matrix of behavior in which these structures exist, and attempt to adduce from observation and experiment an integrated account of communicative behavior. In this enterprise, his attention would be given not only to codes found in natural languages but also to codes and communicative systems which derive from natural languages (for example, systems of writing) or which are several stages removed from natural languages (for example, signaling systems, graphics, mathematical symbolisms, etc.). The study of human cognition and problem solving would be one of the major areas of investigation by the communications generalist.

The work of a communications generalist might extend to any one of a number of practical problems. For example:

(*a*) *Programs of linguistic and area research.*—Research on the languages and cultures of various areas of the world is becoming increasingly necessary, not only for strategic reasons but also for furthering American understanding of other civilizations. The communications generalist could bring to such programs an increased awareness of the interrelations of cultural, psychological, and linguistic factors in the process of understanding and communicating with another civilization. Programs of linguistic and area research are also likely to involve large-scale translation projects in which significant samples of the literatures of other cultures and civilizations are to be put into English. The communications generalist could advise on the technique of translation, both with respect to its mechanical, operational problems and with respect to the subtler problem of insuring that the flavor, spirit, and *Zeitgeist* of a foreign culture are conveyed in a translation as well as they can be.

(*b*) *Technological problems in communications engineering.*—The communications generalist can combine his knowledge of linguistics with his knowledge of natural sciences and statistics in consulting on the design of the various communications devices described on Chapter 7.

(*c*) *The conduct of language education.*—The broad knowledge of a communications generalist would be needed in consulting on the conduct of education in the language arts or in foreign languages, whether in the design of experiments on language education, the construction of measuring devices, or simply in the application of known psychological and pedagogical principles.

Still other areas in which a communications generalist might operate would be: the design of psychological experiments in verbal behavior; the development of special-purpose linguistic codes; the adjustment of linguistic attitudes in a society; the study and use of mass media of communication.

There is no intention here to imply that one person could become really competent to work in *all* the areas described above; it is highly unlikely that one could acquire the range of specialized knowledge necessary for such versatility. Rather, it would be expected that a communications generalist would start from a broad, integrated base and then specialize in one or two particular directions. In every case, however, specialization would take place in several disciplines at once. The communications generalist would have to specialize both in certain areas of linguistics and at the same time in certain areas of psychology and anthropology, for example, depending on the nature of his tasks.

As communications generalists are trained and put into productive work, one could expect the field of language study to develop into a comprehensive, many-sided, but integrated discipline. This expansion, however, is likely to be a slow process. We will have to content ourselves with a number of suggestions as to the immediate steps which can be taken to encourage progress.

THE PRESENT SITUATION AND IMMEDIATE GOALS

Let us recount our major observations on the present state of language studies in order to sharpen our view of the immediate needs.

Linguistic science, we have seen, is highly advanced in methodology. Nevertheless, it still faces certain difficult theoretical problems. There are certain issues in descriptive linguistics, especially in the study of the phoneme, where opposing points of view need somehow to be finally resolved. At the same time, there exist large gaps in our knowledge of the languages of the world. Numerous language structures remain to be described and studied historically by modern techniques. Finally, linguists have made only a beginning in the study of the relations between linguistic and cultural traits.

Interdisciplinary coöperation between various groups concerned with the study of language can be said to be of an extremely limited and localized character. Few psychologists are fully aware of the implications of linguistic science for the study of verbal behavior. Philosophers, educators, communications engineers, and semanticists have been slow to recognize the need for drawing on other disciplines in solving problems concerned with language.

The actual number of linguistic scientists is small; indeed, this is a field in which manpower is in extremely short supply. There is, therefore, need of programs to encourage the development of a larger corps of trained personnel. There are, of course, large numbers of language teachers—teachers of English and of foreign languages—and there has been a distinct surge in the numbers of speech educators. In disciplines like psychology, philosophy, and sociology, however, professional persons concerned with language problems are scattered and difficult to identify.

It remains to point out that there exists a large potential of public interest in language problems, as reflected in the popularity of such relatively nontechnical writings as Stuart Chase's *The Tyranny of Words* (1938), Mencken's *The American Language* (1938), Hayakawa's *Language in Action* (1943), and Bodmer's *The Loom of Language* (1944). Public curiosity about language problems can be satisfied not so much by highly technical studies of specialized interest as by broad studies depicting the role of language in individual behavior and in society.

SOME SPECIFIC RECOMMENDATIONS

The rather broad goals implied in the preceding paragraphs can be achieved only by channeling efforts into certain specific and tangible projects. Some of these projects, designed to support progress toward broad goals rather than toward local, specialized, and "blind-alley" objectives are outlined below. They are listed in the order of their relative priority, although actually many of the priorities are concurrent.

Priority 1. A program for the collection of data on little-known languages and dialects.

Steps should be taken to organize a program for the collection of data on a large number of languages and dialects which have been thus far very imperfectly described. Some of these languages, such as many in Africa and Asia, are of crucial importance in connection with the furtherance of American understanding of foreign cultures and civilizations. Others are moribund languages, spoken in very small speech communities, which can never be studied unless they are studied in the near future.

Such a program would have many advantages. It would provide for the field training and placement of a fairly large number of young linguistic scientists, all of whom will be needed, eventually, to implement the broad goals outlined elsewhere. It would generate a corpus of data which not only will be useful for the future development of linguistics but also is urgently needed for certain types of comparative and historical studies. Previous experience with this type of program shows that the availability of fresh data almost automatically promotes the development of linguistic methodology.

Needless to say, electronic aids (tape recorders, speech stretchers, etc.) should be used to facilitate the collection of data. The whole implementation of the program should be carefully thought out with a view to economy and efficiency.

228

Priority 2. Provision of predoctoral scholarships and fellowships for language studies.

The number of students now undergoing training for the Ph. D. in general linguistics is now so small (probably not over 75 *at most* in the United States at large) that it would be impossible to undertake the priority 1 program above except, initially, on a small scale. It would therefore be necessary to recruit and train a certain number of graduate students every year in order to provide personnel for the larger programs, both for the data-collection program listed as priority 1 and for certain other programs, mentioned below. Difficulties of recruiting young people for graduate study in linguistics are considerable, but they would be reduced materially if a greater number of scholarships and fellowships were established in well-recognized linguistic departments. It is obvious, also, that greater publicity would have to be given about career opportunities in linguistic science. At present, the field of linguistic science is all too unknown among college students.

At the same time, interdisciplinary studies at the graduate level need to be encouraged. Already a number of graduate students have been attracted to a broader program of study than is possible by study in linguistics *as such,* in psychology *as such,* etc. It is among students such as these that we may expect to find the communications generalists of the future.

Interdisciplinary graduate studies will become more practicable if there is some relaxation of the rigorous requirements for doctoral training in each of the several fields. For example, an interdisciplinary student in linguistics might be allowed to substitute appropriate courses in psychology, philosophy, etc. for some of the more specialized courses in linguistics he might otherwise be expected to take. Similar relaxations might be made for students in psychology and other subjects in order to allow time for linguistic studies. Much would depend, of course, on the ability of the student and upon the breadth of his undergraduate training. It would appear that the major obstacle in the way of interdisciplinary graduate studies is the understandable concern of department chairmen over the job-placement possibilities of students. Yet, as seems apparent from our survey of the kinds of things that communications generalists might do, these placement possibilities are not as limited as one might ordinarily assume.

Priority 3. Support of interdisciplinary seminars, surveys, and training institutes.

A start has already been made on the encouragement of interdisciplinary coöperation between linguistics and other fields,[1] but much more needs to be done. Seminars need to be supported not only on a national scale, but also at the local level. Small interdisciplinary groups at various universities could doubtless do much to explore problems of the sort mentioned at various points in the present work.

The same objectives could also be met by the support of special training institutes and surveys.

Priority 4. Greater exploitation of existing sources of funds for fellowships and grants-in-aid for interdisciplinary study and research.

The implementation of interdisciplinary research programs can be supported partly by university and government research funds. There are, however, other sources of funds. Both the American Council of Learned Societies and the Social Science Research Council have postdoctoral fellowships and grants-in-aid; in some cases these are specifically earmarked for persons interested in cross-fertilization between various disciplines. These sources of funds need to be further utilized for interdisciplinary language studies. In the present case, these fellowships and grants-in-aid should not be awarded solely on the basis of the accidents of individual application. Some coördination and positive direction ought to be maintained to insure that efforts are not misdirected into highly specialized approaches of little promise.

Priority 5. Support of specific research and developmental enterprises in linguistics and related disciplines.

Support of specific research projects in linguistics and related disciplines is placed at a low *relative* priority in view of the urgency of developing a large cadre of research personnel and a freer atmosphere for interdisciplinary coöperation. This is not to disparage such research; on the contrary, this kind of support would rise to much higher priority after some years.

There is no need to detail here the kinds of research projects which need to be undertaken. If the preceding chapters have not suggested a host of problems and projects for interdisciplinary research, the writer has indeed failed in his objective.

Research results often have a way of getting tucked away in scientific journals and never applied in practical problems. Sometimes this is by nature of the researches themselves: "pure" science is often called pure simply because it appears not immediately useful. More often, perhaps, it is due to a failure of communication between scientists and the potential consumers of scientific research. Perhaps we should turn our sights onto this failure of communication, as a problem for applied language study. Part of the solution doubtless lies in the establishment of developmental programs of applied science in which the scientist has a direct hand. This has happened in the natural sciences; it can also happen in the social sciences, and in education. It is hoped that the opportunities for the application of scientific studies in language will by now have become somewhat more apparent than formerly.

NOTES AND REFERENCES

NOTES TO CHAPTER 2

1. Other works of interest in the field of gesture are those of Critchley (1939) and Efron (1941).

2. The terms "bow-wow" and "pooh-pooh" as applied to these theories were popularized by Max Müller in his *Lectures on the Science of Language* (1873, p. 358).

3. Voegelin (1944) has demonstrated the admiration of contemporary linguists for Boas's work by rephrasing one of his papers in modern terms. Jakobson (1944) provides an illuminating discussion of Boas's contribution to modern linguistics. Boas's views on language at a later stage of his life can be examined in a chapter he wrote for a compendium on anthropology (Boas, 1938).

4. The present status of Soviet linguistics deserves at least a footnote, if only for its sheer interest. As far as I have been able to determine, Soviet linguistics has until recently been characterized by sound and vigorous development on the side of practical descriptive work. Soviet linguists had produced many reasonably good descriptive grammars of the languages within the borders of the U.S.S.R. On the side of theory, the work of such linguistic students as Vigotsky, Voloshinov, Polivanov, Larin, Bubrikh, Vinogradov, and Shcherba deserves mention. [This statement is made on the authority of R. Jakobson. I am personally acquainted only with the work of Vigotsky (1939).] Some of these writers have particularly well studied the problems of language and thought, of bilingualism, and of the relation of language to social class. As soon as one enters the realm of currently official Soviet linguistic theory, however, one finds a fantastic situation. Until recently, official Soviet linguistic theory was dominated by the theories of Academician N. Ia. Marr, who lived from 1864 to 1934. (This is not to say that other varieties of theory did not exist.) Claiming to base his theories on Marxist teachings, Marr developed a "materialist" doctrine whereby the origin of language was ascribed to gesture ("kinetic language"). He worked out a "Japhetic" theory in which languages were to be classified genealogically according to their status in four stages of development. All languages of the world were claimed to be related; all words in all languages were to be analyzed as containing one or more of four elements, SAL, BER, YON, ROSH, which were alleged to be prehistoric tribal names. Marr also came to the conclusion that "language and thought are dialectically united" and that "language [is] a superstructure which is acted upon by the base through historically developing consciousness." Early in 1950, at a scientific session held on the occasion of the fifteenth anniversary of Marr's death, eulogies of Marr's accomplishments were interlarded with severe criticisms. The ensuing hot debate, which took place in the pages of *Pravda,* culminated with a lengthy statement, patronizing in tone, from none other than Stalin. Marr, said Stalin, "introduced into linguistics an erroneous, un-Marxist formula of language as a superstructure." If language were a superstructure, how could it be, he asked, that the Russian language had not changed essentially since the Russian revolution? "The base is the economic structure of society . . . the superstructure comprises the political, legal, religious, artistic and philosophical views of society and their corresponding political, legal and other institutions." Language cannot be a superstructure, because it does not change as the base changes. Marrism was hence to be completely rejected.

The upshot of Stalin's communication was that many Marrists were thrown out of their positions, and linguists were urged to build a new theory of linguistics. We then find them busily writing "confessions" of past errors, planning the new tasks of "Leninist-Stalinist" linguistics. As one Professor Akhvlediani puts it, "The difficulties will be overcome because Stalinist science is all-powerful. Soviet linguistics will supersede bourgeois science. . . "

For the full report of these events, the reader may be referred to *The Soviet Linguistic Controversy* (Murra *et al.,* 1951) which was my source for the quotations made above. One may also refer to Rubenstein's (1951) recent discussion.

5. I have deliberately substituted the term *lexicography* for what Bloomfield (1933, p. 138) describes as semantics, for two reasons: (*a*) *semantics,* if it has any general, single meaning, refers to the general science of meaning rather than to the specific operation of assigning meanings to forms, as intended here; and (*b*) since I believe that grammatical features can and should be listed and described in much the same manner as lexical items, and together with them, I think it convenient to use *lexicography* to cover the listing of both grammatical and lexical items. Bloomfield seems to imply that grammar, as a branch of semantics, is the statement of the meanings of grammatical features, but this is surely an odd usage.

6. See the numerous "metalinguistic" papers of Sapir (Mandelbaum, 1949).

7. This term was proposed by a group of linguists and psychologists participating in an eight-weeks' seminar during the summer of 1951 at Cornell University (Carroll, 1951).

8. Harris (1951, p. 2) cautions that the linguistic methods he sets forth "do not eliminate nonuniqueness in linguistic descriptions." It is evident, however, that he is speaking of relatively minor differences in the alternative decisions open to the investigator.

9. The complexities of the problem are well illustrated in an article by Togeby (1949). Actually it is likely that the problem may now be regarded as solved, at least in principle; see, for example, the treatments by Harris (1951, index *s.v.* 'word') and Trager and Smith (1951). It is important to note, however, that what is called a word must be defined independently for each language that may be studied.

10. I am informed that in Navaho and Taos, the blue and the green areas are combined in a single term; the term for yellow extends over a small portion of what we call green.

11. One of Whorf's papers on this subject was printed in the proceedings of the Second American Congress on General Semantics (Kendig, 1943). The Spring 1952 issue of *Etc., A Review of General Semantics,* is in fact entirely devoted to "metalinguistic" problems.

12. The substratum theory is not altogether implausible. In certain Spanish-speaking communities in which the influence of English is rising, as in the Philippines, there are indications that the variety of English which is developing is markedly influenced by Spanish phonology. I am also informed that English as spoken in Ireland shows many traces of Irish.

13. We are speaking here of phonetic change, not phonemic change. Phonemic change is undoubtedly saltatory and takes place only when phonetic changes have gone so far as to create a new phonemic pattern.

14. Professor A. H. Marckwardt of the University of Michigan points out that

"there is at present no single history of the English language which sets forth the phonemes of Old English, Middle English, and Modern English respectively" (personal communication).

15. The committee has recently published a "tentative bibliography" of statistical work in linguistics (Trnka, 1950).

16. A description of this project appears in *Language,* 1951, 27, 207–209.

NOTES TO CHAPTER 3

1. For example, the journal *Psychological Abstracts* generally classifies materials on the psychology of language under the heading of social psychology.

2. Watson's view of thinking stimulated a number of investigations to determine whether electrophysiological responses could be observed during the thought process. Jacobson (1932) and Max (1935a, 1935b), for example, were able to observe action potentials in laryngeal and finger muscles which seemed to have some correlations with thought processes as reported by their subjects. However, such experiments cannot be regarded as proof that thought is *identical* with peripheral action potentials, since these might be simply a result of innervation from central mediation processes.

3. Or to use the term adopted here in Chapter 2, in *exolinguistics.*

4. Byers's study is somewhat reminiscent of the study reported by the phonetician Rousselot (1891), who observed the phonetic changes occurring in a single family over a period of time.

5. Meader was a coauthor, with W. B. Pillsbury, of an early book on the psychology of language (Pillsbury and Meader, 1928); Muyskens is a physiologist.

6. Let us rephrase this as "deviation from the dialect of the listener," since dialect geography shows that there are numerous dialects of American English, no one of which could be called "general American."

7. In this paragraph, we are using *information* in the special sense defined by Shannon. See Chapter 7, p. 198.

8. The present writer would urge a slightly different interpretation. Higher-order approximations are easier to remember simply because they are more likely to contain higher-order units of linguistic structure and thus involve relatively fewer selection units.

9. Following the customary practice of linguists, we write phonemic representations of sounds between slant lines. A merely phonetic representation would be written within brackets, as in note 1 to Chapter 4 (p. 239).

10. This would be strikingly true for languages like Turkish, Hungarian, and Finnish which employ the principle of vowel harmony in word formation; the specification of the structural features of vowel harmony in these languages is a much simpler and more direct statement than that which would be obtained by application of the autocorrelation function.

11. It should be pointed out that this diagram, and the conception it represents, is not original with the writer, either in its specific form or in its general content. In its particular form, it was worked out by the members of a seminar in psychology and linguistics in the summer of 1951 at Cornell University. In its general content, it is similar to models presented by a number of other writers, including, to give only recent examples, Wendell Johnson (1946, p. 472), Ruesch and Bateson (1951), and Miller (1951a, Chapter 1). The only novelty, therefore, which may be claimed for the present

treatment is its attempt to identify and describe more fully the nature of each part of the channel as a whole.

12. In Chapter 2, it was suggested that lexicographical procedures can be extended to all linguistic forms and grammatical features. What is of interest here, however, is that by virtue of suggesting the general nature and distinctive features of the reinforcing stimuli for a linguistic item, the lexicographer is stating verbal equivalences. Lexicographers usually try to select verbal equivalences which appeal to elements of human experience that are likely to be common to the individuals who are to use the dictionary, thus enabling a person to learn the "meaning" of a new word purely on a verbal level. The reinforcing stimuli for a linguistic meaning can themselves be verbal stimuli which have been reinforced by still other verbal stimuli, and so on. Such a type of behavior sequence occurs not only when a person is using a dictionary, but also in a multitude of everyday situations. After all, most of our linguistic meanings were never acquired through the use of dictionaries.

13. It would be difficult to show that any linguistic response *as such* is innate or maturational in character. To be sure, Jakobson (1941) has suggested that in the child the various distinctive features of phonemes appear in a characteristic order; nevertheless, this is only to say that the physiological apparatus which makes speech possible matures in a certain developmental sequence. Another argument for the innate character of certain linguistic responses might be made from the phenomenon known as phonetic symbolism. Certain speech sounds appear to have an inherent semantic value; Sapir suggested that the sound [ī] connotes something small, while the sound [ū] connotes something big. It is often observed that many English words beginning with /sp/ connote something being emitted, as in *spit, spray,* etc. It is doubtful, however, whether any general phonetic symbolism exists across various linguistic families, and Sapir's (1929) and S. S. Newman's (1933) studies show at most only that it exists in an artificial experimental situation. Therefore, for this and other reasons, we reject any arguments based on phonetic symbolism.

14. For a somewhat comparable phenomenon in animal learning, we may refer to Skinner's (1948) observations on "superstition" in a pigeon. If a hungry pigeon is placed in an experimental cage and presented with food at regular intervals regardless of the pigeon's behavior, any movement the pigeon *happens* to make just prior to presentation of the food tends to become reinforced, and in later trials the response tends to appear more often, as if the pigeon had acquired the "superstition" that the response would get him food. Thus, a chance response acquires a "meaning" quite unconnected with its inherent nature.

15. Extended discussions of experimental work on thought and concept formation are to be found in reviews by Gibson and McGarvey (1937), Heidbreder (1948), D. M. Johnson (1950), and Vinacke (1951); in R. S. Woodworth's text *Experimental Psychology* (1938, Chap. 30), and in a recent text by Humphrey (1951b). Pre-twentieth-century ideas on language and thought have been reviewed by Mandell (1931).

16. Heidbreder's *Seven Psychologies* (1933) is a useful introduction to some of these psychological theories. For treatments of contemporary positions, see Helson (1951) and Marx (1951).

17. Wickens (1938) found that even when a person is conditioned to extend his finger to escape shock, this conditioning immediately transfers to a flexion movement of the finger to escape shock when the position of the hand is reversed in the apparatus.

The change of experimental conditions is analogous to a change in the environment of a phoneme, and the change in response is analogous to an allophonic variation.

NOTES TO CHAPTER 4

1. There are even suggestions that racial genetics and physical anthropology may have a bearing on linguistic problems. Van Ginneken (1927), for example, proposed that divergent phonetic changes in different subcultures might be accounted for by hereditary factors. Luchsinger (1940) and Tarnóczy (1947) are said to have established the genetic basis for individual differences in the articulatory mechanism. The geneticist Darlington (1947) has discovered a correlation between the frequency of genes for type-O blood in a culture and the presence of what he calls TH sounds (including, apparently, [θ, ð, tʰ, dʰ, tθ, dð] and similar sounds) in the language of the culture. He does not explain how blood grouping could be conceived to have any effect on speech sounds, but assumes that genetic factors in general could make for increased ease or difficulty in the articulation of certain phonetic elements, and hence could lead to preferences for the "easier" sounds. Darlington's results are sufficiently striking to suggest that they could not have occurred by chance; however, they could have occurred through the operation of a third variable, namely, the parallel distribution of linguistic and cultural traits. It is also quite possible that Darlington's classification of the phonetic data was too loose and hence subject to unconscious manipulation on the part of the investigator.

2. Various ethnolinguistic phenomena of this type have been surveyed by Thomas (1937, Chap. IV). Of particular interest is his account of how a Swedish personal pronoun fell from grace. The form *ni,* once a respectable form of address to the second person, acquired a pejorative connotation, with the result that a sentence like "Have you forgotten your cane?" had to be expressed by saying something like "Has Mr. Smith forgotten Mr. Smith's cane?" Circumlocution of this kind came to be so awkward that linguistic reformers seriously proposed that men of good will should wear buttons proclaiming *"Ni* is used here"!

3. This notion is also emphasized by Trager (1949) in his discussion of metalinguistics; see Chapter 2, however, for certain reservations that may be made.

4. Malinowski's objections to linguistic analysis were ill-founded. He confused different levels of analysis, appearing impatient to get to "sociological interpretations" before he had quite grasped the significance of the linguistic structure as such. His essentially antilinguistic position is belied by the fact that the major outlines of a language structure can emerge, through suitable techniques of analysis, even where only the barest reference is made to the specific nonlinguistic traits of the culture. His careless handling of linguistics is illustrated by his claim (1936) that primitive grammatical categories are less precise than those of civilized languages; this is patently an overstatement.

Malinowski's views on meaning are unanswerable because he established his own definition of meaning—but a definition which leads to a vicious particularism in which every utterance must be treated, as it were, by a clinical method which leaves no room for generalization. (One can imagine that he would reject the theory of meaning presented in Chapter 3.) Furthermore, his insistent assertions about the importance of "situational context" do not, on scrutiny, turn out to have much heuristic value. The following is, I think, a fair example of his technique:

At one point in his *Coral Gardens and Their Magic* (1935, Vol. 2, p. 37), he makes much of the fact that a "literal rendering" of a certain utterance can be given a highly

NOTES

meaningful "free translation" only when one is aware of the "contextual specification of meaning." Thus, the "literal rendering"

'Informant's father in child his he see'

becomes, surprisingly,

'Molubabeba in his childhood witnessed a famine.'

This remarkable transformation becomes commonplace, even ridiculous, when we turn back to page 23 and find that the original utterance was a response to Malinowski's asking a group of informants whether any of them had experienced a bad famine. One of the informants had simply replied, in effect, "Molubabeba saw one in his childhood":

Molubabeba	o	gwadi-la	i-gise
(informant's father)	in	child his	he see

It is difficult to see how a descriptive linguist would have had any trouble with this; "contextual specification of meaning" proves to be little more than specification of grammatical antecedents and the satisfaction of mandatory linguistic rules in the language of translation. Note also that Malinowski's literal rendering was not really literal when it supplied "informant's father."

5. See the discussion of Kurath's work, on page 59.

6. In Odum's (1951) history of American sociology, one looks in vain for any reference to sociological studies of language. Linton, in his preface to *The Science of Man in the World Crisis* (a survey of the contributions of various social sciences), has this to say: "That linguistics ultimately will be of great value for the understanding of human behavior and especially of human thought processes can hardly be doubted. However, work along these lines has hardly begun and linguistics is still unable to make any great contribution toward the solution of our present problems" (1945, p. 8). One standard text in sociology which reveals an unusual awareness of the place of language and communication as a societal process is that of Lundberg (1939); however, it contains no citations of specific researches in this area. The task of pointing out the detailed implications of linguistic phenomena in social processes has thus devolved mainly upon linguists and other students of language, such as Schlauch (1942, especially Chap. 10), Lewis (1947), and Bodmer (1944).

7. See, for example, Partridge's *Dictionary of Slang and Unconventional English* (1949) and *Dictionary of the Underworld; British and American; 16th–20th Centuries* (1950), or even a *Dictionary of American Underworld Lingo* compiled with the aid of former convicts (Goldin, O'Leary, and Lipsius, 1950). None of these works are by technical linguists.

8. A fairly recent reference guide to this field has been prepared by Smith, Lasswell, and Casey (1946).

9. Miller's paper is now available in print (1950).

10. A textbook of linguistics specially designed to meet the needs of missionaries has been prepared by Dean Pittman (1948). Its concluding chapters discuss methods of teaching natives to read and problems met in translating the Bible. See, however, a review of this book by Hodge (1950).

11. One of the most active participants in world literacy programs has been Frank C. Laubach; he has published several books on his methods and experiences (1938, 1943).

12. At a UNESCO-sponsored conference in Paris, it was proposed that French and English be established as the two world auxiliary languages (Hart, 1947).

13. Guérard (1922) has written a useful history of the international-language movement. Some contemporary viewpoints are described by Jacob (1947, 1948); see also a review by McQuown (1950).

14. IALA has recently become affiliated with Barnard College as an Institute. An Interlingua dictionary has been published by IALA (1951), and also a grammar (Gode and Blair, 1951).

15. The work was directed by Thorndike and carried out chiefly by Dr. Laura H. V. Kennon. The reference is cited under Division of Psychology, Institute of Educational Research, Teachers College, Columbia University (1933).

16. The operators are *come, get, give, go, keep, let, make, put, seem, take, be, do, have, say, see, send, may, will*. It should be understood that these are used with their normal English inflections.

17. For a detailed discussion on this point, see Walsh (1933).

18. Already I. A. Richards (1942b) has used such a modified form of Basic in his translation of Plato's *Republic*.

NOTES TO CHAPTER 5

1. A summary of Peirce's formulations has been given by Ogden and Richards (1936, Appendix D), to whom several unpublished writings by Peirce were available. There is also a much neglected work by an early American philosopher of language, Alexander Bryan Johnson. This work, first published in 1828, has now been reissued with a critical appraisal by Rynin (A. B. Johnson, 1828).

2. The philosopher John Dewey (1946) has called attention to the possibility that Morris has misinterpreted Peirce's formulation of *semantics*. According to Dewey, Peirce understood semantics to be the study of the relations of equivalent or mutually substitutable signs.

3. H. G. Alexander (1936, 1937) has pointed to some linguistic difficulties in metaphysics, but offers hope that through linguistic analysis a certain degree of metaphysical truth can be achieved by seeing the world from many perspectives. Our review of issues to which a philosophy of language is germane might also extend to questions of ethical values; C. L. Stevenson (1944) has pointed to the semantic components of ethical terms, particularly in respect to their emotive connotations.

4. In 1940, Cassirer came to America, where he exerted considerable influence on philosophical thought. His more recent views on language and symbolism are exemplified in several articles (1945, 1946a) and a book, *Language and Myth* (1946b).

5. For example, Rosenbloom (1950) has a chapter devoted to logical "languages" and their "sentences" in his introduction to mathematical logic.

6. This appears to be the emphasis in several works of Bentley (1932, 1935) and from another standpoint, in the work of Max Black (1949). For a psychological view, see Kantor (1945–50).

NOTES TO CHAPTER 6

1. Committee on the Objectives of a General Education in a Free Society (1946).

2. Quoted from Dora V. Smith, "English Grammar Again," in *English Journal* 27 (1938), p. 647.

3. Integrated treatments of linguistics and related studies as applied in the teaching of English and the language arts may be found in several brochures prepared for the

Modern Language Association (Fries, Sale, and Zeydel, 1940; Pollock *et al.,* 1945; and Lowry *et al.,* 1943).

4. We are not speaking here of the nursery and kindergarten years, but it must be emphasized that these years provide enormous scope for early steps in communication skills, for example, vocabulary building, and the encouragement of speaking and listening skills.

5. For an example of a modern viewpoint, see Strickland (1951).

6. See his introduction to Wilson's *The Miraculous Birth of Language* (1948).

7. Further information on modern educational practices in the teaching of reading may be found in Brickman's review (1950b) and in books and articles by Watts (1947), Witty (1949), and Russell (1949). The psychology of reading has been given a thorough treatment by Anderson and Dearborn (1952). Remedial reading is a particularly challenging field for psycholinguistic research. Reading retardation does not seem to result solely from poor teaching techniques or even always from deficiencies in language symbolization. Hinshelwood (1917) and Cobb (1943) are among psychiatrists who have pointed to neurological and cerebral factors in dyslexia. W. S. Gray (1922) and Monroe (1932) have made extensive case studies and have suggested various kinds of retraining techniques. Eames (1949) has reviewed studies of visual and other physical factors in retarded reading. Tachistoscopic methods of pacing the act of reading by controlling eye movements have been avidly seized upon by many teachers, but they have not been found to be consistently effective. It was early pointed out by Sisson (1937) that poor eye movements may be a result rather than a cause of poor reading habits. Nevertheless, the work of Dearborn and Anderson (1937), using film-projection techniques, is of interest in connection with the role of linguistic units (phrases) in the process of reading. Studies illustrating the complexity of the tasks which research workers face in the field of reading are those by Potter (1949), Rossignol (1949), and Ewers (1950).

8. See, for example, Leonard's (1929) excellent commentary on eighteenth-century views of correctness in English usage. An up-to-date treatment of teaching English usage is Pooley's (1946) book on the subject.

9. Several recent discussions of the problem of correctness do not show a full appreciation of its complexity. For example, Lloyd (1951) rests his case on usage, without explaining why usage should be a criterion and without alluding to the problem of meaning and the efficiency of communication. In the light of Barzun's (1951) rejoinder, Lloyd's arguments fail to be completely convincing. The unreasoned appeal to usage is merely authoritarianism with a new twist.

10. Seashore and Eckerson's (1940) results show that average vocabularies of college students may reach considerably beyond 100,000 items.

11. A discussion of the reasons for the unsatisfactory educational achievements of children leaving school would be much too complicated for the present work. Many failures may perhaps be written off to constitutional differences in mental ability, but this is a counsel of despair—except to suggest that teaching is often directed far above the student's ability. The work of Davis and his associates (1951) gives some reason to believe that difficulties in schooling are due to cultural factors whereby children of lower social status do not get a proper motivation for academic work and lack a suitable linguistic milieu for succeeding in the kind of language study to which they are exposed in school.

12. For an annotated bibliography on readability formulae, see Hotchkiss and Paterson (1950).

13. I may be pardoned for relating my own experiences as a student, as offering some light on the desirability of teaching something of linguistic science fairly early in the educational program. With a strong natural interest in language, even in high-school days I started self-study of a number of languages not ordinarily taught in school. It was also my good fortune at that time to become acquainted with Benjamin Lee Whorf, and through him to be introduced to the marvels of languages like Nahuatl and Maya, as well as to general works like Sapir's *Language* (1921). All of this was done on a highly informal basis—perhaps it was better done in that way. Nevertheless, I should have welcomed more formal instruction in the study of language than I was able to get from the courses in English, Latin, and Greek which I had at high school. At the time, also, few if any colleges and universities offered courses in general linguistics at the undergraduate level.

14. A number of educators (for example, Marckwardt, 1951) have raised doubts as to whether integrated "communications" courses can accomplish anything more than what can be accomplished in a more traditional organization of courses. The teachers of such courses will have to face not only the problems which always arise in language-arts courses, but also a new set of difficulties arising from efforts in integration.

15. A comprehensive bibliography on speech education, including speech pathology and correction, has been prepared by Thonssen and Fatherson (1939; with supplement, 1950). Representative texts, at least for the college level, are those by Gray and Wise (1934; revised edition, 1946) and Baird and Knower (1949). Knower (1951) has indexed the principal journals in the field, the *Quarterly Journal of Speech* and *Speech Monographs*. There is also the *Journal of Speech and Hearing Disorders* and a new journal, *Journal of Communication,* which publish articles relevant to speech education. Gilkinson's (1943) bibliography is useful for locating research studies.

16. It might be added that Ogden and Richards's treatment of the symbolic character of perception deserves renewed attention from psychologists.

17. Among semipopularized treatments of semantics which were influenced by the writings of Ogden and Richards one may cite books by Huse (1933) and Walpole (1941), not to mention the best-seller by Chase (1938).

18. Ogden and Richards do not use even the term semantics, let alone the phrase *general semantics.* Morris (1938, 1946), whose interest in problems of meaning is chiefly philosophical rather than educational, employs the term *semantics* in connection with only one aspect of *semeiotic,* the general science of sign systems. Allen Walker Read (1948) has furnished an account of the various connections in which the word *semantics* has been used.

19. It is hard to find any rigorous evaluation of general semantics in all its aspects. Jeanette Anderson's (1943) tirade is too charged with emotion to be taken seriously. Dunham (1947) expresses doubts as to whether a knowledge of semantic principles can really help one avoid falling into errors of thought and interpretation. Kenneth Burke (1945) and Max Black (1949) find themselves disturbed about the epistemological foundations of general semantics.

20. On this point, see my review (1947) of Wendell Johnson's *People in Quandaries.*

21. To mention only a few works published in the present century, we may cite publications of Sweet (1900), Viëtor (1902), Jespersen (1904), Palmer (1917), West (1926), Huse (1931), and Stott (1946). A series of annotated bibliographies on the subject, initiated by Buchanan and McPhee (1928), has been continued by Coleman and Fife (1933, 1938, 1949) to provide coverage up to the year 1942. Literature since that

NOTES

time has been covered in reviews by Rice (1946), Brickman (1950a), and Carroll and Richards (1952).

22. The conduct of the ASTP language courses has been described and appraised by Agard *et al.* (1944), Angiolillo (1947), and Matthew (1947).

23. Since some of these manuals were not particularly well graded in difficulty and were defective in certain other respects, efforts were made to replace them with improved materials.

24. The report of this committee has been published; in the bibliography it is referenced under Modern Language Journal (1950).

25. In fact, this is the only point at which Basic English necessarily figures in a description of Richards and Gibson's current methods. In their use of Basic English for teaching purposes, they have considerably relaxed Ogden's original strictures about the verb system, admitting to full status as verbs numerous words suggested by other parts of the Basic word list, and even going outside the Basic vocabulary to find useful items.

26. The use of factor analysis theory in the construction of aptitude tests has been reviewed by Wolfle (1940), Guilford (1948), and Carroll and Schweiker (1951).

27. The foreign-language aptitude tests of the Iowa Placement Examinations have been widely used. One of the subtests, which requires the subject to learn a bit of Esperanto, would appear to be a test of some special linguistic aptitude, but in the light of factorial studies of tests of this type it is now certain that it measures nothing more than one or two of the factors of general intelligence, probably reasoning and memory factors.

NOTES TO CHAPTER 7

1. It should be said, however, that current U.S. usage restricts the term *human engineering* to the art of designing machines and systems of machines in order that they can be more efficiently used by human beings in view of human capacities and limitations.

2. Communication theory is not without historical antecedents. Gilchrist (1951) points to a passage (pp. 166–169 of the Blackwell 1941 edition) in Jonathan Swift's *Gulliver's Travels* which describes an imaginary machine for constructing prose by using what communication theorists would now call the statistical structure of the language. To speak on a more serious plane, I may mention an article by the Scottish philosopher and logician Alexander Macfarlane, which I happened to come across in an early volume of the *Proceedings of the Royal Society of Edinburgh* (Macfarlane, 1878–80). In proposing a type of binary coding system and considering its efficiency as compared with that of Morse code, Macfarlane employed a line of thought which clearly foreshadowed contemporary communication theory.

The Russian mathematician A. A. Markov, who developed the mathematical theory of stochastic processes which has been turned to use in modern communication theory, studied the statistical dependencies in a Russian text of 20,000 letters (1913).

Some other historical antecedents of communication theory are reviewed by the British physicist E. Colin Cherry (1951).

3. In Chapter 3, we noted that the hierarchical structure of behavior makes it resistant to the application of the theory of stochastic processes when the analysis must

be based on units of a given order. There is need for the development of a theory of stochastic processes which will show relations between units of different orders.

4. We use the term *random process* in the statistical sense: a random process is the sampling at random from a population of *potential* events.

5. We have reference here to the Sonagraph produced commercially by the Kay Electric Company.

6. Since this was written, such a device has been constructed by Davis, Biddulph, and Balashek (1952) of the Bell Telephone Laboratories in connection with a machine for the automatic recognition of spoken English digits; motion pictures showing the operation of this device were presented at the Speech Analysis Conference, June 1952, at the Massachusetts Institute of Technology.

7. Nevertheless, the recent development of the transistor (Rockett, 1948) promises a reduction in the size of computing machines.

NOTES TO CHAPTER 8

1. It should also be noted that the recent growth of the field of linguistics and the increasing numbers of persons seeking special training in it has prompted the University of Michigan to establish a summer Linguistic Program somewhat similar to the Linguistic Institute. It is possible that the need will eventually become great enough to justify the establishment of summer linguistic programs at still other universities.

2. For a more detailed account of the Linguistic Institute, see the report of a special committee of the LSA concerning it, *Supplement to Language (Bulletin No. 13)*, 1940, 16, No. 1, 83–101.

3. At this writing, bibliographies for the years 1948 and 1949 are available. One should also mention the bibliographies on general linguistics which have appeared annually in the German periodical *Indogermanisches Jahrbuch*.

4. Several individuals, including the present writer, have been regularly contributing abstracts on linguistics, linguistic psychology, communication theory, and related topics.

NOTE TO CHAPTER 9

1. See the present writer's report on a seminar held at Cornell University in the summer of 1951 (Carroll, 1951).

REFERENCES

The date given in parentheses is the reference date used in the text. Where the citation contains two dates, the reference date is generally that of the first edition. Dates suffixed by –a, –b, etc., are used to distinguish between publications of an author in the same year.

Adams, Sidney, and F. F. Powers (1929), "The psychology of language," *Psychological Bulletin* 26: 241–260.

Agard, Frederick B. (1949), "The Cornell language program," *Hispania* 32: 27–34.

——Robert J. Clements, William S. Hendrix, *et al.* (1944), *A survey of language classes in the Army Specialized Training Program.* New York: Commission on Trends in Education of the Modern Language Association of America. 27 p.

——and Harold B. Dunkel (1948), *An investigation of second-language teaching.* Boston: Ginn. vii, 344 p.

Alexander, Hubert G. (1936), "Linguistic morphology in relation to thinking," *Journal of Philosophy* 33: 261–269.

——(1937), "Language and metaphysical truth," *Journal of Philosophy* 34: 645–652.

Allport, Floyd H. (1924), *Social psychology.* Boston: Houghton Mifflin. xiv, 453 p.

American Classical League (1924–25), *The classical investigation.* Princeton: Princeton University Press. Part I: 305 p.; Part III: 203 p. [Part II unpublished.]

Anderson, Irving H., and Walter F. Dearborn (1952), *The psychology of teaching reading.* New York: Ronald Press. x, 382 p.

Anderson, Jeanette (1943), "A critique of general semantics: 'Two times two is the same for everybody. But one never is—,'" *Quarterly Journal of Speech* 29: 187–195.

Angiolillo, Paul F. (1947), *Armed forces foreign language teaching; critical evaluation and implications.* New York: S. F. Vanni. 440 p.

Arsenian, Seth (1945), "Bilingualism in the post-war world," *Psychological Bulletin* 42: 65–86.

Ayer, A. J. (1936), *Language, truth and logic.* New York: Oxford University Press. 254 p.

Baird, A. Craig, and Franklin H. Knower (1949), *General speech; an introduction.* New York: McGraw-Hill. ix, 500 p.

Bales, Robert F. (1950), *Interaction process analysis.* Cambridge: Addison-Wesley Press. xi, 203 p.

Barzun, Jacques (1951), "The retort circumstantial," *American Scholar* 20: 289–293.

Basson, A. H., and D. J. O'Connor (1947), "Language and philosophy; some suggestions for an empirical approach," *Philosophy* 22: 49–65.

Baudouin de Courtenay, Jan (1929), *Einfluss der Sprache auf Weltanschauung und Stimmung.* Warsaw. 71 p.

Baugh, Albert C. (1935), *A history of the English language.* New York and London: Appleton-Century. xiv, 509 p.

Bavelas, Alex (1950), "Communication patterns in task-oriented groups," *Journal of the Acoustical Society of America* 22: 725–730.

Bentley, Arthur F. (1932), *Linguistic analysis of mathematics.* Bloomington, Indiana: Principia Press. xii, 315 p.

————(1935), *Behavior, knowledge, fact.* Bloomington, Indiana: Principia Press. xii, 391 p.

Berkeley, Edmund C. (1949), *Giant brains, or machines that think.* New York: Wiley. xvi, 270 p.

Bertoni, G., and M. G. Bartoli (1925), *Breviario di neolinguistica.* Modena: Società Tipographica Modenese. 126 p.

Birdwhistell, Ray L. (1952), *Introduction to kinesics: an annotation system for analysis of body motion and gesture.* Washington, D. C.: Foreign Service Institute, Department of State. 75 p.

Black, John W. (1946), "Effects of voice communication training," *Speech Monographs* 13: 64–68.

Black, Max (1949), *Language and philosophy; Studies in method.* Ithaca: Cornell University Press. xiii, 264 p.

Bloch, Bernard (1948), "A set of postulates for phonemic analysis," *Language* 24: 3–46.

————(1949), "Leonard Bloomfield [an obituary]," *Language* 25: 87–98.

————and George L. Trager (1942), *Outline of linguistic analysis.* Baltimore: Linguistic Society of America. 82 p.

Bloomfield, Leonard (1914), *Introduction to the study of language.* New York: Holt. x, 335 p.

————(1925), "Why a linguistic society?" *Language* 1: 1–5.

————(1933), *Language.* New York: Holt. ix, 564 p.

————(1939), *Linguistic aspects of science.* Chicago: University of Chicago Press. viii, 59 p. (*International Encyclopedia of Unified Science,* Vol. 1, No. 4.)

————(1942a), "Linguistics and reading," *Elementary English Review* 19: 125–130, 183–186.

————(1942b), *Outline guide for the practical study of foreign languages.* Baltimore: Linguistic Society of America. 16 p.

————(1944), "Secondary and tertiary responses to language," *Language* 20: 45–55.

————(1946), "Twenty-one years of the Linguistic Society," *Language* 22: 1–3.

Boas, Franz (ed.) (1911–22), *Handbook of American Indian languages* (Parts 1 and 2). Washington, D. C.: Government Printing Office. (*Bulletin 40, Bureau of American Ethnology, Smithsonian Institution.*)

————(ed.) (1933–38), *Handbook of American Indian languages* (Part 3). New York: J. J. Augustin, Inc. x, 707 p.

————(ed.) (1938), *General anthropology.* Boston: Heath. 792 p.

Bode, Hendrik, Frederick Mosteller, John Tukey, and Charles Winsor (1949), "The education of a scientific generalist," *Science* 109: 553–558.

Boder, David P. (1940), "The adjective-verb quotient: a contribution to the psychology of language," *Psychological Record* 3: 310–343.

Bodmer, Frederick (1944), *The loom of language* (Lancelot Hogben, ed.). New York: Norton. 692 p.

Böhtlingk, Otto (trans. and ed.) (1887), *Pānini's Grammatik.* Leipzig: Haessel.

Bogatyrev, P. (1937), "Funkcie kroja na Marovskom Slovensku [Functions of folk costume in Moravian Slovakia]," *Spisy Národopisneho Odboru Matice Slovenskej, I.*

Bolinger, Dwight L. (1946), "Visual morphemes," *Language* 22: 333–340.

Bond, Guy L. (1935), *Auditory and speech characteristics of poor readers.* New York: Columbia University, Teachers College, Bureau of Publications. 48 p. (*Contributions to Education,* No. 657.)

REFERENCES

Bonfante, Giuliano (1947), "The neolinguistic position," *Language* 23: 344–375.

Bopp, Franz (1816), *Über das Conjugationssystem der Sanskritsprache.* Frankfurt-am-Main.

Boring, Edwin G. (1946), "Mind and mechanism," *American Journal of Psychology* 54: 173–192.

———(1950), *A history of experimental psychology.* (2nd ed.) New York: Appleton-Century-Crofts. xxi, 777 p.

Bossard, James H. S. (1943), "Family table talk—an area for sociological study," *American Sociological Review* 8: 295–301.

———(1945), "Family modes of expression," *American Sociological Review* 10: 226–237.

———Eleanor S. Boll, and Winogene P. Sanger (1950), "Some neglected areas in family-life study," *Annals of the American Academy of Political and Social Science* 272: 68–76.

Bousfield, W. A., and C. H. W. Sedgewick (1944), "An analysis of sequences of restricted associative responses," *Journal of General Psychology* 30: 149–165.

Brickman, William W. (1950a), "Instruction in foreign languages," *School and Society* 71: 53–60.

———(1950b), "The teaching of reading," *School and Society* 71: 387–394.

Brugmann, Karl, and B. Delbrück (1886–1900), *Grundriss der vergleichenden Grammatik der indogermanischen Sprachen.* (2nd ed., 1897–1911) Strassburg: Trübner.

Buchanan, Milton A., and E. D. McPhee (1928), *An annotated bibliography of modern language methodology.* Toronto: University of Toronto Press. 428 p. (*Publications of the American and Canadian Committees on Modern Languages,* Vol. 8.)

Buck, Carl Darling (1949), *A dictionary of selected synonyms in the principal Indo-European languages; a contribution to the history of ideas.* Chicago: University of Chicago Press. xix, 1515 p.

Bull, William E. (1948), "Natural frequency and word counts; the fallacy of frequencies," *Classical Journal* 44: 469–484.

Burke, Kenneth (1945), *A grammar of motives.* New York: Prentice-Hall. xxiii, 530 p.

Byers, Burton H. (1947), "Regional speech differences in veterans and non-veterans," *Quarterly Journal of Speech* 33: 312–313.

Campbell, Douglas G. (1937), "General semantics: implications of linguistic revision for theoretical and clinical neuro-psychiatry," *American Journal of Psychiatry* 93: 769–807.

Carnap, Rudolf (1928), *Der logische Aufbau der Welt.* Berlin-Schlachtensee: Weltkreis Verlag. xi, 290 p.

Carroll, John B. (1938), "Diversity of vocabulary and the harmonic series law of word-frequency distribution," *Psychological Record* 2: 379–386.

———(1939), "Determining and numerating adjectives in children's speech," *Child Development* 10: 215–229.

———(1941), "A factor analysis of verbal abilities," *Psychometrika* 6: 279–307.

———(1944), "The analysis of verbal behavior," *Psychological Review* 51: 102–119.

———(1947), [Review of Wendell Johnson's *People in Quandaries*] *Journal of Abnormal & Social Psychology* 42: 144–146.

———(1951), "The interdisciplinary summer seminar on linguistics and psychology," *Social Science Research Council Items* 5: 40–42.

REFERENCES

————and S. Earle Richards (1952), "Instruction in foreign languages," *Review of Educational Research* 22: 116–135.

————and Robert F. Schweiker (1951), "Factor analysis in educational research," *Review of Educational Research* 21: 368–388.

Cassirer, Ernst (1923), *Philosophie der symbolischen Formen. Ier. Teil: Die Sprache.* Berlin: Bruno Cassirer Verlag. xii, 293 p.

————(1945), "Structuralism in modern linguistics," *Word* 1: 99–120.

————(1946a), "L'influence du langage sur le développement de la pensée dans les sciences de la nature," *Journal de Psychologie normale et pathologique* 39: 129–152.

————(1946b), *Language and myth* (trans. by S. K. Langer). New York: Harper. x, 103 p.

Castiglione, Salvatore J. (ed.) (1952), "Report of the third annual round table meeting on linguistics and language teaching," *Georgetown University Monograph Series on Linguistics and Language Teaching,* No. 2. v, 105 p.

Chase, Stuart (1938), *The tyranny of words.* New York: Harcourt, Brace. xiv, 396 p.

Cherry, E. Colin (1951), "A history of the theory of information," *Proceedings of the [British] Institution of Electrical Engineers* 98: Part III, No. 55.

Chisholm, Francis P. (1947), *Introductory lectures on general semantics.* Lakeville, Conn.: Institute of General Semantics. v, 126 p.

————(1949), Editorial: "Report of the retiring president, International Society for General Semantics," *Etc., A Review of General Semantics* 7: 38–43.

Chotlos, J. W. (1944), "Studies in language behavior. IV. A statistical and comparative analysis of individual written language samples," *Psychological Monographs* 56: 77–111.

Cobb, Stanley (1943), *Borderlands of psychiatry.* Cambridge: Harvard University Press. xiv, 166 p. (*Harvard University Monographs in Medicine and Public Health,* No. 4.)

Cofer, Charles N. (1951), "Verbal behavior in relation to reasoning and values," pp. 206–217 in Harold Guetzkow (ed.), *Groups, leadership and men.* Pittsburgh: Carnegie Press.

Coleman, Algernon (1929), *Teaching of modern foreign languages in the United States.* New York: Macmillan. 299 p.

————(1933), *An analytical bibliography of modern language teaching, 1927–1932.* Chicago: University of Chicago Press. xiii, 296 p.

————(1938), *An analytical bibliography of modern language teaching, Vol. II (1932–1937).* Chicago: University of Chicago Press. xviii, 561 p.

————and Robert H. Fife (1949), *An analytical bibliography of modern language teaching, Vol. III (1937–1942).* New York: King's Crown Press, Columbia University. xiii, 549 p.

Collinson, William Edward (1937), "Indication; a study of demonstratives, articles, and other 'indicaters,' " *Language Monographs,* No. 17. 128 p.

Comité International Permanent des Linguistes (1949–50), *Bibliographie linguistique des années 1939–1947.* Utrecht and Brussels: Uitgeverij Het Spectrum. 2 vols.

Committee on the Function of English in General Education, Commission on Secondary School Curriculum, Progressive Education Association (1940), *Language in general education.* New York: Appleton-Century. xii, 226 p.

REFERENCES

Committee on the Objectives of a General Education in a Free Society (1946), *General education in a free society*. Cambridge: Harvard University Press. xix, 267 p.

Condon, E. U. (1928), "Statistics of vocabulary," *Science* 67: 300.

Cowan, J Milton (1947), "The Cornell plan of language teaching," *Hispania* 30: 57–60.

Critchley, M. (1939), *The language of gesture*. London and New York: Edward Arnold, Longmans Green. 128 p.

Dale, Edgar, and J. S. Chall (1948), "A formula for predicting readability," *Educational Research Bulletin* 27: 11–20.

Darlington, Cyril P. (1947), "The genetic component of language," *Heredity, An International Journal of Genetics* 1: 269–286.

Davis, Allison, Kenneth Eells, Robert J. Havighurst, Virgil Herrick, and Ralph W. Tyler (1951), *Intelligence and cultural differences*. Chicago: University of Chicago Press. 396 p.

Davis, K. H., R. Biddulph, and S. Balashek (1952), "Automatic recognition of spoken digits," *Journal of the Acoustical Society of America* 24: 637–642.

Dearborn, Walter F., and I. H. Anderson (1937), "A new method for teaching phrasing and for increasing the size of reading fixations," *Psychological Record* 1: 459–475.

Deemer, Walter L., and Phillip J. Rulon (1942), *An experimental comparison of two shorthand systems*. Cambridge: Harvard University Press. xiii, 294 p. (*Harvard Studies in Education*, Vol. 28.)

DeFrancis, John (ed.) (1951), "Report on the second annual round table meeting on linguistics and language teaching," *Georgetown University Monograph Series on Languages and Linguistics*, No. 1. vii, 91 p.

DeLaguna, Grace (1927), *Speech: its function and development*. New Haven: Yale University Press. xii, 363 p.

Delattre, Pierre (1947), "A technique of aural-oral approach; report on a University of Oklahoma experiment in teaching French," *French Review* 20: 238–250, 311–324.

——(1951), "The physiological interpretation of sound spectrograms," *Publications of the Modern Language Association* 66: 864–875.

de Saussure, Ferdinand (1916), *Cours de linguistique générale* (3rd ed.). Paris: Payot, 1931. 331 p.

Dewey, Godfrey (1923), *Relativ frequency of English speech sounds*. Cambridge: Harvard University Press. xii, 148 p. (*Harvard Studies in Education*, Vol. IV.)

Dewey, John (1946), "Peirce's theory of linguistic signs, thought, and meaning," *Journal of Philosophy* 43: 85–95.

Dieth, Eugen (1950), *Vademekum der Phonetik; phonetische Grundlagen für das wissenschaftliche und praktische Studium der Sprachen*. Berne: A. Francke AG. xv, 452 p.

Diringer, David (1948), *The alphabet, a key to the history of mankind*. New York: Philosophical Library. xii, 607 p.

Division of Psychology, Institute of Educational Research, Teachers College, Columbia University (1933), *Language learning; Summary of a report to the International Auxiliary Language Association in the United States, Incorporated*. New York: Bureau of Publications, Teachers College, Columbia University. viii, 59 p.

Dollard, John, and Neal E. Miller (1950), *Personality and psychotherapy; an analysis in terms of learning, thinking, and culture*. New York: McGraw-Hill. xiii, 488 p.

Dreyfus-Graf, Jean (1950), "Sonograph and sound mechanics," *Journal of the Acoustical Society of America* 22: 731–739.

Dunham, Barrows (1947), *Man against myth*. Boston: Little-Brown. xv, 320 p.

Dunkel, Harold B. (1948), *Second-language learning*. Boston: Ginn. vi, 218 p.

Dunn, H. K. (1950), "Calculation of vowel resonances, and an electrical vocal tract," *Journal of the Acoustical Society of America* 22: 740–753.

Eames, Thomas Harrison (1949), "Visual and related factors in reading," *Review of Educational Research* 19: 107–117.

Eaton, Helen S. (1940), *Semantic frequency list for English, French, German, and Spanish; a correlation of the first six thousand words in four single-language frequency lists*. Chicago: University of Chicago Press. xxi, 440 p.

Edwards, Jonathan (1788), *Observations on the language of the Muhhekaneew Indians*. New Haven, Conn.

Efron, David (1941), *Gesture and environment; a tentative study of some of the spatio-temporal and "linguistic" aspects of the gestural behavior of eastern Jews and southern Italians in New York City, living under similar as well as different environmental conditions*. New York: King's Crown Press. x, 184 p.

Eisenson, Jon (1938), *The psychology of speech*. New York: Crofts. xiii, 280 p.

Esper, Erwin Allen (1921), "The psychology of language," *Psychological Bulletin* 18: 490–496.

————(1925), "A technique for the experimental investigation of associative interference in artificial linguistic material," *Language Monographs*, No. 1. 47 p.

————(1933), "Studies in linguistic behavior organization: I. Characteristics of unstable verbal reactions," *Journal of General Psychology* 8: 346–381.

————(1935), "Language," pp. 417–460 in C. Murchison (ed.), *A handbook of social psychology*. Worcester, Mass.: Clark University Press.

Ewers, Dorothea W. F. (1950), "Relations between auditory abilities and reading abilities: a problem in psychometrics," *Journal of Experimental Education* 18: 239–262.

Fairbanks, Gordon H., Helen E. Shadick, and Zulefa Yedigar (1951), *A Russian area reader for college classes*. New York: Ronald Press. v, 204 p.

Fairbanks, Grant, and Wilbert Pronovost (1939), "An experimental study of the pitch characteristics of the voice during the expression of emotions," *Speech Monographs* 6: 87–104.

Fairbanks, Helen (1944), "Quantitative differentiation of samples of spoken language," *Psychological Monographs* 56: No. 2, 19–28.

Fendrick, Paul (1935), *Visual characteristics of poor readers*. New York: Columbia University, Teachers College, Bureau of Publications. 54 p. (*Contributions to Education* No. 656.)

Fife, R. H. (compiler) (1931), *Summary of reports of the modern foreign languages*. New York: Macmillan. 261 p. (*Publications of the American and Canadian Committees on Modern Languages*, Vol. 18.)

Finck, Franz N. (1910), *Die Haupttypen des Sprachbaus*. Leipzig: Teubner. v, 156 p.

Firth, John R. (1937), *The tongues of men*. London: Watts. vii, 160 p.

Fitts, Paul M. (1951), *Human engineering for an effective air-navigation and traffic-control system*. Washington, D. C.: Committee on Aviation Psychology, Division of Anthropology and Psychology, National Research Council. xx, 84 p.

Flesch, Rudolf (1949), *The art of readable writing*. New York: Harper. 237 p.

Fletcher, Harvey (1929), *Speech and hearing*. New York: Van Nostrand. xv, 331 p.

REFERENCES

Flew, Antony G. N. (ed.) (1951), *Essays on logic and language*. New York: Philosophical Library. vii, 206 p.

Foerster, Norman (1941), *Literary scholarship, its aims and methods*. Chapel Hill: University of North Carolina Press. ix, 269 p.

Fortune Magazine (1944), "Science comes to languages," *Fortune* 30: 133–135, 236–240.

Fowler, Henry W. (1926), *A dictionary of modern English usage*. Oxford: Clarendon Press. viii, 742 p.

French, John W. (1951), *The description of aptitude and achievement tests in terms of rotated factors*. Chicago: University of Chicago Press. x, 278 p. (*Psychometric Monograph No. 5*.)

Fries, Charles C. (1940), *American English Grammar; the grammatical structure of present-day English with especial reference to social differences of class dialects*. New York: Appleton-Century. xii, 314 p.

——(1945), *Teaching and learning English as a foreign language*. Ann Arbor: University of Michigan Press. vii, 153 p. (*Publications of the English Language Institute, University of Michigan, No. 1*.)

——(1952), *The structure of English; an introduction to the construction of English sentences*. New York: Harcourt, Brace. ix, 304 p.

——with the coöperation of W. M. Sale and Edwin H. Zeydel (1940), *Language study in American education*. New York: Commission on Trends in Education of the Modern Language Association of America. 40 p.

——and Aileen A. Traver (1940), *English word lists; a study of their adaptability for instruction*. Washington, D. C.: American Council on Education. ix, 109 p.

Gabelentz, G. von der (1891), *Die Sprachwissenschaft; ihre Aufgaben, Methoden, und bisherige Ergebnisse*. Leipzig: Weigel. xx, 502 p.

Gardiner, A. H. (1932), *The theory of speech and language*. Oxford: Clarendon Press. x, 332 p.

Garvin, Paul L. (1948), "Esquisse du système phonologique du Nambikwara-Tarunde," *Journal de la Société des Américanistes* 37: 133–189.

Gelb, Ignace J. (1952), *A study of writing*. Chicago: University of Chicago Press. 298 p.

Gibson, Eleanor J., and H. R. McGarvey (1937), "Experimental studies of thought and reasoning," *Psychological Bulletin* 34: 327–350.

Gilchrist, J. C. (1951), "Communications theory: an historical note," *American Psychologist* 6: 689–690.

Gilkinson, Howard (1943), *Outlines of research in general speech*. Minneapolis: Burgess. ii, 80 p.

——and Franklin H. Knower (1940), "Individual differences among students of speech as revealed by psychological tests," *Quarterly Journal of Speech* 26: 243–255.

Gilliéron, J. L., and E. Edmont (1902–10), *Atlas linguistique de France*. Paris: Champion. (35 parts.)

Gode, Alexander, and Hugh E. Blair (1951), *Interlingua: a grammar of the international language*. New York: Storm Publishers. x, 118 p.

Goldin, Hyman E., Frank O'Leary, and Morris Lipsius (eds.) (1951), *Dictionary of American underworld lingo*. New York: Twayne Publishers. 327 p.

Goldstein, Kurt (1948), *Language and language disturbances: aphasic symptom complexes and their significance for medicine and theory of language*. New York: Grune & Stratton. xii, 374 p.

Gould, G. T., Jr. (1951), "Design of an apparatus for speech stretching," *Technical Data Digest* 16(5): 14–19.

Gray, Giles Wilkeson, and Claude Merton Wise (1934), *The bases of speech*. New York: Harper. xvii, 439 p. [rev. ed., 1946; xiv, 610 p.]

Gray, Louis H. (1939), *Foundations of language*. New York: Macmillan. xvi, 530 p.

Gray, William S. (1922), *Remedial cases in reading*. Chicago: University of Chicago Press. vii, 208 p. (*Supplementary Educational Monographs*, No. 22.)

———(1948), *On their own in reading*. Chicago: Scott, Foresman. xv, 268 p.

Greenberg, Joseph H. (1948), "Linguistics and ethnology," *Southwestern Journal of Anthropology* 4: 140–147.

———(1949), "The logical analysis of kinship," *Philosophy of Science* 16: 58–64.

Gregoire, Antoine (1950), "La renaissance scientifique de la linguistique enfantine," *Lingua* 2: 355–398.

Grove, Victor (1950), *The language bar*. New York: Philosophical Library. v, 160 p.

Guérard, Albert Léon (1922), *A short history of the international language movement*. New York: Boni & Liveright. 268 p.

Guilford, J. P. (1948), "Factor analysis in a test development program," *Psychological Review* 55: 79–94.

Guillaume, P. (1927), "Les débuts de la phrase dans le langage de l'enfant," *Journal de Psychologie* 24: 1–25.

Haas, Mary R. (1943), "The linguist as a teacher of languages," *Language* 19: 203–208.

Haber, Tom Burns (1948), "The present status of Basic English in the United States," *Quarterly Journal of Speech* 34: 483–488.

Hall, Robert A., Jr. (1944), "Hungarian grammar," *Language Monographs*, No. 21. 91 p.

———(1946), "Bàrtoli's 'Neolinguistica,'" *Language* 22: 273–283.

———(1948a), "French," *Language Monographs*, No. 24. 56 p. (*Structural Sketches I.*)

———(1948b), *Descriptive Italian grammar*. Ithaca: Cornell University Press and Linguistic Society of America, 1948. xi, 228 p. (*Cornell Romance Studies*, Vol. 2.)

———(1950), *Leave your language alone!* Ithaca: Linguistica. xi, 254 p.

———(1951), "American linguistics 1925–1950," *Archivum Linguisticum* 3: 101–125.

Hamilton, D. Lee, and Ernest F. Haden (1950), "Three years of experimentation at the University of Texas," *Modern Language Journal* 34: 85–102.

Harris, Zellig S. (1946), "From morpheme to utterance," *Language* 22: 161–183.

———(1951), *Methods in structural linguistics*. Chicago: University of Chicago Press. xv, 384 p.

———(1952), "Discourse analysis," *Language* 28: 1–30.

Hart, Donn V. (1947), "UNESCO studies one-world language problems," *French Review* 21: 317–319.

Hartley, Eugene L., and Ruth E. Hartley (1952), *Fundamentals of social psychology*. New York: Knopf. 832 p.

Hartog, Philip (1947), *Words in action*. London: University of London Press. xvi, 275 p.

Haugen, Einar (1951), "Directions in modern linguistics," *Language* 27: 211–222.

Hayakawa, S. I. (1941), *Language in action*. New York: Harcourt, Brace. xiii, 345 p.

———(1949), *Language in thought and action*. New York: Harcourt, Brace. x, 307 p.

———(1950), "Linguistic science and the teaching of composition," *Etc., A Review of General Semantics* 7: 97–103.

REFERENCES

Heidbreder, Edna (1924), "An experimental study of thinking," *Archives of Psychology* (*New York*), No. 73. 175 p.

——(1933), *Seven psychologies.* New York: Appleton-Century. viii, 450 p.

——(1948), "Studying human thinking," pp. 96–123 in T. G. Andrews (ed.), *Methods of psychology.* New York: Wiley.

Helmholtz, H. von (1863), *Die Lehre von den Tonempfindungen.* (1st ed.) Brunswick: Viewig. xi, 605 p.

Helson, Harry (ed.) (1951), *Theoretical foundations of psychology.* New York: Van Nostrand. 787 p.

Henmon, V. A. C., *et al.* (1929), *Prognosis tests in the modern foreign languages.* New York: Macmillan. xxvi, 363 p. (*Publications of the American and Canadian Committees on Modern Languages,* Vol. 14.)

Hinshelwood, James (1917), *Congenital word blindness.* London: Lewis. ix, 112 p.

Hjelmslev, Louis (1943), *Omkring sprogtheoriens grundlæggelse.* [*Concerning the foundations of linguistic theory.*] Copenhagen. 112 p.

Hockett, Charles F. (1948a), "Biophysics, linguistics, and the unity of science," *American Scientist* 36: 558–572.

——(1948b), "Implications of Bloomfield's Algonquian studies," *Language* 24: 117–131.

——(1950), "Age-grading and linguistic continuity," *Language* 26: 449–457.

——(1951a), [Review of Martinet's *Phonology as functional phonetics*], *Language* 27: 333–342.

——(1951b), [Review of DeFrancis's *Nationalism and language reform in China*], *Language* 27: 439–445.

Hodge, Carleton T. (1950), [Review of Pittman's *Practical Linguistics*], *Language* 26: 149–152.

Hohlfeld, John Maurice (1950), *An experiment employing two methods of teaching Spanish to college freshmen.* Doctor's thesis. Philadelphia: University of Pennsylvania. 88 p.

Hoijer, Harry (1951), "Cultural implications of some Navaho linguistic categories," *Language* 27: 111–120.

——*et al.* (1947), *Linguistic structures of native America.* New York: Viking Fund. 423 p. (*Viking Fund Publications in Anthropology,* No. 6.)

Hollingworth, H. L. (1935), "The conditions of verbal configuration," *Journal of Experimental Psychology* 18: 299–306.

Horn, Ernest (1942), "Language and meaning," pp. 377–413 in Nelson B. Henry (ed.), *The psychology of learning.* Part II, Forty-First Yearbook of the National Society for the Study of Education. Chicago: University of Chicago Press. xiv, 463 p.

Hotchkiss, Sanford N., and Donald G. Paterson (1950), "Flesch readability reading list," *Personnel Psychology* 3: 327–344.

Huebener, Theodore (1949), "Vocational opportunities for foreign language students," *Modern Language Journal, Supplementary Series* No. 1 (3rd rev. ed.). 35 p.

Hull, Clark L. (1920), "Quantitative aspects of the evolution of concepts," *Psychological Monographs* 38, No. 123. 85 p.

——(1934), "The concept of the habit-family hierarchy and maze learning," *Psychological Review* 41: 33–54, 134–152.

——(1943), *Principles of behavior.* New York: Appleton-Century-Crofts. x, 422 p.

Hultzén, Lee S. (1947), "Phonetics, phonemics, and teachers of speech," *Quarterly Journal of Speech* 33: 202–206.

Humboldt, Wilhelm von (1836–39), *Über die Kawi-Sprache auf der Insel Java, nebst einer Einleitung über die Verschiedenheit des menschlichen Sprachbaues und ihren Einfluss auf die geistige Entwickelung des Menschengeschlechts.* Berlin: Druckerei der König. akad. Wiss. 3 vols.

Humphrey, George (1951a), "There is no problem of meaning," *British Journal of Psychology* 42: 238–245.

———(1951b), *Thinking: an introduction to its experimental psychology.* New York: John Wiley and Sons. vii, 331 p.

Huse, Howard R. (1931), *The psychology of foreign language study.* Chapel Hill: University of North Carolina Press. viii, 231 p.

———(1933), *The illiteracy of the literate; a guide to the art of intelligent reading.* New York: Appleton-Century. x, 272 p.

Hyneman, Charles S. (1945), "Post-war significance of the wartime area and language courses," *Bulletin of the American Association of University Professors* 31: 441–447.

International Auxiliary Language Association (1945), *General Report.* International Auxiliary Language Association, Suite 1808, 420 Lexington Avenue, New York 17, N. Y.

———(1951), *Interlingua-English; a dictionary of the international language.* Prepared by the research staff of the IALA under the direction of Alexander Gode, Ph. D. New York: Storm Publishers, Inc. lxiv, 415 p.

Iordan, Iorgu (1937), *An introduction to Romance linguistics, its schools and scholars.* Rev., trans. and in parts recast by John Orr. London: Methuen. xi, 403 p.

Irwin, Orvis C. (1941), "Research on speech sounds for the first six months of life," *Psychological Bulletin* 38: 277–285.

———(1947), "Development of speech during infancy: curve of phonemic frequencies," *Journal of Experimental Psychology* 37: 187–193.

Jacob, H. (1947), *A planned auxiliary language.* London: Dennis Dobson. 160 p.

———(1948), *On language making.* London: Dennis Dobson. 16 p.

Jacobson, E. (1932), "Electrophysiology of mental activities," *American Journal of Psychology* 44: 677–694.

Jakobson, Roman (1928), "Quelles sont les méthodes les mieux appropriées à un exposé complet et pratique de la grammaire d'une langue quelconque?" *Actes du Ier Congrès International de Linguists du 10–15 avril, 1928:* pp. 33–36.

———(1941), *Kindersprache, Aphasie und allgemeine Lautgesetze.* Uppsala: Almqvist & Wiksell. 83 p. (*Språkvetenskapliga Sällskapets i Uppsala Förhandlingar, 1940–42.*)

———(1944), "Franz Boas' approach to language," *International Journal of American Linguistics* 10: 188–195.

———(1949), "On the identification of phonemic entities," *Travaux du Cercle Linguistique de Copenhague* 5: 205–213.

———C. Gunnar M. Fant, and Morris Halle (1952), *Preliminaries to speech analysis; the distinctive features and their correlates.* Cambridge: Acoustics Laboratory, Massachusetts Institute of Technology, Technical Report No. 13. viii, 58 p.

———and John Lotz (1949), "Notes on the French phonemic pattern," *Word* 5: 151–158.

255

REFERENCES

Jespersen, Otto (1904), *How to teach a foreign language*. New York: Macmillan. 194 p.

───(1922), *Language; its nature, development and origin*. London: Allen and Unwin. 448 p.

───(1937), *Analytic syntax*. Copenhagen: Munksgaard. 170 p.

───(1941), *Efficiency in linguistic change*. Copenhagen: Munksgaard. 90 p.

Jóhanneson, Alexander (1948), "Origin of language," *Nature (London)* 162: 902.

Johnsen, Julia E. (compiler) (1944), *Basic English*. New York: Wilson. 234 p. (*The Reference Shelf*, Vol. 17, No. 1.)

Johnson, Alexander Bryan (1828), *A treatise on language*. Edited, with a critical essay on his philosophy of language, by David Rynin. Berkeley and Los Angeles: University of California Press, 1947. ix, 443 p.

Johnson, Donald M. (1950), "Problem solving and symbolic processes," *Annual Review of Psychology* 1: 297–310.

Johnson, Palmer O., and Jerzy Neyman (1936), "Tests of certain linear hypotheses and their application to some educational problems," *Statistical Research Memoirs* 1: 57–93.

Johnson, Wendell (1939), "Language and speech hygiene; an application of general semantics," *General Semantics Monographs*, No. 1, Institute of General Semantics, Chicago. v, 54 p.

───(1946), *People in quandaries; the semantics of personal adjustment*. New York: Harper. xiv, 532 p.

Joos, Martin (1936), [Review of Zipf's *Psychobiology of Language*], *Language* 12: 196–210.

───(1948), "Acoustic phonetics," *Language Monographs*, No. 23. 136 p.

Judd, C. H., *et al.* (1936), *Education as the cultivation of the higher mental processes*. New York: Macmillan. 206 p.

Kaeding, F. W. (1897–98), *Häufigkeitswörterbuch der deutschen Sprache*. Steglitz bei Berlin: Selbstverlag des Herausgebers. vi, 671 p.

Kainz, Friedrich (1941–43), *Psychologie der Sprache*. Stuttgart: Ferdinand Enke Verlag. 2 vols.

───(1946), *Einführung in die Sprachpsychologie*. Vienna: Verlag der Ringbuchhandlung A. Sexl. 149 p.

Kantor, J. R. (1922), "An analysis of psychological language data," *Psychological Review* 29: 267–309.

───(1936), *An objective psychology of grammar*. Bloomington: Indiana University Publications. xvi, 344 p.

───(1945–50), *Psychology and logic*. Bloomington: Principia Press. Vol. I: xviii, 363 p.; Vol. II: xvi, 359 p.

Kempelen, Wolfgang von (1791), *Le mécanisme de la parole, suivi de la description d'une machine parlante*. Vienna: B. Bauer. [See also Homer Dudley and T. H. Tarnóczy, "The speaking machine of Wolfgang von Kempelen," *Journal of the Acoustical Society of America* 22: 151–166 (1950).]

Kendig, Marjorie M. (ed.) (1943), *Papers from the second American congress on general semantics, University of Denver, August 1941; non-Aristotelian methodology for sanity in our time*. Chicago: Institute of General Semantics. xxiv, 581 p.

Keyser, Cassius J. (1934), "Mathematics and the science of semantics," *Scripta Mathematica* 2: 247–260.

Kluckhohn, Clyde, and Dorothea Leighton (1946), *The Navaho*. Cambridge: Harvard University Press. xx, 258 p.

Knower, Franklin H. (1938), "A study of speech attitudes and adjustments," *Speech Monographs* 5: 130–203.

———(1951), *Table of contents of the Quarterly Journal of Speech, 1915–1950, and Speech Monographs, 1934–1950*. The Speech Association of America. 53 p.

Korzybski, Alfred (1921), *The manhood of humanity; the science and art of human engineering*. New York: Dutton. xv, 264 p.

———(1933), *Science and sanity; an introduction to non-Aristotelian systems and general semantics*. Lancaster: Science Press. xx, 798 p.

Krapp, George Philip (1925), *The English language in America*. New York: Century. 2 vols.

Kroeber, A. L. (1941), "Some relations of linguistics and ethnology," *Language* 17: 287–291.

———and C. D. Chrétien (1937), "Quantitative classification of Indo-European languages," *Language* 13: 83–103.

———(1939), "The statistical technique and Hittite," *Language* 15: 69–71.

Kruszewski, N. (1881), *Über die Lautabwechslung*. Kasan, Russia: Universitätsbuchdruckerei. 41 p.

Kurath, Hans (1949), *A word geography of the eastern United States*. Ann Arbor: University of Michigan Press. x, 88 p., 163 maps.

———with Marcus L. Hansen, Julia Bloch, and Bernard Bloch (1939), *Handbook of the linguistic geography of New England*. Providence: Brown University. xii, 240 p.

Lado, Robert (1950), *Measurement in English as a foreign language with special reference to Spanish-speaking adults*. Doctor's Thesis. Ann Arbor: University of Michigan. [Abstract in *Microfilm Abstracts*, 10, No. 4: 114–115. (1950).]

———(1951), "Phonemics and pronunciation tests," *Modern Language Journal* 35: 531–542.

Lasswell, Harold, Nathan Leites, *et al.* (1949), *Language of politics: studies in quantitative semantics*. New York: Stewart. vii, 398 p.

Laubach, Frank C. (1938), *Toward a literate world*. New York: Columbia University Press. 174 p.

———(1943), *The silent billion speak*. New York: Friendship Press. vi, 201 p.

Leary, William G. (1952), "Studies in language and culture in the training of foreign service personnel: the School of Languages and Linguistics of the United States Department of State," *Etc., A Review of General Semantics* 9: 192–202.

Lee, Bernard S. (1950), "Effects of delayed speech feedback," *Journal of the Acoustical Society of America* 22: 824–826.

Lee, Dorothy D. (1943), "The linguistic aspect of Wintu·' acculturation," *American Anthropologist* 45: 435–440.

———(1950a), "Notes on the conception of the self among the Wintu Indians," *Journal of Abnormal and Social Psychology* 45: 538–543.

———(1950b), "Lineal and nonlineal codifications of reality," *Psychosomatic Medicine* 12: 89–97.

Lee, Irving J. (1941), *Language habits in human affairs: an introduction to general semantics*. New York: Harper. xxvii, 278 p.

———(1950), "On the varieties of research in general semantics," *Etc., A Review of General Semantics* 7: 170–179.

REFERENCES

Leonard, Sterling A. (1929), *The doctrine of correctness in English usage, 1700–1800.* Madison: University of Wisconsin. 361 p. (*University of Wisconsin Studies in Language and Literature,* No. 25.)

———(1932) *Current English usage.* Chicago: National Council of Teachers of English. xxii, 232 p. (*English Monographs,* No. 1.)

Leopold, Werner F. (1948), "The study of child language and infant bilingualism," *Word* 4: 1–17.

———(1952), *Bibliography of child language.* Evanston, Illinois: Northwestern University Press. v, 115 p.

Leskien, August (1876), *Die Declination im Slavisch-Litauischen und Germanischen.* Leipzig: Hirzel. xxix, 158 p.

Lévi-Strauss, Claude (1949), *Les structures élémentaires de la parenté.* Paris: Presses Universitaires. xiv, 639 p.

———(1951), "Language and the analysis of social laws," *American Anthropologist* 53: 155–163.

Lewis, M. M. (1947), *Language in society.* London: Nelson. vi, 249 p.

Liberman, A. M., P. Delattre, and F. S. Cooper (1952), "The rôle of selected stimulus-variables in the perception of the unvoiced stop consonants," *American Journal of Psychology* 65: 497–516.

Licklider, J. C. R., and George A. Miller (1951), "The perception of speech," pp. 1040–1074 in S. S. Stevens (ed.), *Handbook of experimental psychology.* New York: Wiley.

Lindesmith, A. R., and A. L. Strauss (1949), *Social psychology.* New York: Dryden Press. xvi, 549 p.

Linton, Ralph (ed.) (1945), *The science of man in the world crisis.* New York: Columbia University Press. xiv, 532 p.

Lloyd, Donald J. (1950), "A 'linguistic' approach to English composition," *Language Learning* 3: 109–116.

———(1951), "Snobs, slobs, and the English language," *American Scholar* 20: 279–288.

Lorge, Irving (1937), "The English semantic count," *Teachers College Record* 39: 65–77.

———(1949), *The semantic count of the 570 commonest English words.* New York: Institute of Psychological Research, Teachers College, Columbia University (distributed by the Bureau of Publications). x, 186 p.

Lotz, John (1950), "Speech and language," *Journal of the Acoustical Society of America* 22: 712–717.

Lowry, Howard F., with Oscar J. Campbell, Henry Grattan Doyle, Marjorie Hope Nicolson, and others (1943), *Literature in American education.* New York: Commission on Trends in Education of the Modern Language Association. 29 p.

Luchsinger, R. (1940), "Die Sprache und Stimme von ein- und zwei-eiigen Zwillingen in Beziehungen zur Motorik und zum Erbcharakter," *Archiv der Julius Klaus Stiftung* 15: 461–527.

Lundberg, George A. (1939), *Foundations of sociology.* New York: Macmillan. xx, 556 p.

Macfarlane, Alexander (1878–80), "Suggestions on the art of signalling," *Proceedings of the Royal Society of Edinburgh* 10: 698–700.

Malinowski, Bronisław (1935), *Coral gardens and their magic; a study of the methods of tilling the soil and of agricultural rites in the Trobriand Islanders.* London: Allen and Unwin. 2 vols.

REFERENCES

———(1936), "The problem of meaning in primitive languages," Supplement I, pp. 296–336 in Ogden and Richards, *The meaning of meaning,* 3rd edition. New York: Harcourt, Brace.

———(1937), "The dilemma of contemporary linguistics" [Review of M. M. Lewis's *Infant Speech*], *Nature (London)* 140: 172–173.

Mandelbaum, David G. (ed.) (1949), *Selected writings of Edward Sapir in language, culture, and personality.* Berkeley and Los Angeles: University of California Press. xv, 617 p.

Mandell, Sybil (1931), "The relation of language to thought," *Quarterly Journal of Speech* 17: 522–531.

Marckwardt, Albert H. (1951), "A critique of communications in general education," *Journal of Higher Education* 22: 1–9.

———and Fred G. Walcott (1938), *Facts about current English usage.* New York: Appleton-Century. viii, 144 p. (*English monograph* No. 7; A publication of the National Council of Teachers of English.)

Markov, A. A. (1913), "Essai d'une recherche statistique sur le texte du roman 'Eugène Onĕgin,' illustrant la liaison des épreuves en chaine," *Bulletin de l'Academie Impériale des Sciences de St. Petersbourge,* Sixth Series, 7: 153–162. [Text in Russian.]

Marquis, D. G., Harold Guetzkow, and R. W. Heyns (1951), "A social psychological study of the decision-making conference," pp. 55–67 in H. Guetzkow (ed.), *Groups, leadership, and men.* Pittsburgh: Carnegie Press.

Martinet, André (1946), "Au sujet des *Fondements de la Théorie Linguistique* de Louis Hjelmslev," *Bulletin de la Société de Linguistique de Paris* 42: 19–42. (Fascicule 1, No. 124.)

Marx, Melvin H. (ed.) (1951), *Psychological theory: contemporary readings.* New York: Macmillan. 598 p.

Mathews, Mitford M. (ed.) (1951), *A dictionary of Americanisms—on historical principles.* Chicago: University of Chicago Press. 2 vols., 1966 p.

Matthew, Robert John (1947), *Language and area studies in the armed services; their future significance.* Washington, D. C.: American Council on Education. xix, 211 p.

Max, L. W. (1935a), "An experimental study of the motor theory of consciousness, I," *Journal of Comparative Psychology* 19: 469–486.

———(1935b), "An experimental study of the motor theory of consciousness, II," *Journal of General Psychology* 13: 159–175.

McCarthy, Dorothea (1946), "Language development in children," pp. 477–581 in L. Carmichael (ed.), *Manual of child psychology.* New York: Wiley.

McGranahan, Donald V. (1936), "The psychology of language," *Psychological Bulletin* 33: 178–216.

McQuown, Norman A. (1950), [Review of Jacob's *A planned auxiliary language*], *Language* 26: 175–185.

Mead, George H. (1904), "The relation of psychology and philology," *Psychological Bulletin* 1: 375–391.

———(1934), *Mind, self and society from the standpoint of a social behaviorist.* Ed. with an introduction by Charles W. Morris. Chicago: University of Chicago Press. xxxviii, 400 p.

REFERENCES

Meader, Clarence L., and John H. Muyskens (1950), *Handbook of biolinguistics.* Toledo: Weller. xxi, 330 p.

Meillet, Antoine (1921–1938), *Linguistique historique et linguistique générale.* Paris: Champion. 2 vols.

Meinhof, Carl (1912), *Die Sprachen der Hamiten.* Hamburg: Friederichsen. xv, 256 p.

Mencken, H. L. (1938), *The American language* (4th ed.). New York: Knopf. xi, 769, xxix p. *Supplement I* (1945): xviii, 740, xxxvi p.; *Supplement II* (1948): xiii, 890, xliii p.

Menzerath, Paul (1950), "Typology of languages," *Journal of the Acoustical Society of America* 22: 698–701.

Mercier, Louis J.-A. (1930), "Is the Coleman Report justified in its restatement of objectives for modern language?" *French Review* 3: 397–415.

Milewski, Tadeusz (1947), *Zarys językoznawstwa ogólnego. I: Teoria językoznawstwa.* [Outline of general linguistics. Part I: Theory of linguistics.] Lublin: Naklad i wydawnictwo.

Mill, John Stuart (1843), *A system of logic, ratiocinative, and inductive; being a connected view of the principles of evidence and the methods of scientific investigation.* New York: Harper, 1874 (8th ed.). xv, 659 p.

Miller, George A. (1950), "Language engineering," *Journal of the Acoustical Society of America* 22: 720–725.

———(1951a), *Language and communication.* New York: McGraw-Hill. xiii, 298 p.

———(1951b), "Speech and language," p. 789–810 in S. S. Stevens (ed.), *Handbook of experimental psychology.* New York: Wiley.

———and Frederick C. Frick (1949), "Statistical behavioristics and sequences of responses," *Psychological Review* 56: 311–324.

Modern Language Association (1900), *Report of the Committee of Twelve.* Boston: Heath. vi, 99 p.

Modern Language Journal (1950), "The college requirement for proficiency in a foreign language," *Modern Language Journal* 34: 593–603.

Monroe, Marion (1932), *Children who cannot read; the analysis of reading disabilities and the use of diagnostic tests in the instruction of retarded readers.* Chicago: University of Chicago Press. xvi, 207 p.

Morris, Charles W. (1938), *Foundations of the theory of signs.* Chicago: University of Chicago Press. vii, 59 p. (*International Encyclopedia of Unified Science,* Vol. I, No. 2.)

———(1946), *Signs, language, and behavior.* New York: Prentice-Hall. xii, 365 p.

Mowrer, O. Hobart (1950), *Learning theory and personality dynamics; selected papers.* New York: Ronald Press. xviii, 776 p.

Müller, Friedrich (1876–88), *Grundriss der Sprachwissenschaft.* Vienna: Holder. 4 vols.

Müller, Max (1873), *Lectures on the science of language* (2nd ed.). New York: Scribner, Armstrong. 416 p.

Murra, John V., Robert M. Hankin and Fred Holling (trans.) (1951), *The Soviet linguistic controversy.* New York: King's Crown Press. 98 p.

Murray, Elwood (1944), *The speech personality* (rev. ed.). Philadelphia: Lippincott. xii, 517 p.

Newman, Edwin B. (1951), "The pattern of vowels and consonants in various languages," *American Journal of Psychology* 64: 369–379.

REFERENCES

Newman, Stanley S. (1933), "Further experiments in phonetic symbolism," *American Journal of Psychology* 45: 53-75.

———(1941), "Behavior patterns in linguistic structure: a case study," pp. 94-106 in L. Spier *et al.* (eds.), *Language, culture, and personality: essays in memory of Edward Sapir.* Menasha, Wisconsin: Sapir Memorial Publication Fund.

———(1944), "Cultural and psychological features in English intonation," *Transactions of the New York Academy of Science* 7: 45-54.

———and Vera G. Mather (1938), "Analysis of spoken language of patients with affective disorders," *American Journal of Psychiatry* 94: 913-942.

Nida, Eugene A. (1946), *Morphology: the descriptive analysis of words.* Ann Arbor: University of Michigan Press. xii, 221 p. (*University of Michigan Publications in Linguistics,* Vol. 2.)

———(1948), "The analysis of grammatical constituents," *Language* 24: 168-177.

Odum, Howard W. (1951), *American sociology: the story of sociology in the U. S. through 1950.* New York: Longmans, Green. vi, 501 p.

Ogden, Charles K. (1930a), *Basic English; a general introduction with rules and grammar.* London: K. Paul, Trench, Trubner. 100 p.

———(1930b), *The Basic vocabulary; a statistical analysis, with special reference to substitution and translation.* London: K. Paul, Trench, Trubner. 96 p.

———(1932), *The Basic dictionary, being the 7,500 most useful words with their equivalents in Basic English, for the use of translators, teachers, and students.* London: K. Paul, Trench, Trubner. xx, 106 p.

———(1934), *The system of Basic English.* New York: Harcourt, Brace. ix, 322 p.

———(1935), *Counter-offensive; an exposure of certain misrepresentations of Basic English.* Cambridge, England, and Peiping, China: The Orthological Institute. 207 p., plus an appendix of 53 pages reproducing in its entirety the monograph by West *et al., A critical examination of Basic English.*

———and Ivor A. Richards (1936), *The meaning of meaning.* (3rd ed.) New York: Harcourt, Brace. xxii, 363 p. [First published in 1923.]

Olmsted, David L. (1950), *Ethnolinguistics so far.* Norman, Okla.: Battenburg Press. 16 p. (*Studies in Linguistics, Occasional Papers,* No. 2.)

Osgood, Charles E. (1952a), "The nature and measurement of meaning," *Psychological Bulletin* 49: 197-237.

———(1952b), "The role of representational mediation processes in behavior," *Psychological Review* [in press].

Osthoff, Hermann, and Karl Brugmann (1878-90), *Morphologische Untersuchungen auf dem Gebiete der indogermanischen Sprachen.* Leipzig: Hirzel. 5 parts.

Oswald, Victor A., Jr., and Stuart L. Fletcher, Jr. (1951), "Proposals for the mechanical resolution of German syntax patterns," *Modern Language Forum* 36: 61-104.

Palmer, Harold E. (1917), *The scientific study and teaching of languages.* Yonkers-on-Hudson: World Book Co. 328 p.

Panel on Psychology and Physiology (1949), *A survey report on human factors in undersea warfare.* Washington, D. C.: National Research Council. x, 541 p.

Partridge, Eric (1949), *A dictionary of slang and unconventional English* (3rd ed.). London: Routledge & Kegan Paul. xvi, 1230 p.

———(1950), *A dictionary of the underworld, British and American; being the vocabularies of crooks, criminals, racketeers, beggars, and tramps; 16th-20th centuries.* London: Routledge. xv, 804 p.

REFERENCES

Partridge, Eric, and John W. Clark (1951), *British and American English since 1900.* New York: Philosophical Library. x, 341 p.

Paul, Hermann (1880), *Prinzipien der Sprachgeschichte* (1st ed.). Halle: Niemeyer. vii, 288 p. [2nd ed., *Principles of the history of language,* trans. by H. A. Strong. New York: Macmillan, 1889. xlvii, 512 p.]

Paul, Wilson B., Frederick Sorensen, and Elwood Murray (1946), "A functional core for the basic communication course," *Quarterly Journal of Speech* 32: 232–244.

Payne, Stanley L. (1951), *The art of asking questions.* Princeton: Princeton University Press. xiv, 249 p.

Pedersen, H. (1931), *Linguistic science in the nineteenth century* (trans. by J. Spargo). Cambridge: Harvard University Press.

Pei, Mario A. (1946), "It comes to languages—but is it science?" *Modern Language Journal* 30: 421–428.

Pike, Kenneth L. (1943), *Phonetics; a critical analysis of phonetic theory and a technic for the practical description of sounds.* Ann Arbor: University of Michigan Press. ix, 182 p.

————(1946), *The intonation of American English.* Ann Arbor: University of Michigan Press. xi, 200 p.

Pillsbury, W. B., and C. L. Meader (1928), *The psychology of language.* New York: Appleton. vii, 306 p.

Pittman, Dean (1948), *Practical linguistics.* Cleveland: Mid-Missions (314 Superior Avenue). xiii, 229 p.

Pollock, Thomas C., with William C. DeVane and Robert E. Spiller (1945), *The English language in American education.* New York: Commission on Trends in Education of the Modern Language Association of America. viii, 32 p.

Pooley, Robert C. (1946), *Teaching English usage.* New York: Appleton-Century-Crofts. xi, 265 p. (*English Monographs,* No. 16.)

Pop, Sever (1950), *La dialectologie: Aperçu historique et méthodes d'enquêtes linguistiques.* Louvain: Chez l'auteur. lv, 1134 p.

Potter, Muriel Catherine (1949), *Perception of symbol orientation and early reading success.* New York: Columbia University, Teachers College, Bureau of Publications. 69 p. (*Contributions to Education* No. 939.)

Potter, Ralph K., George A. Kopp, and Harriet C. Green (1947), *Visible speech.* New York: Van Nostrand. xvi, 441 p.

Powell, John W. (1880), *Introduction to the study of Indian languages, with words, phrases, and sentences to be collected* (2nd ed.). Washington, D. C.: Smithsonian Institution, Bureau of Ethnology. xi, 228 p.

Powers, F. F. (1929), "Psychology of language learning," *Psychological Bulletin* 26: 261–274.

Pronko, N. H. (1946), "Language and psycholinguistics," *Psychological Bulletin* 43: 189–239.

Read, Allen Walker (1948), "An account of the word 'semantics,'" *Word* 4: 78–97.

Reed, David W. (1949), "A statistical approach to quantitative linguistic analysis," *Word* 5: 235–247.

Reichenbach, Hans (1947), *Elements of symbolic logic.* New York: Macmillan. xiii, 444 p.

Reiss, Samuel (1950), *The rise of words and their meanings.* New York: Philosophical Library. 301 p.

262

REFERENCES

Révész, G. (1946), *Ursprung und Vorgeschichte der Sprache*. Berne: Francke. 279 p. [Also, a French translation: *Origine et préhistoire du langage*. Paris: Payot, 1950. 234 p.]

————(1950), "Thought and language," *Archivum Linguisticum* 2: 122–131.

Rice, Winthrop H. (1946), "Foreign language instruction," *Review of Educational Research* 16: 139–160.

Richards, Ivor A. (1929), *Practical criticism*. New York: Harcourt, Brace. xiii, 375 p.

————(1938), *Interpretation in teaching*. New York: Harcourt, Brace. xii, 420 p.

————(1942a), *How to read a page; a course in effective reading, with an introduction to a hundred great words*. New York: Norton. 246 p.

————(1942b), *The Republic of Plato, a new version founded on Basic English*. New York: Norton. 218 p.

————(1943), *Basic English and its uses*. New York: Norton. 143 p.

————(1945), *The pocket book of Basic English; a self-teaching way into English with directions in Spanish, French, Italian, Portuguese, German*. New York: Pocket Books. xxx, 334 p.

————and Christine Gibson (1945), *Learning Basic English; a practical handbook for English-speaking people*. New York: Norton. 116 p.

————M. H. Ilsley, and C. Gibson (1950), *French self-taught with pictures*. New York: Pocket Books. xxvii, 274 p.

————Ruth C. Metcalf, and Christine Gibson (1950), *Spanish self-taught through pictures*. New York: Pocket Books. xiv, 270 p.

Rockett, Frank H. (1948), "The transistor," *Scientific American* 179(3): 52–55.

Rosenbloom, Paul C. (1950), *The elements of mathematical logic*. New York: Dover. iv, 214 p.

Ross, Alan S. C. (1950), "Philological probability problems," *Journal of the Royal Statistical Society* (Series B) 12: 19–59.

Rossignol, Lois J. (1949), *Relationships among hearing acuity, speech production, and reading performance in Grades 1A, 1B, and 2A*. New York: Columbia University, Teachers College, Bureau of Publications, 50 p. (*Contributions to Education*, No. 936.)

Rouse, Irving (1939), "Prehistory in Haiti; a study in method," *Yale University Publications in Anthropology*, No. 21. 202 p. and plates.

Rousselot, abbé Jean (1891), *Les modifications phonétiques du langage, étudiées dans le patois d'une famille de Cellefrouin (Charente)*. Thèse. Paris.

Rubenstein, Herbert (1951), "The recent conflict in Soviet linguistics," *Language* 27: 281–287.

Ruesch, Jurgen, and Gregory Bateson (1951), *Communication; the social matrix of psychiatry*. New York: Norton. vi, 314 p.

Rundle, Stanley (1946), *Language as a social and political factor in Europe*. London: Faber & Faber. 207 p.

Russell, David H. (1949), "Reading and child development," pp. 10–32 in *48th Yearbook*, Part II, of the National Society for Study of Education. Chicago: University of Chicago Press.

Sanford, Fillmore H. (1942a), "Speech and personality: a comparative case study," *Character and Personality* 10: 169–198.

————(1942b), "Speech and personality," *Psychological Bulletin* 39: 811–845.

263

REFERENCES

Sapir, Edward (1921), *Language; an introduction to the study of speech.* New York: Harcourt, Brace. vii, 258 p.

———(1929), "A study in phonetic symbolism," *Journal of Experimental Psychology* 12: 225–239.

———(1930), "Totality," *Language Monographs,* No. 6. 28 p.

———(1944), "Grading: a study in semantics," *Philosophy of Science* 11: 93–116. [Also in Mandelbaum (1949), pp. 122–149.]

———*et al.* (1925), "The problem of an international auxiliary language," *Romanic Review* 16: 244–256.

———and Morris Swadesh (1932), "The expression of the ending-point relation in English, French, and German," *Language Monographs,* No. 10. 125 p.

Schlauch, Margaret (1942), *The gift of tongues.* New York: Modern Age Books. ix, 342 p.

Schleicher, August (1863), *Die Darwinsche Theorie und die Sprachwissenschaft* (2nd ed.). Weimar: Böhlau, 1873. 33 p.

Schuchardt, H. (1885), *Über die Lautgesetze.* Berlin. vi, 39 p.

Sears, Robert R. (1936), "Functional abnormalities of memory with special reference to amnesia," *Psychological Bulletin* 33: 229–274.

———(1951), "A theoretical framework for personality and social behavior," *American Psychologist* 6: 476–483.

Seashore, Robert H., and Lois D. Eckerson (1940), "The measurement of individual differences in general English vocabularies," *Journal of Educational Psychology* 31: 14–38.

Sebeok, T. A. (1943), "The phonemic system of Santali," *Journal of the American Oriental Society* 63: 66–68.

Semmelmeyer, Madeline (1940), *The application of general semantics to a program for promoting reading readiness.* Chicago: Institute of General Semantics. 16 p. (Mimeographed.)

Shannon, Claude E., and W. Weaver (1949), *The mathematical theory of communication.* Urbana: University of Illinois Press. vi, 117 p.

Sheehan, Joseph G. (1951), "The modification of stuttering through non-reinforcement," *Journal of Abnormal and Social Psychology* 46: 51–63.

Shenton, Herbert N. (1933), *Cosmopolitan conversation; the language problems of international conferences.* New York: Columbia University Press. xviii, 803 p.

Sievers, Eduard (1876), *Grundzüge der Lautphysiologie zur Einführung in das Studium der Lautlehre der indogermanischen Sprachen.* Leipzig: Breitkopf & Härtel.

Sisson, E. Donald (1937), "The role of habit in eye movements in reading," *Psychological Record* 1: 159–168.

Skinner, B. F. (1936), "The verbal summator and a method for the study of latent speech," *Journal of Psychology* 2: 71–107.

———(1938), *The behavior of organisms; an experimental analysis.* New York: Appleton-Century. ix, 457 p.

———(1947), *Verbal behavior.* William James Lectures, Harvard University. [To be published.]

———(1948), " 'Superstition' in the pigeon," *Journal of Experimental Psychology* 38: 168–172.

264

REFERENCES

Smith, Bruce Lannes; Harold D. Lasswell, and Ralph D. Casey (1946), *Propaganda, communication and public opinion; a comprehensive reference guide.* Princeton: Princeton University Press. 442 p.

Smith, Caldwell P. (1951), "A phoneme detector," *Journal of the Acoustical Society of America* 23: 446–451.

Soffietti, James Peter (1949), *Phonemic analysis of the word in Turinese.* New York: [Author]. 71 p.

Spitzer, Leo (1948a), *Essays in historical semantics.* New York: Vanni. xvii, 316 p.

————(1948b), *Linguistics and literary history; essays in stylistics.* Princeton: Princeton University Press. vi, 236 p.

Steinthal, H. (1860), *Characteristik der hauptsächlichsten typen der Sprachbaues.* Berlin: Dümmler. ix, 335 p.

Stern, Gustaf (1931), *Meaning and change of meaning, with special reference to the English language.* Göteborg. 456 p.

Stevenson, Charles L. (1944), *Ethics and language.* New Haven: Yale University Press. xi, 338 p.

Stott, D. H. (1946), *Language teaching in the new education.* London: London University Press. 100 p.

Strickland, Ruth G. (1951), *The language arts in the elementary school.* Boston: Heath. xiv, 370 p.

Sturtevant, Edgar H. (1947), *An introduction to linguistic science.* New Haven: Yale University Press. 173 p.

Swadesh, Morris (1939), "Edward Sapir" [an obituary], *Language* 15: 132–135.

————(1948), "On linguistic mechanism," *Science and Society* 12: 254–259.

Sweet, Henry (1877), *A handbook of phonetics.* Oxford: Clarendon Press. xx, 215 p.

————(1900), *The practical study of language; a guide for teachers and learners.* New York: Holt. xiv, 280 p.

Tagliavini, Carlo (1949), *Introduzione alla glottologia* (4th ed.). Bologna: Pàtron. 506 p.

Tarnóczy, T. H. (1947), "Physical characteristics of speech sounds and some aspects of their anthropological relations," *Acta Anthropobiologica (Budapest)* 1: 1–43.

Taylor, Calvin W. (1947), "A factorial study of fluency in writing," *Psychometrika* 12: 239–262.

Thomas, William I. (1937), *Primitive behavior; an introduction to the social sciences.* New York: McGraw-Hill. ix, 847 p.

Thompson, Laura (1950), "Science and the study of mankind," *Science* 111: 559–563.

Thomson, G. H., and J. R. Thompson (1915), "Outlines of a method for the quantitative analysis of writing vocabularies," *British Journal of Psychology* 8: 52–69.

Thonssen, Lester, and Elizabeth Fatherson (1939), *Bibliography of speech education.* New York: Wilson. 800 p. [A supplement was published in 1950.]

Thorndike, Edward L. (1932), *A teacher's word book of the twenty thousand words found most frequently and widely in general reading for children and young people.* New York: Bureau of Publications, Teachers College, Columbia University. vii, 182 p.

Thurstone, L. L. (1938), *Primary mental abilities.* Chicago: University of Chicago Press. ix, 121 p. (*Psychometric Monograph* No. 1.)

REFERENCES

Titchener, E. B. (1909), *Lectures on the experimental psychology of the thought processes.* New York: Macmillan. xi, 318 p.

Togeby, Knud (1949), "Qu'est-ce qu'un mot?" *Travaux du Cercle Linguistique de Copenhague* 5: 97–111.

Tolman, Edward C. (1932), *Purposive behavior in animals and men.* New York: Century. xiv, 463 p.

Trager, George L. (1949), *The field of linguistics.* Norman, Okla.: Battenburg Press. 8 p. (*Studies in linguistics, Occasional Papers* No. 1.)

———and Henry Lee Smith, Jr. (1951), *An outline of English structure.* Norman, Okla.: Battenburg Press. 92 p. (*Studies in Linguistics, Occasional Papers* No. 3.)

Trnka, Bohumil (1950), *A tentative bibliography* [of statistical linguistics]. Utrecht: Spectrum. 22 p.

Trubetskoy, N. S. (1939a), "Grundzüge der Phonologie," *Travaux du Cercle Linguistique de Prague,* No. 7. 271 p.

———(1939b), "Wie soll das Lautsystem einer künstlichen internationalen Hilfsprache beschaffen sein?" *Travaux du Cercle Linguistique de Prague* 8: 5–21.

Ullmann, Stephen (1951a), *Words and their use.* New York: Philosophical Library. 110 p.

———(1951b), *The principles of semantics.* Glasgow: Jackson. vii, 314 p. (*Glasgow University Publications,* No. 84.)

Urban, Wilbur M. (1939), *Language and reality; the philosophy of language and the principles of symbolism.* New York: Macmillan. 755 p.

United Nations Educational, Scientific, and Cultural Organization (1949), *Fundamental education; description and programme.* Paris: UNESCO Publication No. 363. 85 p.

———(1951), *The Haiti pilot project; phase one.* Paris: UNESCO. 79 p. (*Monographs on Fundamental Education, IV.*)

Van Ginneken, J. (1927), "Die Erblichkeit der Lautgesetze," *Indogermanische Forschungen* 45: 1–44.

Viëtor, Wilhelm (1902), *Die Methodik der neusprachlichen Unterrichts; ein geschichtlicher Ueberblick in vier Vorträgen.* Leipzig: Teubner. 56 p.

Vigotsky, L. S. (1939), "Thought and speech," *Psychiatry* 2: 29–54.

Vinacke, W. Edgar (1951), "The investigation of concept formation," *Psychological Bulletin* 48: 1–31.

Voegelin, C. F. (1942a), [Review of works by Buechel and Vogt], *Language* 18: 69–73.

———(1942b), "Sapir: insight and rigor," *American Anthropologist* 44: 322–324.

———(1944), "Continuation of International Journal of American Linguistics," *International Journal of American Linguistics* 10: 109–112.

———(1948), "Distinctive features and meaning equivalence," *Language* 24: 132–135.

———(1949), "A decade of American Indian linguistics studies," *Proceedings of the American Philosophical Society* 93: 137–140.

Von Foerster, Heinz (ed.) (1951), *Cybernetics: circular causal and feedback mechanisms in biological and social systems.* New York: Josiah Macy, Jr. Foundation. (*Transactions of the Seventh Conference, October 23–24, 1950, New York.*)

———(1952), *Cybernetics: circular causal and feedback mechanisms in biological and social systems.* New York: Josiah Macy, Jr. Foundation. (*Transactions of the Eighth Conference, March 15–16, 1951, New York.*)

266

REFERENCES

Walpole, Hugh R. (1941), *Semantics; the nature of words and their meanings*. New York: Norton. 264 p.

Walsh, Chad (1933), "The verb system in Basic English," *American Speech* 8: 137–143.

Warner, W. L., and P. S. Lunt (1941), *The social life of a modern community*. New Haven: Yale University Press. xx, 460 p.

Watson, John B. (1919), *Psychology from the standpoint of a behaviorist*. Philadelphia: Lippincott. xi, 429 p.

———(1920), "Is thinking merely the action of language mechanisms? (V)," *British Journal of Psychology* 11: 87–104.

Watts, A. F. (1947), *The language and mental development of children; an essay in educational psychology*. Boston: Heath. 354 p.

Weiss, Albert Paul (1925), "Linguistics and psychology," *Language* 1: 52–57.

———(1929), *A theoretical basis of human behavior*. Columbus, Ohio: Adams. xvii, 479 p.

Welby, Victoria (1903), *What is meaning? Studies in the development of significance*. London: Macmillan. xxxi, 321 p.

Wellek, René, and Austin Warren (1949), *Theory of literature*. New York: Harcourt, Brace. x, 403 p.

Werner, Heinz, and Edith Kaplan (1950), "Development of word meaning through verbal context: an experimental study," *Journal of Psychology* 29: 251–257.

West, Michael P. (1926), *Learning to read a foreign language; an experimental study*. New York: Longmans, Green. xi, 56 p.

———E. Swensen, and others (1934), *A critical examination of Basic English*. Toronto: University of Toronto Press. 53 p. (*Toronto University, Department of Educational Research, Bulletin No. 2.*)

Whitney, William Dwight (1867), *Language and the study of language*. New York: Scribner, Armstrong, 1885. (5th ed.) xi, 505 p.

———(1874), *Oriental and linguistic studies* (2nd Series). New York: Scribner, Armstrong. ix, 431 p.

———(1875), *The life and growth of language; an outline of linguistic science*. New York: Appleton. vii, 326 p.

Whorf, Benjamin Lee (1933), *The phonetic value of certain characters in Maya writing*. Cambridge: Harvard University Press. ix, 48 p. (*Papers of the Peabody Museum of American Archaeology and Ethnology, Harvard University.*)

———(1935), "The comparative linguistics of Uto-Aztecan," *American Anthropologist* 37: 600–608.

———(1939), "Science and linguistics," *The Technology Review* 42: 229–231, 247–248.

———(1940a), "Linguistics as an exact science," *The Technology Review* 43: 61–63, 80–83.

———(1940b), "Languages and logic," *The Technology Review* 43: 250–252, 266–272.

———(1941), "The relation of habitual thought and behavior to language," pp. 75–93 in L. Spier *et al.* (eds.), *Language, culture, and personality: essays in memory of Edward Sapir*. Menasha, Wisconsin: Sapir Memorial Publication Fund.

———(1949), *Four articles on metalinguistics*. Washington, D. C.: Foreign Service Institute, Department of State. [Reprinted from Whorf, 1939, 1940a, 1940b, 1941.]

REFERENCES

Wickens, D. D. (1938), "The transference of conditioned excitation and conditioned inhibition from one muscle group to the antagonistic muscle group," *Journal of Experimental Psychology* 22: 101–123.

Wiener, Norbert (1948), *Cybernetics, or control and communication in the animal and the machine.* New York: Wiley. 194 p.

————(1950), *The human use of human beings; cybernetics and society.* Boston: Houghton Mifflin. 241 p.

Willis, Robert (1830), "On the vowel sounds, and on reed organ pipes," *Transactions of the Cambridge Philosophical Society* 3: 231–268.

Wilson, Richard Albert (1948), *The miraculous birth of language.* With a preface by George Bernard Shaw. New York: Philosophical Library. 256 p.

Witty, Paul (1949), *Reading in modern education.* Boston: Heath. xvi, 319 p.

Wolfle, Dael Lee (1932), "The relation between linguistic structure and associative interference in artificial linguistic material," *Language Monographs,* No. 11. 55 p.

————(1940), *Factor analysis to 1940.* Chicago: University of Chicago Press. vii, 69 p. (*Psychometric Monographs,* No. 3.)

Woodworth, Robert S. (1938), *Experimental psychology.* New York: Holt. xi, 889 p.

Wundt, Wilhelm (1900–09), *Völkerpsychologie; eine Untersuchung der Entwicklungsgesetze von Sprache, Mythen und Sitte.* Leipzig: Englemann. 3 vols.

————(1901), *Sprachgeschichte und Sprachpsychologie, mit Rücksicht auf B. Delbrücks 'Grundfragen der Sprachforschung.'* Leipzig: Engelmann. 110 p.

Yule, G. Udny (1944), *The statistical study of literary vocabulary.* Cambridge, England: Cambridge University Press. ix, 306 p.

Zipf, George K. (1935), *The psycho-biology of language.* Boston: Houghton Mifflin. ix, 336 p.

————(1949), *Human behavior and the principle of least effort.* Cambridge, Mass.: Addison-Wesley Press. xi, 573 p.

INDEX

INDEX

Numbers in *italics* identify citations in the References.

INDEX

attitude, 77, 89
attitudinal disposition, 93
audiovisual aids in language teaching, 180,
   182, 184, 186, 188, 191, 206–208
audition, 83
aural comprehension tests, 177, 195
Australia, languages of, 56
autocorrelation function, 86, 237(n)
automatic recognizer, 210, 245(n)
auxiliary languages, 122, 125-132, 240(n)
Ayer, A. J., 133, 246
Aztecan language, 58

Babylonián language, 55
Baird, A. C., 243(n), 246
Balashek, S., 245(n), 250
Baldwin, J. M., 162
Bales, R. F., 87, 246
Baltic languages, 54
Bantu language, 43, 57, 116
Bartoli, M. G., 51, 247
Barzun, J., 242(n), 246
"basic communicese," 212
Basic English, 126, 128–132, 163f, 184,
   203, 241(n), 244(n)
Basson, A. H., 48, 138, 246
Bateson, G., 237(n), 263
Baudouin de Courtenay, J., 19, 45, 246
Baugh, A. C., 65, 246
Bavelas, A., 86, 88, 246
behavior, decoding, 91, 99
   encoding, 89, 92f
   innate, 94, 238(n)
   intentive, 89, 99
   interpretive, 91
   and language, 14
   operant, 78, 100, 107, 188
   of philosophers, 139
   purposive, 107
   respondent, 107
   structure of, 106
   verbal, 69–111
behaviorism, 74f, 81f, 88f, 106
behavioristics, statistical, 107
Bell Telephone Laboratories, 206, 209,
   245(n)
Bentley, A. F., 241(n), 246
Berber language, 55

Berkeley, E. C., 210, 247
Berlitz system of language teaching, 169f
Bertoni, G., 51, 247
bibliography, foreign language teaching
   243f(n)
   linguistics, 54, 216, 245(n)
   psychology of language, 71
   speech education, 243(n)
   statistical linguistics, 237(n)
Biddulph, R., 245(n), 250
bilingualism, 99
binary digit ("bit"), 198, 200, 203
binary number system, 199
binary opposition, 22, 202f
biolinguistics, 80
Biological Abstracts, 216
Birdwhistell, R. L., 14, 35, 247
bit, information unit, 198, 200, 203
Black, J. W., 79, 247
Black, M., 241(n), 243(n), 247
Blair, H. E., 241(n), 252
Bloch, B., 15, 23, 36, 51, 67, 147, 215,
   247, 257
Bloch, J., 257
blood grouping and sounds, 239(n)
Bloomfield, L., 15, 19–23, 27, 30, 39, 49,
   52f, 57, 65, 75, 80–82, 97, 135, 141–
   143, 146–148, 151, 172–174, 220,
   236(n), 247
Boas, F., 20, 57f, 61, 81, 215, 220, 235(n),
   247
Bode, H., 225, 247
Boder, D. P., 101, 247
Bodmer, F., 228, 240(n), 247
Böhtlingk, O., 16, 247
Bogatyrev, P., 35, 247
Bolinger, D. L., 13, 247
Boll, E. S., 248
Bond, G. L., 150, 247
Bonfante, G., 51, 248
Bopp, F., 16, 18, 248
Boring, E. G., 71, 89, 248
borrowing, linguistic, 50, 52, 112
Borst, J. M., 209
Bossard, J. H. S., 119, 248
Bousfield, W. A., 98, 248
"bow-wow" theory, 17

INDEX

Herodian, 16
Herrick, V., *250*
Heyns, R. W., 87, *259*
Hindustani language, 54
Hinshelwood, J., 242(n), *254*
Hispania, 218
Hispanic Review, 217
historical linguistics. *See* comparative linguistics
history, 3
  cultural, 52, 59, 65, 116
  and language, 5
  of peoples and cultures, 50, 58
Hittite language, 9, 18, 49f, 55
Hjelmslev, L., 22, *254*
Hocart, A. M., 75
Hockett, C. F., 13, 22, 42, 49, 62, 100, 135, *254*
Hodge, C. T., 240(n), *254*
Hohlfeld, J. M., 179, *254*
Hoijer, H., 48, 58, *254*
Holling, F., *260*
Hollingworth, H. L., 110, *254*
Hopi language, 44, 47, 57
Horn, E., 142f, 167f, *254*
Hotchkiss, S. N., 242(n), *254*
Hottentot language, 57, 116
Huebener, T., 223, *254*
Hull, C. L., 94, 101, 106, *254*
Hultzén, L. S., 160, *255*
human engineering, 196, 244(n)
humanities, 26, 29, 65, 112
Humboldt, W. von, 18, 45, 56, *255*
Humphrey, G., 95, 238(n), *255*
Hungarian language, 237(n)
Huse, H. R., 100, 243(n), *255*
Husserl, E., 162
Hyneman, C. S., 175, *255*

IALA. *See* International Auxiliary Language Association
idea, 71, 77, 88, 92, 95
ideational fluency, 101
idiolect, 10
Ido, auxiliary language, 128
illiteracy, 121–124
Ilsley, M. H., 185, *263*
image, 72, 89, 95

imageless thought, 74
imagination, 70
imitation, tests, 194
immediate constituents, 37, 39
India, languages of, 55, 123
Indiana University, 214, 221
Indic languages, 3
individual differences, 46, 64, 69, 144, 150
  language behavior, 101
  language usage, 66
  school achievement, 242(n)
  second-language students, 170
  speech, 87
Indo-European languages, 18, 35, 48–50, 52, 54f, 62
Indo-European linguistics, 21, 23
Indogermanisches Jahrbuch, 245(n)
Indo-Iranian languages, 54
Indonesia, languages of, 56
infant speech, 98
infinitive, split, 151
informant, language teaching, 173, 191
information, amount in speech, 84f
  in behavior sequences, 89, 92, 103
  definition, 198, 237(n)
  measurement, 196
  theory of, 6, 88, 196–205
innate behavior, 94, 238(n)
Institute of General Semantics, 166
Institute of Languages and Linguistics, Georgetown University, 182
instrumental learning, 78
intelligence, and second-language learning, 170, 194, 244(n)
  tests, 4
intelligibility, of languages, 8
  of speech, 5, 79, 83, 87, 196
  of words, 85
Intensive Language Program, 173, 175–177, 182, 190, 192, 220
intentive behavior, 89, 99
interdisciplinary coöperation, 1, 212, 227, 230
interdisciplinary studies, 229f
Interlingua, auxiliary language, 127, 132, 241(n)
international auxiliary language, 123, 125–132, 241(n)

as catalog of environment, 11, 43–48, 114
of the child, 4, 34, 78, 88, 95, 98f, 111, 188, 238(n)
and culture, 14, 26, 48, 112, 116
definition, 7–12, 67, 77
and education, 140–195, 226
expression theory, 77, 92
families, 23, 25, 49, 54, 62, 114
as metascience, 135
and national traits, 81
origin, 14, 17, 81, 100f
psychology, 4, 18, 69–111, 158
and science, 27
as social control, 5
and social science, 5, 112–132
and sociology, 117
and speech, 12f, 116
speech vs. writing, 13, 110, 141, 144, 191, 202
spoken, 13
statistical structure, 204
as system, 8, 10, 13, 76
and thought, 45, 47, 67, 103–105, 142
typology, 14, 25, 42f, 62, 67, 203
language and area studies, 175, 225
language arts, in education, 4
teaching, 123, 141–168, 226, 241(n)
Language Dissertations, 215
language engineering, 5, 113, 121f
Language Guides, 174
Language Learning, 218
Language Monographs, 215
language teaching. *See* foreign-language teaching
language teachers, 2
organizations, 217
language systems, 8, 10, 23
efficiency, 13
languages, dead, 9, 13
international auxiliary, 123, 125–132, 241(n)
moribund, 8, 228
number of, 53
See also under specific languages
langue, la, 11, 64
Larin, B. A., 235(n)
Lasswell, H. D., 119f, 240(n), *257, 265*

Latin language, 16, 18, 39, 49, 54, 124, 156
Laubach, F. C., 124, 240(n), *257*
law, Grimm's, 18
Zipf's frequency-rank, 64
laws, frequency-distribution, 63
of behavior, 69
linguistic, 79
phonetic, 18, 49f
learning, 26, 69, 106
instrumental, 78
of language, 94–100, 144, 168–192
learning theory, 92, 97, 108, 111
and origin of language, 100
and stuttering, 103
Leary, W. G., 182, *257*
Lee, B. S., 103, *257*
Lee, D. D., 48, *257*
Lee, I. J., 165, 167, *257*
Leibnitz, G. W., 162
Leighton, D., 48, 115, *257*
Leites, N., *257*
Leonard, S. A., 152, 154, 242(n), *258*
Leopold, W. F., 98, *258*
Leskien, A., 50, *258*
Lettish language, 54
Lévi-Strauss, C., 35, *258*
Lewis, M. M., 240(n), *258*
lexicography, 24f, 28, 32, 66, 90, 92, 236(n), 238(n)
lexicon, 25, 118, 192
and culture, 114
in mechanical translation, 211
Libby, W. F., 63
Liberman, A. M., 209, *258*
Licklider, J. C. R., 83f, *258*
Lindesmith, A. R., 118, *258*
Linguaphone, 170
linguistic analysis, 21, 53, 84, 122, 137
and communication theory, 203
in foreign-language teaching, 180, 185, 189
and psychology, 82
linguistic change, 14, 49, 59, 62, 80, 100f, 144, 151
Linguistic Circle of New York, 214f
linguistic codes, 2, 11, 27, 36, 64, 90, 198, 201

INDEX

Mather, V. G., 102, *261*
Mathews, M. M., 66, *259*
Matthew, R. J., 244(n), *259*
Max, L. W., 237(n), *259*
Maya language, 17, 58, 210
McCarthy, D., 98, *259*
McConnel, O., 124
McGalliard, J. C., 15
McGarvey, H. R., 238(n), *252*
McGranahan, D. V., 71, *259*
McPhee, E. D., 243(n), *248*
McQuown, N. A., 241(n), *259*
Mead, G. H., 71, 118, *259*
Meader, C. L., 80, 237(n), *260*, *262*
meaning, 9, 27, 70, 77f, 82, 88–90, 94–97,
  100, 105, 111, 133f, 138, 142–144,
  157, 161–164, 239(n)
  categories, 36
  connotative, 95–97
  denotative, 95–97
  dimensions, 97
  extensional, 97
  learning of, 94–97, 167, 184, 188
  and linguistic analysis, 21, 24–29, 31f
  of linguistic forms, 24–29, 34, 38
  structural, 38, 40
measurement, educational and psychological, 158, 192–195
Meillet, A., 15, *260*
Meinhof, C., 116, *260*
Meinong, A., 162
memory, 89
  and meaningfulness, 86
Mencken, H. L., 65, 228, *260*
mental chemistry, 73
mental health, 108f, 161, 165
mentalism, 72, 75, 77, 81, 89
Menzerath, P., 43, *260*
Mercier, L. J.-A., 172, *260*
message as component in communication
  system, 90
metalinguistics, 26–29, 43, 182, 239(n)
metaphysics, 6, 135, 137–139, 241(n)
Metcalf, R. C., 185, *263*
methodology, comparative linguistics, 48–
  52
  linguistic, 25, 29–40, 67
Mexico, languages of, 49, 58

Middle English, 66
Milewski, T., 23, *260*
Mill, James, 73
Mill, J. S., 73, *260*
Miller, E., 87
Miller, G. A., 70f, 78, 83–87, 95f, 107, 121,
  203, 237(n), 240(n), *258*, *260*
Miller, N. E., 102, 106, 108f, 115, 250
mimicry-memorization method, 99, 169,
  176, 180, 188, 191
mimicry span, tests, 194
mind, 71–73, 89
Minoan language, 210
missionaries, 121
Mithridates, 17
model of communication process, 88
Modern Language Association, 177, 216,
  242(n), *260*
Modern Language Journal, 217
Modern Language Notes, 217
Modern Language Study, 171f, 187, 193
Modern Philology, 217
Mon-Khmer languages, 56
Monroe, M., 242(n), *260*
mood, grammar, 76
morpheme, 21, 24f, 30–32, 36f, 40, 42
morphology, 21, 24f, 31, 35–41, 76
  child language learning, 98
morphophonemics, 21, 24f, 86
Morris, C. W., 134–136, 243(n), *259f*
Morse code, 244(n)
Mosteller, F., 225, *247*
motivation, 69–70
Mowrer, O. H., 106, *260*
Müller, F., 18, *260*
Müller, M., 162, 235(n), *260*
multiple factor analysis, 101, 193f, 244(n)
Munda languages, 56
Murra, J. V., 236(n), *260*
Murray, E., 143, 159, *260*, *262*
musical responses, 104
Muyskens, J. H., 80, 237(n), *260*

Nahuatl language, 58
naming ability, 101
National Council of Teachers of English,
  153, 217

282

INDEX

Santali language, 75
Sapir, E., 15, 20–23, 29, 39–43, 45, 48f, 57, 61, 65, 75, 81f, 114, 127, 220, 223, 236(n), 238(n), 264
Scandinavian languages, 54
Schlauch, M., 240(n), 264
Schleicher, A., 75, 264
scholarships, 229
School of Language and Linguistics, 181f
Schuchardt, H., 50, 264
Schweiker, R. F., 244(n), 249
science, and language, 20, 27
   unity of, 134, 137
scientific generalist, 225
Scripture, E. W., 4
Sears, R. R., 106, 108, 264
Seashore, R. H., 242(n), 264
Seashore musical ability tests, 194
Sebeok, T. A., 75f, 264
second language. See foreign language
Sedgewick, C. H. W., 98, 248
selection of verbal behavior units, 93
semantic change, 52
semantic count, 63
semantics, 15, 76, 131, 134, 160f, 236(n), 241(n), 243(n)
   and communication theory, 202
   general, 6, 47f, 103, 162, 164–168, 243(n)
semeiotic, 134f, 243(n)
   systems, 11f, 14
seminar, psychology and linguistics, 245(n)
Semitic-Hamitic languages, 55–57
Semmelmeyer, M., 168, 264
sensation, 74, 89
"sen-sit," 184
sentence, 35, 37f, 40, 73
sentences, logical, 241(n)
sentence-types, 93, 106
Serbo-Croatian language, 54
set, psychological, 74, 77, 89, 92f
Shadick, H. E., 180, 251
shall and will, usage, 151
Shannon, C. E., 4, 84, 86, 88, 111, 197f, 201, 203, 212, 237(n), 264
Shaw, G. B., 146, 268
Shcherba, L. V., 235(n)
Sheehan, J. G., 103, 264

Shenton, H. N., 125, 264
shorthand, 63, 179
Siamese (Thai) language, 56, 173
Sievers, E., 32, 264
sign, 78
sign language, 87
signal-to-noise ratio, 201
signals, 12, 87
significs, 162
signs, theory, 133f, 138
simplification of language, 156
simultaneous translation, 182
Sino-Tibetan languages, 56
Siouan language, 57
Sisson, E. D., 242(n), 264
Skinner, B. F., 70, 78, 106f, 188, 238(n), 264
slang, 65, 118
Slavic languages, 54
Slavic linguistics, 215
Smith, B. L., 240(n), 265
Smith, C. P., 211, 265
Smith, D. V., 241(n)
Smith, H. L., Jr., 39, 55, 174, 181, 183, 236(n), 266
social attitudes, 106
social class and language, 112, 124
social control, language in, 112, 118
social groups, and dialect, 118
   study, 117
social psychology, 3, 18, 70
Social Science Research Council, 219f, 230
social sciences, 5, 11, 26, 29, 52, 66, 112–132
social status, 114
sociobiology, 135
sociology, 5, 117–119, 240(n)
   organizations and periodicals, 219
Socrates, 16
Soffietti, J. P., 34, 265
Sonograph. See sound spectrograph
Sorensen, F., 143, 262
sound spectrograph, 26, 33, 205–207, 245(n)
   playback device, 209
sounds of language, 24f, 31–35, 84
South America, languages of, 58
Soviet linguistics, 55, 235(n)